THE
MURDER OF
BIGGIE SMALLS

THE
MURDER OF
BIGGIE
SMALLS

Cathy Scott

PLEXUS PUBLISHING LONDON

Copyright © 2001 by Cathy Scott
Published by Plexus Publishing Limited
55a Clapham Common Southside
London SW4 9BX
First printing

British Library Cataloguing in Publication Data

Scott, Cathy
  The murder of Biggie Smalls
  1.Notorious B.I.G. 2.Rap musicians - United States -
  Biography 3. Murder - California - Los Angeles
  I.Title
  364.1'523'0979494

ISBN 0 85965 307 2

Printed in Great Britain
Cover photograph by Guy Aroch/Corbis Outline

10 9 8 7 6 5 4 3 2 1

*To Voletta Wallace for her incredible generosity
in sharing the memories of her only child,
the late Christopher Wallace, aka Biggie Smalls,
with a grateful journalist*

CONTENTS

ACKNOWLEDGMENTS

It was Ernest Hemingway who once described the craft of writing as a lonely process. And while I penned this manuscript alone, there were many people who stood by me. I thank them now.

And to those who hung in there through a situation that unfortunately occurred while I was in the midst of writing the manuscript, thank you all for your encouragement as I fought the dastardly demons. A colleague once told me that journalists should ask themselves this question: If they were not reporters, would the people they call their friends still be there? It's a good question.

To my friends: Carolyn Oberlander for her prayers; Karin Fantus for putting me up in her Upper West Side Manhattan apartment; Vickie Pynchon, my friend and counselor, as always, for a lifetime of friendship; writer Steve Waterstrat for a shoulder to lean on; former UPI reporter Myram Borders for her journalistic advice; author Lora Shaner for her camaraderie; Teresa Moody for her steadfast support; and author and poet Kevin Powell for his generous recommendation—I owe you big time. Thanks also to Susan Gembrowski, Linda Ballantyne, Jim and Kathleen Kelley-Markham, Karen Finkelstein, Candy Greene, Sandy Smith, Sheryl Carlton, Marty Parker, Carole Bowers, Charlene Fern, Jodi Dewey, Kae Reed, Jim and Karen Campbell, and Randy Dotinga.

To my friend and neighbor Brett Gall, you give me hope; to Sean Neary at *George* magazine; Hoag Levins and Ed Levine with APBNews.com; Geoff Schumacher with *Las Vegas CityLife*; Patricia Cunningham with Sheridan Broadcasting; Ginger Tafoya with *Las Vegas* magazine; Albert Jones (formerly at Borders bookstore); Kent Lauer with the Nevada Press Association; author and *Las Vegas*

Review-Journal columnist John L. Smith; *Review-Journal* columnist Steve Sebelius; Ben Mohr with KVBC (NBC) in Las Vegas; Christine Mahoney with Las Vegas's *Fox 5*; *Dummies* writers Andy and Tina Rathbone (I want *your* royalties, Andy); Larry Henry (formerly with the *Las Vegas Sun*); Jon Moser with jonnymo.com; the Society of Professional Journalists' national board, as well as its regional director, Mark Scarp; and my attorney, Robert Kossack.

To detectives and beat officers with the New York City, Los Angeles, Compton, Inglewood, and Las Vegas Police Departments, who filled in the many blanks; the Brooklyn–Clinton Hills residents for sharing their stories about their friend Chris Wallace; and to my sources within the music industry and police departments.

Much gratitude goes to my agent, Frank Weimann, with the Literary Group, and my editors, Dana Albarella and Elizabeth Beier, at St. Martin's Press.

Special thanks to Voletta Wallace for her patience and generosity.

For being there: my parents, Eileen Rose Busby and my late stepfather Richard Busby, and Jim and Helen Scott; my son, Raymond Somers Jr. (who also happens to be my Web master for www.cathyscott.com); my twin sister, Cordelia Mendoza; my brother, J. Michael Scott; my stepsister Nancy Whitlock; and my cousin Covert Corey; and to the rest of my family for their support.

To my late friend Patrick Falk, who told me twenty-five years ago that I should be an investigator because I ask so many questions. (Or did he say *too* many questions?)

And, finally, to my late grandmother, Esther Rose, who, thankfully, questioned everything and passed down that trait to me.

INTRODUCTION

ALMOST SIX MONTHS TO THE DAY after rap star Tupac Shakur was gunned down on a Las Vegas street, someone else got away with murder—at least for the time being. This time it was the drive-by shooter of hip-hop rapper Christopher Wallace, who recorded and performed both as Biggie Smalls and the Notorious B.I.G.—the Bad Boy Entertainment record label's number one performer.

The day after Biggie was gunned down in Los Angeles on Sunday, March 9, 1997, police there were confident they would make an early arrest. The third anniversary has now come and gone. No arrests have been made and no charges have been filed. But it's not because of a lack of effort on the part of the Los Angeles Police Department; they hit the case hard from the beginning. And police continue to express confidence they'll solve the crime.

I learned of Biggie Smalls's death when I was awakened early on that Sunday, March 9, just hours after the shooting, by a phone call from a *Philadelphia Inquirer* entertainment writer seeking a comment. I had covered Tupac Shakur's murder extensively six months earlier for a Las Vegas paper and was in the throes of writing a book about the Vegas slaying. Here was another, almost identical case of a rapper gunned down in a drive-by shooting.

With Biggie's murder, the world of rap took yet another hit. The rap nation has endured a deadly war. Some say it was a bicoastal rivalry, with Tupac Shakur on the West Coast and Biggie Smalls the rival rapper on the East Coast. Some go further, saying it was Death Row Records in the West versus Bad Boy Entertainment in the East. Like Tupac's murder, Biggie's killing was another example of black-on-black violence, the leading cause of death among young black men in

America. Police in both cases identified the shooters as black males. And they said the drive-by killings appeared to be planned, professional hits. Both Tupac and Biggie, with their deaths, left behind them a web of intrigue.

This story—and the interviews and research—took me to New York City: Upper West Side, Times Square, and midtown Manhattan and Brooklyn's Clinton Hill and Bedford-Stuyvesant; and, in California, to Compton and Los Angeles. I didn't take a taxi to Biggie Smalls's old Brooklyn neighborhood; I rode the New York City subway and the crowded city buses. I walked the streets where he grew up. I visited police precincts and headquarters in Los Angeles and New York City, and the L.A. Corner's Office, where Biggie's body was taken after he was shot. I also went to LAPD's Robbery-Homicide Division headquarters.

I visited Bad Boy Entertainment's offices in midtown Manhattan, and Quad Studios in Times Square, where Tupac was shot the first time and where many contend the bad blood between Biggie and Tupac began. Twice I went to the scene of the crime, to the Petersen Automotive Museum in Los Angeles's Wilshire District. I went upstairs to the room where Biggie had left a party just minutes before the shooting. I drove the same route from the museum to the hospital where Biggie was taken and where he was pronounced dead.

The conclusions drawn in this book are observations made as the result of interviews gathered throughout my eighteen months of research. I interviewed many people repeatedly. The dialogue comes either from people who heard it, or were there when it was said. All court quotations come from court documents. Statements by police officers are from conversations and interviews with officers and from police reports and documents.

I have reviewed scores of newspaper and magazine articles—literally hundreds of them—and culled and verified facts about Biggie Smalls and related topics from those articles. I listened to radio interviews and watched hours of TV and video footage on Biggie and Tupac and the East Coast–West Coast rift. I also used my own materials from articles I wrote for the *Las Vegas Sun* while I worked for that paper, and from an in-depth piece I wrote for *George* magazine (October 1998) about both cases.

I also drew from statements made by Frank Alexander, Tupac's personal bodyguard and witness to his murder, in his book *Got Your Back: The Life of a Bodyguard in the Hardcore World of Gangsta Rap*. Other books I used for reference were Martin Roth's *Strictly Murder, A Writer's Guide to Criminal Homicide*; Chuck D's *Fight the Power: Rap, Race, and Reality*; Nathan McCall's *Makes Me Wanna Holler*; Kevin Powell's *Keepin' It Real*; and LL Cool J's *I Make My Own Rules*.

I have read and listened to most if not all of Biggie's lyrics about the gangsta lifestyle, violence in the streets and in the ghetto. But I do not profess to be an expert on gangsta hip-hop. I came into this story as a journalist interested in a murder case, wanting to tell the public what happened, not as a fan interested in a rap star, and certainly not as a music critic.

Like the Tupac Shakur case, this was another unsolved murder story I felt needed to be told. It was in the same spirit as my earlier book, *The Killing of Tupac Shakur*, that I wrote this manuscript—to tell one man's tragic story, along with his human frailties, of how he came to such a violent and very public death. This is a story about the rise of a rap star and the professional hit that brought him down. I hope the following pages depict Christopher Wallace for who he was: a young man, an only son, a husband, a father of two, and one of the most successful and notorious rap performers the industry has ever seen. This is his story.

—Cathy Scott
March 2000

THE SHOOTING

IN THE WEE HOURS OF A SPRING DAY, at exactly 12:49 in the morning, six to ten bullets flashed into the darkness. The lone trigger man, using a semiautomatic handgun, sprayed the side of the dark-green 1997 GMC Suburban. Then, in a lightning-quick moment, as suddenly as it had started, it was over. Inside the Suburban, Biggie Smalls lay motionless. Outside on the street, frightened people ducked for cover.

It was March 9, 1997, a day that would forever be emblazoned in the minds of hip-hop music fans across the nation, if not the world.

Several hours before the deadly shooting, on the afternoon of Saturday, March 8, Biggie Smalls had picked up the phone in his plush Regent Beverly Wilshire hotel suite on Wilshire Boulevard in Beverly Hills. He dialed his mother's number in New York. It was evening on the East Coast when his mother answered her phone. Biggie told her he was in Los Angeles.

"What are you doing in L.A.?" a surprised Voletta Wallace asked her son. "I thought you left for London."

He told her no, and explained that his plans to leave for Europe that morning had changed, and that he wouldn't be going on a London promotional tour after all, for his soon-to-be released double album, *Life After Death . . . 'Til Death Do Us Part.*

"Puffy wanted me here," Biggie told his mother. "Europe's canceled. Puff told me I could do telephone interviews instead of makin' the trip over there."

He was referring to Sean "Puffy" Combs, the head of Biggie's record label, Bad Boy Entertainment. Earlier in the day, at ten o'clock, Biggie was in an L.A. recording studio finishing tracks for Puffy's debut solo album, *Hell Up in Harlem* (the title was later changed to *No*

Way Out). Biggie was also in L.A. to promote his new CD, and to shoot a video with Puffy for the single "Hypnotize."

Before he called his mother, Biggie phoned his friend Lance "Un" Rivera in New York. "His whole mood," Rivera would say later, "was that March 25 [his album's release date] is gonna change the world. He wanted to be known as the nicest MC ever." That's why the music awards were so important to Biggie. It was recognition for his rhymes.

To *Vibe* magazine writer Cheo Hodari Coker the night before, Biggie said he was still in L.A. because he was enjoying himself. "He canceled, he told me, because he was having too much fun in Cali," Coker said.

During his telephone conversation with his mother, Biggie told her all about being a presenter the night before, at the Eleventh Annual *Soul Train* Music Awards.

She didn't know it then, but that call would be the last conversation Voletta Wallace would ever have with her only son. The fans didn't know it then, either, but that night would also mark Biggie's last public appearance.

As he walked onto the stage at the famous Los Angeles Shrine Auditorium and Expo Center to present an award, the crowd started booing. Given the circumstances, Biggie bent over the mike and, as cheerfully as he could muster, he asked, "Wha's up, Cali?"

He waited for the booing to stop.

It didn't.

From the cheap seats, some in the audience flashed Westside hand signals, denoting their West Coast street-gang affiliations. As he opened the envelope to announce the winner—Toni Braxton for Best Female R&B/Soul Album—the chorus of boos continued, which could partly explain Biggie's melancholy mood the next day when he called his mother. The loud booing marked the divisive turf war in the East Coast–West Coast rap feud. And Biggie was well aware of it.

He was in good company at the awards ceremony. Biggie felt honored to be invited. Also taking center stage during the live two-hour telecast were co-hosts Gladys Knight, LL Cool J, and Brandy, with fellow presenters Snoop Doggy Dogg, Aaliyah, Immature, Tisha Campbell, and Heavy D.

The night's biggest award, for Best R&B/Soul or Rap Album, went posthumously to Biggie's onetime rival, the late Tupac Shakur, for his multiplatinum double disc *All Eyez on Me*.

The *Soul Train* Music Awards each year honors the industry's hottest entertainers. It's a black-tie, star-studded event showcasing the best in R&B, rap, gospel, and jazz. Being booed at such a prestigious event in front of his peers was an embarrassment for Biggie, especially since Biggie was trying to distance himself from the so-called rap turf war.

On the phone, Biggie told his mother that he and the Bad Boy group had moved in and out of about five different hotels during their four-week stay in the City of Angels. A month earlier he had called her from his suite at the Westwood-Pacific Hotel in West L.A., where the group had been staying for a few days. His stay in L.A. was almost over, he told his mother.

Biggie also said, "We're goin' to a party tonight." Attending the music-industry bash would prove to be a deadly decision.

Biggie mentioned that he was not especially up for going out that night. Being booed the night before had gotten to him. Plus he was tired from all the recording they had been doing. But he was going to the party anyway, out of obligation to his record label, because Puffy Combs had asked him to. Once there, however, witnesses would later say, Biggie looked to be having a good time. He tried sloughing off the booing from the night before by saying, "That's okay. Just wait till March 25. They'll see." He was proud that his new album was about to drop.

Biggie told his mother it was just as well he wasn't going to London because he didn't feel enough bodyguards had been lined up in advance. Voletta was relieved. If Biggie was worried about his safety while in the U.K., then so was she.

On the other hand, Biggie assured his mother, he had plenty of bodyguards while in L.A. "We have off-duty cops guarding us," he told her. He must have felt safe, she thought to herself after she hung up, or he wouldn't stay there. She never gave it another thought—not until afterward, when it was too late.

Puffy Combs once told a reporter that Biggie was always concerned about safety. "That's why we took precautions," he told *MTV News* in March of '97. "You know, like hiring off-duty police officers. We thought that was the safest way to do it. And people that defend the city, we thought we was gonna hire them to protect and defend us."

Other than hiring security guards, there were no outward signs of fear or concern during Biggie's entire stay on the West Coast, nor any hesitation from anyone in the Bad Boy Entertainment group, even though in the past East Coast rappers had been worried about traveling to southern California because of bad blood between rappers on opposite coasts.

Not all rappers were as relaxed. A cautious Snoop Doggy Dogg canceled a concert tour shortly after Tupac Shakur was fatally gunned down in September of '96. Snoop didn't want to be next. Friends later said Biggie should have been just as apprehensive, especially about spending time in the L.A. area. It was considered Tupac's territory, and Tupac had been killed in the West, in Las Vegas, just six months earlier.

For his part, Biggie was beginning to feel at home in L.A. He shopped with a Realtor for a vacation home while he was there, looking for a West Coast getaway. "Yes, Christopher was comfortable in L.A.," Voletta conceded after her son's death. "Maybe he was *too* comfortable."

Biggie presented himself as a reluctant participant in the bicoastal rap feud. However, his reported contacts with gang members in Los Angeles in the days before his death would later prove to be a scenario for police, as one of a handful of possible motives for his murder.

When Biggie got dressed for the post-awards party in L.A. that night, he put on faded blue jeans and a long-sleeved, button-up black velour shirt. The weather on the eighth was a typical March day for the Los Angeles basin: a bit cloudy and windy because of a small storm sweeping through the area, but no rain. The temperature at midday reached 63 degrees Fahrenheit—not exactly shorts weather. But it wasn't cool enough for a jacket, either. And a heavy bulletproof vest was out of the question; it wasn't something he even traveled with. As usual, Biggie took his walking cane. He'd been doing that ever since he injured his knee in a New Jersey car accident six months earlier, in September. A steel pin was surgically implanted into his leg and it was taking time to heal.

Around his neck on a heavy gold chain hung a large solid-gold Jesus

Christ pendant: not the prized Bad Boy Entertainment gold medallion and logo with a baby wearing a baseball cap and workboots. He wore sunglasses, even though the party was indoors and at night. He wanted to look cool, sharp. And, of course, he wore one of his trademark hats, this one a casual riding cap.

Biggie was known for wearing brimmed one-hundred-percent–wool felt bowler hats to match his designer suits. His suits were similar to those worn in the 1930s by mobsters. He liked having the look of a mob wiseguy when he rapped his gangsta/playa lyrics. But that night he wasn't playing the "Notorious B.I.G." role. No tough-guy act that night. He was, simply, Biggie.

The night marked the end of a lengthy recording session in L.A. for Puffy and Biggie and the Bad Boy company. It also turned out to be an important promotion for Biggie's *Life After Death* album, to be released in just two weeks. On the heels of all that work, all Biggie wanted to do that night was relax in the company of friends.

About eight o'clock, guests began arriving at 6060 Wilshire Boulevard at Fairfax Avenue for the post-awards celebration. The Petersen Automotive Museum is on Museum Row on the Miracle Mile in the Wilshire District near Hollywood. The Miracle Mile is one of the busiest business districts in the world; included with the automotive museum along this stretch are the La Brea Tar Pits, the Wiltern Theater, and the Farmers Market.

The music-industry party was hosted by *Vibe* magazine and Qwest Records (both operated by Quincy Jones) and Tanqueray gin. The guest list read like a who's who of the hip-hop genre. The list included many of the same celebrities who attended the awards ceremony the night before. Invitees who showed up included rappers Heavy D, Busta Rhymes, Chris Tucker, Da Brat, Yo-Yo, Jermaine Dupri, and, of course, Biggie Smalls and Puffy Combs. Also attending was Quincy Jones's daughter Kidada, Tupac Shakur's girlfriend, who was with him in Las Vegas the night he was killed.

A noteworthy, if not a surprise, attendee was Orlando Anderson, the reputed Crips gang member who had been roughed up by Tupac and Suge Knight just hours before Tupac was gunned down in Las Vegas. Orlando was once detained by police for questioning about

Tupac's death. Orlando was the reason Suge Knight, Puffy Combs's music rival, was later incarcerated. Police would later say that Orlando's appearance had no significance for them, and ruled out Orlando in the murder-scene scenarios.

In their rented cars (during their stay in L.A. Bad Boy Entertainment had rented GMC Suburbans from Budget Rent a Car of Beverly Hills), Puffy and Biggie arrived at the party just after nine o'clock, intentionally timed so they would be fashionably late. Accompanying Biggie in his rented Suburban were his roommates—James Lloyd, who performed as Little Caesar (Lil' Cease) in Junior M.A.F.I.A., and Damien "D-Rock" Butler, Biggie's best friend and road manager— who both lived with him in his Teaneck, New Jersey townhouse. They drove to the covered garage at the valet area near the entrance to the museum. But they were met by a sign saying the valet parking garage was full. So they drove around the block and found street parking on Fairfax Avenue, a block or so away.

The group, with the moonlighting cops in tow as their personal bodyguards, got out of their GMC Suburbans and paraded back up the street to the museum, then walked up the three steps leading to the entrance. They showed their invitations, and a doorman opened one of the four all-glass doors and let them in.

Once inside, they continued toward the elevators about twenty-five yards away, past the security office on the right near the front entrance. Working alone in the security dispatch office on swing shift that night, and monitoring the museum's five surveillance consoles, was a female dispatcher. She watched on the cameras as the group approached the information desk. "Where do we go for the *Vibe* party?" Puffy asked an employee. "Upstairs, second floor. Use the elevator or the escalator," the museum employee answered.

Puffy, Biggie, and their group walked past the information desk to two elevators. They got in an elevator and rode to the next floor. Upstairs, they walked past the immaculately polished, shiny chromed muscle cars, to the Grand Salon, a larger exhibition hall where the party was being hosted. More exhibitions of race cars, classic cars, hot rods, motorcycles, movie and celebrity vintage and antique cars were on display there. The dance floor was in the center of the room, surrounded by tables fronting the automobiles.

The crowd was up. Everyone was still pumped from the awards ceremony the night before. It was a mostly celebrity crowd. Puffy was surprised to see such a large group. He had been told it was going to be a private party. He had been expecting a much smaller, intimate crowd—that's what he told Biggie when he talked him into going with him.

By nine-thirty P.M. the party really began to take off. It was about that time, witnesses would later recall, that Biggie was seen having a good time, talking and laughing with friends. He sat at a table on the rim of the dance floor, directly in front of an early model Düsseldorf, with Puffy and record producer–rapper Jermaine Dupri. And he chatted with other friends who stopped by his table. Russell Simmons, CEO of Def Jam Records, sat across from Biggie's table. Russell clowned around with Biggie for appearing so calm, cool, and collected as overtly flirtatious women approached Biggie. Just before midnight, the DJ put on "Hypnotize," the single track from Big's new album.

Biggie felt like he was getting the star recognition and love he deserved—his just due, he thought. It had been more than two years since his first album had dropped. And this album had been cut while he was still in a wheelchair. People walked up to his table and congratulated him on his soon-to-be-released second album. Women sat on his lap and also danced in front of him. He couldn't get up and dance with them because his injured leg was still healing. He signed autographs and people snapped his photograph. He was pleased his music was well received, especially on the heels of the negative reception and booing he'd gotten at the awards ceremony the night before.

More and more people crowded onto the second floor of the museum. By midnight the room was packed. About thirty minutes later, at 12:35 A.M., Los Angeles fire marshals, already standing by and on swing-shift duty at the museum for the special event, announced they were breaking up the party. The building was dangerously overcapacity with, by that time, an estimated two thousand in attendance. Another two hundred people milled around outside hoping to catch a glimpse of a celebrity or two. The building needed to be evacuated immediately, the fire marshals announced abruptly.

"This party is over. Please leave in an orderly manner. Immediately!" barked a fire marshal's voice over the loudspeaker. The four glass doors opened and the guests, some of them drunk, poured out into the first-floor garage. Fire marshals upstairs opened the stairwell door, and some guests walked down the stairs. Others crowded the escalator and elevators. Los Angeles police officers, also assigned to the special event, were on duty for traffic control and posted outside the museum.

As people left, Biggie and Puffy stayed upstairs waiting for the crowd to disburse. Biggie had to take it slowly because of his leg. While they waited upstairs, Puffy and Biggie posed together for a last-minute photo. They both mugged and wore deadpan looks on their faces. It would be the last photograph taken of Biggie alive.

By 12:40 A.M., the guests spilled onto the streets. Others waited in the garage for valet service. Fans continued gathering outside on the street. Within a matter of minutes, everyone would be in for a tragic surprise.

Biggie and Puffy emerged from the building through the crowd and stood at the valet stand for a few minutes. They talked with friends who were waiting for their cars to be driven around. Puffy and Biggie made arrangements to meet at an after-party at a private residence owned by Interscope Records executive Steven Stoute (whom Puffy would rough up two years later, over a music-video dispute). Biggie smiled to his friends and said, "See y'all at the next party." Then he turned and walked away.

The Bad Boy group walked out of the garage and past the museum's toll parking booth to Fairfax Avenue where their SUVs were parked on the street. (Afterward, police confiscated the museum's surveillance videotapes on which the group was clearly seen walking out of the garage, hanging a left on Fairfax, rendering them out of sight of the cameras' lenses as they headed to their vehicles.)

Puffy, his driver, and friends got into their GMC Suburban while Biggie and his crew got into their dark-green one. That the vehicles used by the Bad Boy group were nearly identical would later form another crime scenario for Los Angeles police investigators.

Biggie got into the front passenger seat. Just like Tupac six months before him, he was sitting shotgun. He was a perfect target.

Biggie's driver, a bodyguard and friend identified only as Greg, got behind the wheel. (Biggie had never learned to drive because he didn't see the need. After all, he grew up in Brooklyn using the public bus and subway systems. When he needed to go somewhere, he was chauffeured by either a car or limo service, or friends would pick him up and drive him.) Lil' Cease and Damien Butler climbed into the backseat of the Suburban.

Puffy and his entourage left first, with Biggie's utility vehicle close behind as it pulled away from the curb and onto the crowded street. Blaring from the Suburban's stereo was a tape of Biggie's new album. A Ford Blazer fell in behind Biggie's Suburban. The Blazer was carrying the group's personal bodyguards—all off-duty cops from the Inglewood Police Department, the same pool of moonlighting cops from which Suge Knight (Tupac Shakur's record producer) had drawn. One of those off-duty cops was behind the wheel of the Blazer.

The drivers of the Suburbans and the Blazer got onto Fairfax and headed toward Wilshire Boulevard. The line of three sport-utility vehicles came to a dead stop at a red signal light at the intersection of Wilshire and Fairfax, about a hundred yards away from the driveway entrance to the museum. Puffy's Suburban was still in front of Biggie's as they all sat waiting for the light to turn green.

Another car, described as a dark-green or dark-color sedan, drove up on the right. The dark sedan came to a halt next to Biggie's vehicle. The sedan's driver, a black man in his early twenties wearing a dress shirt, suit, and bow tie, pulled a silver automatic pistol, stuck it out the car window, and opened fire. More than half a dozen shots were pumped from the 9-millimeter handgun into the passenger side of Biggie's car.

For a fleeting moment, Biggie had a look of surprise on his face. He was the only one hit.

In a reflex action, everyone in both Suburbans ducked. They

thought the crack of gunfire they heard was just shots being fired into the air, a common occurrence at previous parties they'd attended. They realized they were wrong when they heard people in the crowd holler, "They hit up Biggie's car, they hit up Biggie's car!"

Inside Biggie's Suburban, Damien and Lil' Cease had dropped to the floor. Lil' Cease didn't get but a quick look at the shooter. "He was driving with his left hand and had to come across with the gun in his right," he would later tell the *Los Angeles Times*. "All I could see was that he [the shooter] was black and had a receding hairline. He had a bow tie on and a suit. The guy was already set the second he drove up. As fast as you could turn around, he was just shooting up the car."

Both Lil' Cease and Damien, however, saw enough of the shooter to provide details for two composite sketches—one drawn by a police artist the day after the shooting, and the next, eighteen days later. Damien, too, saw Biggie try to dodge the bullets as they began to fly.

"Biggie ducked and stayed all the way down," Damien told the *Los Angeles Times*. "If he had made it, I could see by the look on his face that he could tell you who the shooter was. But he didn't have time to say a word. He didn't say, 'Ouch.' He didn't say, 'Yo, look out.' He didn't say nothin'." That revelation—that Biggie appeared to recognize the assailant—unfortunately wouldn't help investigators later because Biggie didn't live to tell them about it.

Puffy immediately jumped out of his Suburban and ran toward Biggie's GMC where Lil' Cease and Damien were with Biggie. Biggie was slumped forward in his seat—he, too, had tried to dodge the bullets; instead, he took them in his chest. He lost consciousness almost immediately.

"He just laid there," Damien told the *L.A. Times*, "looking at me in my face. He died in my arms."

2

THE CRIME SCENE

THE SMELL OF GUNPOWDER filled the air. Panic broke out. People started screaming. The shooting was a brazen attack in front of hundreds of people, including Biggie's estranged wife, rhythm-and-blues singer Faith Evans, and Mark Pitts, Biggie's manager. Many people on the street ran toward the garage to take cover, away from the gunfire.

The first call made to the Los Angeles Police Department's emergency 911 line came in at 12:49 A.M. Police squad cars were immediately dispatched to the scene of the crime. "Shots fired. Reported at the Petersen Automotive Museum, 6060 Wilshire Boulevard. All units in the area respond." Officers were dispatched from the Wilshire Community Police Station at 4861 West Venice Boulevard a few miles away.

One woman ran into the museum's security dispatch office, screaming, "Someone call the police!" She was told by the dispatcher that police officers were already on the scene, taking charge, and that more were on the way.

Puffy opened Biggie's passenger door. Frantically, he and others in their group tried to pull Biggie out of his seat, to the ground. But they couldn't budge him because of his size. He was deadweight.

Puffy, who had gotten on his knees next to Biggie, was visibly distraught. Puffy tried again to lift Biggie, and more people went over to the car to help roll him over in his seat, but he was simply too heavy and too large. Because they couldn't move him, they also couldn't see just how badly he'd been injured.

Puffy pushed the now unconscious Biggie to the side, propping him up in his seat, and closed the passenger-side door. Instead of reclining Biggie's seat and staying there, where police were already on the scene and to where an ambulance had been dispatched, Puffy and his crew left. In a split-second decision, they had opted to deliver the injured rapper themselves to Cedars-Sinai Medical Center, less than two miles away.

Many in the black community say they're accustomed to ambulances not always arriving quickly. Perhaps this was one of the reasons Puffy chose to leave. He and his crew knew where the hospital was because they'd driven past it many times during their extended stay in L.A. And they were in a panic to get medical help as soon as possible for Biggie.

Greg—the bodyguard—jumped into the driver's seat of Biggie's Suburban and drove toward Cedars-Sinai, leaving the scene of the crime. Lil' Cease and Damien were in the backseat. Puffy, with a driver, followed closely in his Suburban. They headed out onto South Fairfax, turning left on Wilshire Boulevard, driving the three blocks to San Vicente Boulevard, and veering right. The driver hammered the remaining twelve blocks to the hospital. In good traffic, the less-than-two-mile route is a four- or five-minute drive. The driver gunned the GMC's V-8 engine and made it there in almost half that time. Puffy and his crew repeated out loud, even though Biggie was in another vehicle and couldn't hear them, "C'mon, man, hold on. Hold on, B.I.G."

When they arrived with Biggie at Cedars-Sinai at 8700 Beverly Boulevard a few minutes later, Greg, the driver, honked the SUV's horn as it flew into the emergency driveway to the hospital off of Gracie Allen Drive. Everyone jumped out of the Suburbans and ran to the doors of the emergency room, frantically calling out for help. Emergency-room attendants sprang into action. Within moments, they were by Biggie's side.

Hospital attendants, with Puffy and others helping, lifted Biggie's still body onto a gurney. As he was wheeled into the hospital, Puffy whispered in his ear, uttering prayers. Inside, emergency-room personnel examined Biggie. This was a modern ER, which is classified as a trauma center equipped with the latest in modern medical equipment. The doctors and nurses used everything at their disposal.

Still, it looked hopeless. Biggie had stopped breathing.

He had suffered massive injuries. He'd taken seven shots in his chest and abdomen. He was bleeding internally and had lost a lot of blood. For about twenty minutes, doctors and ER personnel tried to save him. They tried resuscitating him. But he had been mortally wounded. They couldn't bring him back. "They tried everything in the hospital to revive him," Voletta Wallace said about their efforts. "Everything."

"They told me that he was already deceased, that he had died immediately," Puffy Combs would later tell the *New York Daily News*.

Biggie was classified as DOA, dead on arrival.

At 1:15 A.M. on Sunday, March 9, 1997, twenty-four-year-old Christopher George Latore Wallace was pronounced dead by doctors at Cedars-Sinai Medical Center. At the hospital with Puffy when officials made the announcement was Biggie's wife, Faith Evans, with whom he shared his youngest child, Christopher Jr., who was just five months old at the time of his father's death. Biggie's oldest child, T'Yanna, from a previous relationship, was three years old at the time.

A doctor walked out of the surgical room and approached Puffy Combs and Faith Evans. He told them there was nothing more the ER medical staff could do for Biggie. He was gone. No one, besides hospital personnel, got to see him to say good-bye.

Sitting still at the emergency entrance, with the passenger door ajar and the seat eerily vacant, was Biggie's bullet-riddled Suburban with "B.I.G." stickers on the wheels and bumper stickers on the back that read, "Think B.I.G. March 25, 1997"—promotion stickers for his upcoming *Life After Death* album.

Back at the 6060 Wilshire Boulevard crime scene, a team of SWAT officers clad in riot gear and armed with heavy artillery arrived and surrounded the area to prevent what police thought might turn into an out-of-control melee as distraught friends and fans learned the bad news that Biggie had been fatally wounded. By that time, the media began to converge on the scene and the first local news satellite trucks showed up.

No such melee broke out. Instead, after hearing the news, dozens of concerned friends and fans left the museum, and instead of going to the after-party as many had originally planned, they drove to the Cedars-Sinai hospital and gathered for hours early Sunday in the parking lot, near where Biggie's Suburban sat. Also arriving at the hospital were Biggie's manager, Mark Pitts.

The crowd of friends and fans in the parking lot left only after hospital officials confirmed for them that Biggie had passed.

Meanwhile, after learning that Biggie had been driven in a private car to the hospital, detectives and crime-scene analysts were dispatched to Cedars-Sinai. Upon their arrival, police immediately cordoned off the Suburban in the hospital's parking lot. Crime-scene analysts went over every inch of Biggie's vehicle and studied the bullet holes—five were visible on the passenger-side front door—before they towed it to a police impound yard.

Immediately following the gunfire, the shooter simply drove away. Some of the off-duty Inglewood Police Department officers who were moonlighting for the night as personal security for the Bad Boy group took off in their Blazer after the gunman. They followed the getaway vehicle down Wilshire Boulevard.

But their efforts were unsuccessful; the shooter sped away into the night, disappearing. The off-duty cops did not get a license-plate number. There were some reports that a man on foot first approached Biggie's car and that when Biggie unrolled the window to talk to the man, a trigger man in a nearby car opened fire. (Ironically, a stunned Biggie had told a *Vibe* reporter, after Tupac Shakur was fatally gunned down in Las Vegas: "I couldn't believe it. When you're making so much money, a drive-by shooting ain't supposed to happen. You're supposed to have flocks of security; not even supposed to be sitting by no window.") Reports of a suspect on foot, however, were never substantiated.

Within hours, police stopped a man in the area whose vehicle fit early descriptions of a black Jeep seen by witnesses. The man carried a gun. Police booked him on suspicion of firing it into the air shortly after the murder. But they did not consider him a suspect in Biggie's murder. Based upon later eyewitness accounts, police believed the assailant's car was a dark full-sized sedan, specifically a Chevrolet Impala, not a truck or sport-utility vehicle as was initially reported.

Speculation surfaced early on that Biggie may not have been the intended target. Was it possible the shooter had believed Puffy Combs was sitting next to the window in the car and that Combs, not Biggie Smalls, had been the intended target and he had shot the wrong man? Could the shooter have thought he was aiming at Puffy, and not Biggie, who had been sitting unsuspecting in the passenger seat? After all, the windows in both Suburbans were tinted, making it difficult to see in from the outside. It's a theory the police, more than three years later, did not rule out; many theories were, but not that one. Puffy and Biggie were passengers in two cars that looked almost identical, making that theory a plausible one for investigators.

Also, why were the bodyguards, who were well-trained police officers, unable to take down even a partial license-plate number of the getaway car, or at least a good, usable description of the car and the shooter for police? This, too, was an angle police would later explore.

Back inside the hospital, everyone knew that someone had to notify Biggie's mother. They were hesitant. No one wanted to make that call, to be the bearer of such devastating news. And they didn't know quite how to say it. Should the doctor do it? The police? Should it be Damien? Or Puffy? Or Biggie's manager, Mark? They passed the phone around. Someone had to do it. Finally, it was Damien, Biggie's closest friend, who took the phone and dialed Voletta Wallace's number.

It was nearly dawn on the East Coast when the sound of a telephone ringing startled Voletta Wallace awake. Without thinking, she automatically looked at the clock. She would forever remember the exact time. The clock read 5:21 A.M. Eastern Standard Time. Voletta quickly switched on the lamp on her bedstand and answered the phone. She immediately recognized the voice on the other end as Damien's. But he was upset and crying. And she could hear other people in the background. "The only thing I heard was screaming," Voletta would later recall.

Damien, sobbing, kept repeating, "Mrs. Wallace, Mrs. Wallace. Is there anyone there with you? Oh, Mrs. Wallace."

"I screamed, 'What's wrong with you, Damien? What's wrong?' " Voletta said. "My sister-in-law was staying with me and she heard me screaming and came into my room and took the phone from me."

What Damien was about to say was the most awful news Voletta Wallace would ever hear. It would shatter her world. Still crying,

Damien blurted out to Voletta's sister-in-law that Biggie was dead. He told her that Biggie had been shot to death in a drive-by. "I knew the call had to be [about] Christopher," Voletta later said. "I knew it had to be bad news. That was very heart-wrenching for Damien. Their hearts were ripped apart [because] someone had to tell me."

For the second time in just a few hours, Voletta Wallace had taken a call from Los Angeles. Shortly after the last call, she boarded a plane and flew to Los Angeles to identify her only child's body and to make arrangements to bring him back to his native New York, to bring him home to Brooklyn.

3

BROOKLYN

There's a tree that grows in Brooklyn. Some people call it the Tree of Heaven. No matter where its seed falls, it makes a tree which struggles to reach the sky. It grows in boarded up lots and out of neglected rubbish heaps. It grows up out of cellar gratings.

It is the only tree that grows out of cement. It grows lushly . . . survives without sun, water, and seemingly without earth. It would be considered beautiful except that there are too many of it.

       —Betty Smith, *A Tree Grows in Brooklyn*

CHRISTOPHER WALLACE, a chunky, awkward fourteen-year-old, sat in the lobby of New York City Police Department's Eighty-eighth Precinct and wept. NYPD officers in Brooklyn North's Patrol Borough, at the Eighty-eighth, had been through this before with Christopher. The routine was the same: They would haul him in for questioning about petty crimes. He would start crying. Then they would drive him home and hand him over to his mother. They never charged him with a crime. This particular time, though, Christopher, with tears still rolling down his face but fighting hard to compose himself, told the detectives, "I'm gonna be famous one day. You wait'n see. I'm gonna be *big*."

The cops weren't impressed. "We'd say, 'Get outta here. Shut up,' " said NYPD detective Andre Parker, who at the time worked out of the Eighty-eighth at 298 Classon Avenue in a turn-of-the-century redbrick building. "If we looked at him cross-sides, he would cry. Yeah, he'd have a fit when we brought him in. He'd cry and say, 'I ain't doin' nothin'. I swear it.' He was just this chunky kid. A scared kid."

Brooklyn's Eighty-eighth Precinct covers the working-class neighborhood in which Christopher Wallace, who later changed his name to

Biggie Smalls, grew up in a row-house apartment building on a tree-lined street. There weren't any front yards with grass or lawns to play on in this Brooklyn neighborhood—just concrete sidewalks with trees every few feet.

Christopher was raised by his mother, Voletta Wallace. She was a single parent and a preschool teacher who worked two jobs to support the household. The modest neighborhood they lived in was what Voletta described as "racially mixed." Voletta herself was from Trewany, Jamaica. She moved to New York in 1959, when Jamaica was still a British colony. Ten years after arriving in the U.S., she became a naturalized citizen. "I fell in love with the United States," said Voletta, who forty years later still speaks with a strong and distinct Jamaican accent. "I adopted America as my home." Two years later, in the United States, she met Christopher's father, George Latore.

Latore, a politician and a businessman who was also Jamaican-born, left them before Christopher's second birthday. Biggie's mother never remarried. The last time Biggie saw his father was about four years after he had abandoned them, when Biggie was about six years old. They never got close, and Biggie was left with no childhood memories of his father.

On Monday, March 4, 1996, George Latore died. It was exactly one year and five days before his estranged son was murdered. Voletta said the news of his father's death did not affect Biggie. He never really knew his father. His mother described the divorce as "a clean break" where "we parted ways and got on with our lives."

Biggie claimed in his music and during interviews that because his father moved out when he was a baby, he never had a male role model or father image to look up to. But his mother said otherwise. "His grandfather was a father figure for him," Voletta Wallace said, "even though he lived fourteen hundred miles away in Jamaica. Biggie loved and adored and respected him." He and his grandfather were buddies. Every year until Biggie was fifteen, he flew with his mother to Jamaica, back to his roots, for summer vacations. Jamaica, known for its eternal summer, has dense tropical forests, rivers, and miles of white beaches bordered by the Caribbean Sea. The setting was an ideal tropical atmosphere for Biggie to spend summers with his grandfather. It is also the island, with its rich cultural background, where reggae music was born, popularized by the late Bob Marley.

Fourteen hundred miles away, in a Brooklyn neighborhood, was where Voletta Wallace chose to raise her son. Besides relatives in Jamaica, Biggie also had aunts and an uncle living in New York City who spent time with him. The apartment his mother rented was in a "fairly decent" Brooklyn neighborhood. Voletta explained: "A lot of people talk about ghettos. It wasn't a rough neighborhood where I was afraid to go out my door, in other words." Still, an iron door installed at the front stoop barred any uninvited guests from entering their apartment building.

Voletta Wallace didn't move out of their Brooklyn walk-up until two years after her son became successful, around 1995. That was when what she described as "the real money" began pouring in. Voletta sublet the apartment to her brother. Three years later, the name Wallace remained on a label marking a buzzer for apartment 3L at the front-porch stoop of a brownstone at 226 Saint James Place.

The Wallaces' apartment, a third-floor walk-up in that tenement building on Saint James, near busy Fulton Street in Clinton Hill, was just half a block away from the stores and bars the kids hung out at. It was an inner-city neighborhood just up the street from the towering public housing projects where Biggie played as a child. As a teenager, Biggie ventured farther away, up Fulton at North Street, to one of the roughest sections of Brooklyn, called Bedford-Stuyvesant, just a ten-minute walk north.

The Fort Greene section in Brooklyn's Clinton Hill was where Voletta Wallace and her husband chose to have their child. They rented the apartment just before their son was born.

Christopher George Latore Wallace—he was given two middle names, after his father—was born in Brooklyn on Sunday, May 21, 1972. He weighed an even eight pounds. Voletta brought her baby boy—she called him "Chrissy-pooh"—home from Cumberland Hospital when he was eleven days old; home to the third-floor apartment he would grow up in; home to Clinton Hill, which, in 1972, was still a good neighborhood.

Bounded by the Brooklyn-Queens Expressway, and Classon, Atlantic, and Vanderbilt Avenues, the neighborhood was developed in the mid–nineteenth century for prosperous merchants squeezed out of Brooklyn Heights. By 1880 Clinton Avenue had become an aristocratic neighborhood known as Millionaires' Row, or "the Fifth Avenue of Brooklyn." The Fort Greene area was a silk-stocking district in the 1890s. Back then, Clinton Avenue and the surrounding streets were fashionable addresses. But when the Interborough Rapid Transit Subway, or the IRT, opened the neighborhood to commuters in 1908, many of the patrician inhabitants began to move away.

By the 1920s most of the former brownstone mansions were either destroyed, or divided and converted into rooming houses and furnished apartments, becoming the Clinton Hill of Biggie's boyhood. Not far from Biggie's neighborhood was the noisy Brooklyn Navy Yard on Flushing Avenue.

Biggie once described the Brooklyn of his youth as waking up to the warmed-over aroma of Chinese takeout and the clashing sounds of children squealing and of construction workers building and tearing down. There were trash-strewn vacant lots and buildings badly in need of rejuvenation that were, instead, havens for crime. "It's not a large area," NYPD detective Andre Parker commented, "but it covers a lot of people."

Christopher, like other kids who hung out on the streets of Brooklyn, was well known around the neighborhood to just about everyone there. As he got older, his mother called him Chris or Christopher. But to the neighborhood kids he was "Big." The name would help carry him into one of the shortest but most successful rap careers in the history of hip-hop. He would become notorious, the Notorious B.I.G. The streets toughened him up.

A lot of kids in the neighborhood were tagged with nicknames when they were growing up. By the time Christopher was about ten years old, his friends had begun calling him Big. The name caught on. Even at five years old, his size had intimidated his classmates. "He was always bigger than everyone else," Voletta Wallace recalled. As a result, the kids respected him, she said. As a teenager, he grew to be even bulkier, but not obese. He gained the bulk of his girth, his mother and childhood friends said, after he became famous and after he entered into a short-lived and rocky marriage in 1995 to singer Faith Evans. At the time of his death on March 9, 1997, Biggie carried nearly four hundred pounds on his six-foot-two-inch frame and wore triple-extra-large shirts and size 14EEE shoes. (Biggie, in 1995, once talked about his weight problem to *MTV News*: "It's a lot for a big person to get up on stage and rap, man . . . 'cause we get tired quick. For real, man, we be breathing hard." Besides his weight, latent childhood asthma also contributed to Biggie's labored breathing.)

When Biggie was about ten, he made his mother proud. His school had a Father's Day celebration and the kids talked about their fathers. "I remember he said to me, 'Ma, what their fathers did for them is what you did for me.' "

A single, working parent, she tried to instill a strong work ethic in her son.

By the time he was eleven, Biggie was bagging groceries at Met Foods, a corner market at Fulton and Saint James, just a block and a half up the street from his apartment building. Three years later, still hanging on a wall inside Met Foods was a photo with the caption "The Notorious B.I.G." It was Biggie's stage name. Inscribed were the words, "We'll always love you, Big Poppa." He worked there as a bag boy for about two years.

Most of the kids from Biggie's neighborhood rapped. It was characteristic of life on the streets of black America, kids rapping a combination of different rhymes and stories which became a national anthem of sorts for the streets, something they could identify with. Biggie was a product of that life in the 'hood in the 1980s and 1990s.

No other kids in that mostly poor Brooklyn neighborhood ever seriously expected they would actually become a rap star—except Biggie. He wanted to turn his rapping from a casual pastime into a big-time moneymaker. It was his ticket beyond his street, out of the 'hood and into the world of entertainment.

"I'm gonna be big one day. I'm gonna be a famous rapper," he once told the police at the Eighty-eighth after they picked him up. Detective Andre Parker recalled the exact moment that he learned Biggie actually *had* made it big. It was after Biggie's first album was released. "You remember that punk kid we used to have in here? He has an album out. Can you believe it? He *did* make it big,' " Parker recalled a fellow officer saying.

Once he became successful, he often went back to his old neighborhood to visit. Because Biggie knew firsthand just how tough it could be growing up in Clinton Hill, he never forgot the kids he left behind on the streets of Brooklyn. Several teenagers whom he saw street-hustling just like he used to, he hired for odd jobs. It got them off the streets. They became part of the group of many who surrounded the famous Notorious B.I.G., making up his entourage.

The kids looked up to Biggie as a hero figure. They wanted to make it, too, just like he had. To them, he was living proof that there was a way out of the ghetto. He also took a group of teenagers—including Kimberly Jones (performing as Lil' Kim), whom Biggie had mentored and was rumored to have once dated; Little Caesar (later known as Lil' Cease); Chico Delvico; Capone; Nino Brown; and Bugsy—and started a rap group. He named them Junior M.A.F.I.A., after the real street gang from "do or die" Bed-Stuy, and used them as backup singers. The group would go on to release albums of their own.

"After he made it, he always came back home," Detective Parker said, "once a week. He was good with the kids around here. The kids loved him. My nephew who lives in the neighborhood was crazy about him."

Even during his early years, Biggie was fiercely independent and self-assured. As a young boy, his favorite bedtime stories were *Christopher Robin* and *Winnie-the-Pooh* (thus the nickname Chrissy-pooh). Biggie and his mother regularly read nursery rhymes and biblical Scriptures together. As a youngster, Biggie wrote songs, rhyming them like the nursery rhymes he once read with his mother. What made Biggie stand out from the other neighborhood rhymers was that he never put the songs on paper. He kept them all in his head.

Even though Biggie may have been a mama's boy at home, being read to and coddled, in the neighborhood he had a tough exterior. But he didn't start hustling on the streets until he hit his teens. He loved playing basketball on the neighborhood courts. He attended local basketball games with his friends, and watched college and pro basketball games on TV. Still, he never played any organized school sports.

Puffy Combs once described what it was like watching Biggie play basketball. "A lot of people don't know that he had a set shot," Puffy told MTV shortly after Biggie's death. "It bugged me out one day. We were out in L.A. recording in a studio, and there was a basketball court and Biggie was taking shots and making shots, and I just couldn't believe that. That was something that was funny to me, that he was a real good basketball player. Nobody, nobody knows that, though."

The kids in the neighborhood knew it. Besides having a set shot, Biggie was larger than them and able to push his weight around on the court. But while Biggie may have been bigger than his classmates, he always looked younger, with his pudgy face and bassett-hound eyes. "He never had hair on his face. He had a baby face," his mother said. "Even as an adult, he couldn't grow a beard."

By the time Biggie was a teenager, he gave up his grocery-store job and childhood games to hustle $5 and $10 bags of weed on the corner for bigger pocket change. To MTV, Biggie explained: "I was a full-time, one hundred-percent hustler. Sellin' drugs, wakin' up early in the morning, hittin' the set selling my shit 'til the crack of dawn. My mother goin' to work would see me out there in the morning. That's how I was on it."

Biggie later rapped on his 1994 *Ready to Die* album about Pop from Brother Mike's Barber Shop at 932 Fulton Street. The barbershop was just half a block from the corner where the kids hung out. From that corner the kids would sell a little reefer, drink malt liquor, Moët, and a concoction of Alize liqueur mixed with Hennessy cognac coined "Thug's Passion" by Tupac Shakur.

"He was trying to fit in," said Wakeem Widdi, owner of the corner market where Biggie's mother did most of her grocery shopping and where Biggie once worked. "He smoked [marijuana] occasionally. He wasn't as bad as people think. He was sweet to everybody."

When Biggie was fifteen, Detective Parker recalled, police hauled him into the New York City's Eighty-eighth Precinct again, this time for questioning about a local murder. Biggie wasn't a suspect; but detectives thought he might have witnessed the crime. They merely wanted to talk to him. Biggie told them he "didn't see nothin'." Biggie evoked the so-called "code of silence," a rule he learned early on the streets which would ironically spill over into his own murder investigation a decade later.

"We had one homicide we brought him in for," Detective Parker said. "That was the worst crime we ever questioned him about. Everything else was petty. We brought all the kids in for questioning who were in the area at the time of the murder. The block that he grew up on, most of the people who live there own their own homes. But that corner where he lived is rough. There have always been drugs on that corner—heroin, crack, you name it."

According to the Brooklyn cops who knew him, Biggie was never a full-on drug dealer. He hustled some on the streets, selling small quantities of drugs—nickel bags and dime bags, as the officers call them. Brooklyn cops insisted that Biggie didn't have anything to do with "the real dealers" in the area, those who dealt in heavier drugs and larger quantities.

"It was small-time stuff he was doing," Detective Parker said. "He was just a neighborhood guy out there hustling. You'd hear his records, about how he would rob people. He didn't do nothin' like that. He was just a kid comin' up. He was a scared kid. He wasn't a roughneck. For the most part, he was a good kid. He wasn't one of the ones we considered bad. He would be on the corners selling like nickels and dimes. To be a drug dealer you have to be selling and supplying to other drug dealers. He wasn't doing nothin' like that. If you want to call somebody selling weed and nickel bags a drug dealer, go ahead. But he wasn't what *we* called a drug dealer."

A uniformed beat officer who patrolled Biggie's Brooklyn neighborhood, and who asked that his name not be used, said borough officers knew Biggie as just a regular kid. "He wasn't a thug. He was just a street kid," the officer said.

Voletta Wallace explained it further. "The story with Christopher is this: He knew a lot of people who did things, bad things. He hung out with them [because they were] from his life, his neighborhood. He would come home from school, do his jobs in the house, then hang out with those guys. I think Chris may have been the lookout for them. I know he wasn't out there selling drugs. He hated jail. It was not something he looked up to. It was something he detested. There were so many times the cops came to my house and said, 'Miss Wallace, I know you. I know your son. He's hanging out with the wrong crowd.' "

Even in that environment, with the violence and street crimes going on around him, not to mention his personal involvement in drug hustling, Biggie excelled in school, receiving top grades. His mother enrolled him in a private Catholic school and took him with her regularly to her church prayer meetings. Biggie attended Brooklyn-area Catholic schools until high school. He was always a good student, especially in math, science, and art. He maintained high-enough marks to make the honor roll each semester.

When he was four, his mother had enrolled him in the Quincy-Lexington Open Door Day Care Center in Brooklyn. Then, from age six until he entered middle school at Queen of All Saints, he had attended St. Peter's Claver Elementary School. From Queen of All Saints he attended Westinghouse High School. However, over his mother's strong objections, he dropped out of school during his junior year, when he was seventeen.

"He received an English award, math award, you name it. Every year he was in school he received academic awards," Voletta said. That was why she was more than perplexed when her son decided to become a high-school dropout. Biggie had shown academic promise. And she had always emphasized the importance of an education.

One of the things Biggie enjoyed most about school was taking art classes. He loved to draw. What's more, he was good at it. "He could look at you and sketch you, and you would come out perfect as a peach," his mother said. "I always thought he was going to be a graphic artist."

But Biggie's visions of one day becoming a commercial artist dissolved when he no longer saw a lucrative financial future in it. Once he started hanging out on the streets and hustling, everything changed. "He loved money," Voletta said—and high school, to him, didn't hold the promise of cash; hustling on the streets did.

"I had fire coming out of my ears," his mother explained. After all, she had been attending night college classes to further her own education. She would have preferred seeing Biggie finish high school and continue on to college. It was what she had always envisioned for him and what she had prepared him for. She saw school, not rap, as a way out of the neighborhood for her son. "I asked him, 'What's the matter with you? You *have* to stay in school.' " Robert Izzo, coordinator of student affairs at Westinghouse High, said he didn't know Biggie had dropped out of school until afterward. Biggie was a volunteer in Izzo's Big Brother program. "He worked well with the kids, the younger ones. He didn't talk down to them." He said that Biggie and other students "used to hang out in my office and talk about music. He wasn't the bad guy everybody made him out to be."

But continuing in school was not to be. School bored Biggie. For Biggie, it was just the opposite; he saw street action as a way out. While he was tied strongly to his mother and respected her opinions, he told her he was quitting school anyway so he could "do something that's more challenging. I'm gonna make you proud of me."

His mother couldn't talk any sense into him, so she gave up. She knew she couldn't fight him because his mind was already made up. Biggie was his mother's son—strong-willed—and once his mind was made up, he was hard to budge. She allowed him to drop out.

After quitting high school when he was still seventeen, Biggie, who hated the idea of going to jail, was arrested for selling crack during a visit with friends in North Carolina. He stayed in jail a few days until his mother was able to wire $25,000 to a bail bondsman; Voletta used a portion of a $90,000 lawsuit settlement against New York City for a broken foot Biggie had suffered after falling out of a public bus. "It [the settlement] was money for him," Voletta said. "It belonged to him." After Biggie's release, Voletta said she called the bondsman and asked for the posted bail money to be returned. "He [the bondsman] said it was his," Voletta said. "We never got it back."

Aside from hustling drugs, Biggie became known in the neighborhood for his rap skills. The same year he dropped out of school, he got heavy into rap—and he wrote his own rhymes. Biggie always enjoyed music, his mother said. "All I know is he was making a lot of noise in the house at a very young age," she said. "I would tell him, 'I wish you would stop that noise, all that banging, all that talking.' He would say, 'Ma, it's not noise. One of these days this noise is gonna make you rich.' But to me it was noise, you know? Christopher was rapping always, but he started taking it seriously when he was seventeen or eighteen."

During those years, Biggie hung out a lot with his friend, Chico Delvico, who lived two doors up. They MCed in a small back room using two Technics turntables, compliments of Chico's mother. Biggie often ate his favorite meal, breakfast—a combination of waffles, ice cream, and bacon—at Chico's house. Chico's back room was where Biggie got serious about rap. He perfected his use of a playful banter with his lyrics, what back then was considered to be simple rap.

"I remember bits and pieces of it," Chico's sister, Jessie Lyons, told a reporter. "But [the songs] always ended the same, with Biggie talking about how he was going to make it big . . . having money and success, and going away from here."

But soon the lyrics would change, and gangsta rap would become all the rage. With it came a sense of menace in the lyrics. Biggie's playful, bantering lyrics became passé. Rapping about expensive cars and neighborhood girls gave way to rapping about Uzis, whores, and hustlers. If Biggie wanted to get in the game, he would have to stand out from his competitors. He would have to develop his own style of stage presence and revise his lyrics to reflect the latest hardcore nature of rap—specifically, gangsta rap.

He did. He had the drive to excel, to rise to the top of the rap genre at the time. He became one of the founding fathers of gangsta rap. Biggie worked hard at perfecting his own style of delivery, using his husky-voiced, harsh sound to rap the tough lyrics he wrote himself. He liked the street stories from Clinton Hill he could tell in his songs.

Besides hanging out with Chico, he also palled around and sang with the OGB Crew—or the Old Gold Brothers—from nearby Bedford Avenue. They weren't rappers, but their soulful style helped Biggie's versatility and expanded his repartee. Using Chico's back room as a makeshift studio, Biggie—who back then called himself Quest—cut some demo tapes of his own original rhymes. It was a defining moment for Biggie. At age nineteen, it would launch his career and forever change his life. Biggie would go from rapping on a street corner to recording in a sound studio. He would literally become an overnight success. Biggie stood on the crest of a wave, just within reach of diving headfirst into a lucrative musical career.

4

THE MUSIC

IN EARLY 1992, Biggie's homemade demo tapes were circulated throughout the Clinton Hill and Bedford-Stuyvesant neighborhoods to folks who already knew who he was. A music store, the Culture Lion on Fulton Street, just two blocks from Biggie's apartment building, sold the cassettes. People liked what they heard, and his music was an instant hit in the 'hood. But people outside the neighborhood still didn't know who he was.

A neighborhood pal, who MCed with Biggie as 50 Grand, gave a demo tape to Mister Cee, who at the time was working with Big Daddy Kane, a well-known fast-speed rapper, also from Brooklyn, who grew up there several years before Biggie.

Mister Cee saw Biggie's potential. He befriended him and told him about a column in the magazine *The Source* called "Unsigned Hype." It featured new artists. Mister Cee wanted to give columnist Matt Life (known professionally as Matty C) one of Biggie's demo tapes. Biggie didn't think the tape was that good, but he told Mister Cee, "Fuck it. Send it in." But first, Biggie remade a cleaner copy of the demo, then Mister Cee gave that one to Matt Life. It worked. The columnist liked the sound and mentioned it, alongside Biggie's photo, in the magazine's March 1992 edition. That modest mention marked Biggie's first national publicity.

About the same time, Sean "Puffy" Combs, who by then was a young, energetic newcomer to the music scene, was working for Uptown Records. He had ambitions of his own to make a mark in the industry. He was always scouting for new talent. He called Mister Cee, inquiring about some possible new rap acts and demo tapes to listen to. At the time, Puffy was Uptown's national director of A&R. Mister Cee told

Puffy he had a couple of new tapes, including a demo from "this kid from the 'hood" who was still unsigned. "He's big. He's hot," Mister Cee told Puffy when he described Biggie to him. Puffy directed Mister Cee to send along the tape.

Puffy, too, liked what he heard. He later told MTV that he listened to the tape over and over and couldn't stop listening. "As soon as I put it on, it just bugged me out," he said. "I listened to it for days and days, hours and hours. And his voice just hypnotized me."

Puffy was anxious to meet Biggie, but he didn't have his telephone number. Mister Cee didn't have it, either. So Puffy started looking for Biggie. He called people he knew in Brooklyn, and he drove down Fulton Street, asking around for Biggie. He eventually tracked him down and arranged to meet him for lunch that week in a Brooklyn cafe. During the meeting, Puffy told Biggie he thought they would make a good team and that he could make him rich. Puffy told him, "It sounds like you could rhyme forever. I wanna sign you."

What Puffy was proposing to him was a music contract. Biggie was beside himself. He knew this was the break he'd been waiting for. But he tried not to show his elation. He just sat there, calmly and quietly listening, with a deadpan look on his face.

Puffy, too, was excited, but he showed it. He wanted to sign Biggie and he didn't hold back his enthusiasm. He had just finished working on records for Jodeci and Mary J. Blige, Father C, and Heavy D. He was looking for a new project, an undiscovered, fresh new artist he could promote. He was ready to break in a new talent, someone who had the makings to become a big star. Puffy believed he'd discovered that new talent in Biggie. At the same time, he thought to himself, "How am I gonna market him? He looks like a liquor-store robber." So he decided to capitalize on that look, emphasizing it rather than trying to cover it up.

Biggie's mobster look was born. Puff felt he could be the producer who could put Biggie—the total package of look and sound—on the rap map. He would present Biggie as the rapper mob don.

But Biggie's mother felt otherwise. She was afraid her son was about to be exploited. Even though it was the break in Biggie's career he had been waiting for, his mother didn't see it that way. "I resented the fact that they saw this young kid [and] they wanted to make him rich. Mister Cee discovered Christopher when he was about nineteen and introduced him to Puffy. I figured if I ever met Puffy, I would strangle him. I wanted to meet Puffy. I wanted Christopher to do his music and excel in it, but at the same time, get an education. I wanted to tell Puffy that. But, evidently, Christopher never wanted an education. He was promised to be made rich. Puffy told him, 'Look, with this type of material, I can make you a millionaire,' and that's exactly what happened."

Puffy presented Biggie with an Uptown contract and Biggie signed on the dotted line.

Now that he had a contract and a record producer, Biggie officially changed his performing name from "Quest," and his childhood nickname of "Big," to "Biggie Smalls." The name was fashioned after a character of the same name in the film *Uptown Saturday Night*, starring Sidney Poitier and Bill Cosby; that became his moniker, his tag.

Abraham Widdi, Biggie's longtime friend from his old neighborhood, said it was Biggie who made Puffy famous, not the other way around. Abraham believed because Biggie was so talented, eventually he would have been discovered. Puffy just happened to be the first to find him, he said. "If it wasn't for B.I.G., Puff wouldn't be who he is or where he is today," Abraham emphasized. Whatever the impetus, the ambitious Puffy rose quickly at Uptown from an A&R director to vice president.

Simultaneously, Biggie's star was also rising. In 1993, Biggie contributed to Mary J. Blige's *What's the 411?* album. Biggie was recognized for it. He was making a real name for himself in the rap scene. And he cut his now classic debut single, "Party and Bullshit." He was a fast-rising star.

Together, Puffy and Biggie completed Biggie's first album. However, in 1991, before it could be released, Puffy was ousted from Uptown. He was let go after a management dispute with Uptown's CEO, Andre Harrell. Rumors on the street said the firing was for insubordination.

Puffy, however, landed on his entrepreneurial feet in 1995 by scoring a $15 million distribution deal with Arista Records to take his Bad Boy Entertainment record label, which Uptown Records had started for him, to another level. Without Puffy, Uptown decided they no longer wanted Biggie on their label, so they dropped him, too. Not too long after that, Puffy brought Biggie over to the Bad Boy family.

There was an unknown rapper also named Biggie Smalls who was active in the music scene in California when Biggie signed on at Bad Boy. Puffy Combs once explained to a reporter, "There was another rapper called Biggie Smalls, so we couldn't use that [name]. Biggie wanted to call himself 'Notorious.' " To prevent confusion with the other Smalls, Biggie devised a new moniker by simply adding "Notorious" in front of his nickname "Big." (After the release of Biggie's hit single "Big Poppa," he began referring to himself as Big Poppa as well. That moniker, too, caught on, giving him two stage names.)

All of Biggie's attention was now on his musical career. He saw his fan base swell. Life, as a result, was changing fast for the onetime street hustler. He was on his way up. He had money in his pockets and women on his arms. Before he became a well-known rapper, he was shy with women and never had a long-term girlfriend. Now he could take his pick.

People on the street were starting to recognize Biggie. "When I was in the 'hood," he told an MTV reporter as he stood on a corner in his old neighborhood, "and, like, I'm hustlin' and a car pull up, you know what I'm sayin'? [I'm] starin'. I'll probably grip up on my joint, you know what I'm sayin'? Not knowin' what's the deal, y'know? But now, me being a rapper, there a car pull up, it could be a fan, you know. They could want an autograph. Y'know, it's kind of sickie but it's cool."

Well-known or not, Biggie continued hanging out with his friends in Brooklyn. He and Damien would go to Biggie's friend Abraham Widdi's house and work out with weights in the basement. At night they would go out to kick it at CC's Club in Manhattan. Or they would stay in Brooklyn and throw dice and drink beer at Hodgie's, a corner saloon on Fulton Street. Tupac Shakur, already a star in his own right in the rap community, would sometimes show up to throw dice with them.

"Biggie would call me up and say, 'C'mon, Abraham, party with me. I'll pick ya up in an hour.' He would show up in a stretch limo and we'd cruise Brooklyn," Abraham said, adding, "He was fun to be around." It was just friends—not stars—hanging out together, he said. "Tupac and B.I.G. were good friends."

In September 1994, Biggie's debut solo album *Ready to Die* was released on Puffy's new Bad Boy label. It was produced by Easy Mo Bee and was an instant hit. It had two No. 1 singles—"Big Poppa" and "One More Chance"—that went double platinum after they each sold more than two million copies. And "One More Chance" was named *Billboard*'s Rap Single of the Year.

The album also included other hit songs: "Juicy," "Me and My B*tch," "Warning," and "The What." "Juicy" was a celebratory song about one man's rise from life on the streets. It was an instant hit because kids could identify with its visual street lyrics. That was the impetus that seemed to draw listeners to Biggie's music—real-life tales straight from the street.

In June of 1995, Biggie released a maxi-single that included two different remixes of "One More Chance / Stay with Me," which originally appeared on the *Ready to Die* album. The single debuted on the *Billboard* R&B Top 40 chart; in 1995, Biggie won Best Rap Artist and Best Rap Single for the track at the *Billboard* Awards. "One More Chance" debuted at number 5 on the *Billboard* list, tying Michael Jackson's "Scream / Childhood" as the highest debuting single ever.

The success of *Ready to Die* was everything Biggie and Puffy had hoped for.

Besides recording his own hits, Biggie also shared studio time with Michael Jackson, appearing as a guest rapper on Michael's *HIStory— Past, Present and Future Book 1* album. He also appeared on R. Kelly's debut album. Then, appearing alongside Sticky Fingers and MC Lyte, Biggie played himself on an episode of the TV series *New York Undercover*. He was branching out.

He was becoming known not only on the East Coast, but on the West, as well. He was said to be single-handedly responsible for the crossover success of East Coast rap because his music had appeal for rap fans on both coasts. His songs were considered to be ghetto anthologies, no matter what the geography. Biggie intensified New York's style of rap and its emphasis on machismo by focusing even more on the criminal life, thus his emphasis on gangsta rap. In the East, rappers dreamt of leaving the projects in Brooklyn and moving up to pricey Manhattan. Conversely, the vision in the West was dramatically different. The sheer physical differences from coast to coast created sharply contrasting ghetto communities. In L.A. they dreamt of staying put, staying close to the streets they came from, with their rhymes reflecting the values of their neighborhoods. In contrast to Biggie, Tupac was a product of staying close to the 'hood, to L.A.

Biggie rapped about robbing and killing—the inner-city thug life—and about how much conditions had deteriorated in his neighborhood during his lifetime, a period when he said fistfights had been replaced with semiautomatic gunfire. His rhymes conjured up visions of homies, hard liquor, 'hood rats, and gats.

His style was a mix of old soul and gangsta rap, setting him apart from other artists, such as the pioneers of West Coast rap: Ice Cube, Too Short, Eazy-E, and Tupac. Gangsta/playa rap was born with Biggie's style. He dressed and rapped like an old-time mobster. He owned the look.

But not all was a bed of roses for Biggie. In March of 1993, his mother, Voletta Wallace, underwent a mastectomy of her right breast. Biggie never went to see her. It was said he was so upset by it that he couldn't face visiting her in the hospital. (Voletta since has made a full recovery.)

Then, Biggie had several run-ins with the law on charges ranging from alleged beatings to drugs and weapons possession.

Next, in an accusation that would haunt Biggie until his death, the word on the street was that he, along with Puffy Combs, helped set up the 1994 ambush robbery and shooting of Tupac Shakur in Manhattan, a rumor both men vehemently denied. The two were never charged and the case was never solved; but the rumors never died.

The same year, Biggie and his entourage were accused of beating Nathaniel Banks, a music promoter. The altercation happened after one of Biggie's concerts was canceled in Camden, New Jersey. On Wednesday, January 8, 1995, after Biggie failed to show up in court, an arrest warrant was issued in Camden, charging Biggie with assault and robbery. Biggie was thrown in jail for four days, but he was later acquitted. His mother explained that Biggie hadn't been present when the crime took place. "The show was canceled, so he didn't go," Voletta Wallace said. "A fan was upset, and that's how it all got started."

Even though he was acquitted in criminal court two years later, on Monday, January 27, 1997, Biggie suffered a legal setback in the case when a civil-court jury awarded Banks $41,000 in damages plus $1,700 in medical bills (Banks's jaw was broken), ordering Biggie to pay.

Biggie's legal wrangles would continue, most of which were caused by his own doing. In March 1995, as he and a friend were leaving the Palladium, a nightclub in Manhattan's Union Square, a crowd of autograph-seekers harassed them, and, after some words were exchanged, two of the fans hopped in a cab to leave. Biggie and the friend followed the cab. When they caught up with it, they took base-ball bats and smashed the windows. Biggie pleaded guilty to criminal mischief and fourth-degree harassment. He was ordered to perform one hundred hours of community service.

In August 1996, Biggie was charged with gun and marijuana pos-session after police, who said they were checking out a parking com-plaint in the neighborhood (Biggie later expressed skepticism about that claim) found weapons in his Teaneck, New Jersey, condominium. The year before, Biggie had moved into a townhouse at the Courts of Glenpointe condominium complex, a private gated community in Tea-neck, about twenty-five miles from Brooklyn. Property records show that Biggie purchased the condominium in November 1995 for $310,000. According to real-estate listings for the complex when the condominiums were built in the 1980s, that was the price for a three-bedroom triplex with amenities such as a private elevator and a Jacuzzi.

Police had staked out Biggie's residence, then raided it. Undercover officers confiscated an infrared rifle, among other firearms. Besides the infrared rifle, designed for use at night, and marijuana, the raid netted a cache of weapons, including a submachine gun, several semiauto-matic handguns, a pistol, and a large quantity of ammunition, includ-ing hollow-point bullets, as outlined in the police report.

Officer Robert McCabe, who processed Biggie at the Teaneck PD's jail, said Biggie was "very cooperative." "I photographed and fingerprinted him," he said. "He was very pleasant. He took a snooze in his cell block. He was in for quite a few hours before his paperwork could be done and he was released."

Biggie continued making trouble for himself. Next, on Sunday, September 15, 1996 (coincidentally, two days after Tupac's death), Biggie and fellow rappers were caught smoking weed while sitting on a Brooklyn street in Biggie's parked "luxury car," as police described it in their report. An anonymous tip led police to Biggie's vehicle. After officers arrived, all three occupants of the car were issued summonses to appear in court. They were each charged with drug possession. Biggie, along with his friends, was released from custody on his own recognizance. The outcome of the case was pending when Biggie was killed.

In the midst of his scrapes with the law, Biggie became a father at the age of twenty. He had had an affair with a young woman from his old Brooklyn neighborhood and she got pregnant and had a baby girl. While Biggie took the responsibility of being a father, he chose not to marry his daughter's mother. They named their baby T'Yanna.

Also in the middle of his legal troubles, Biggie met his future wife, Faith Evans. It was on Thursday, August 31, 1995, during a Bad Boy Family photo shoot in midtown Manhattan, home of Bad Boy's headquarters. The two performers had never met before, even though they both had contracts with Bad Boy Entertainment. Although Faith had signed with Bad Boy in 1994 after Puffy Combs discovered her while she was singing backup for Al B. Sure in L.A., she didn't know who Biggie was.

Faith, who originally was from Newark, New Jersey, was impressed with Biggie. She did most of the talking that night while he listened. Biggie was reserved, in part because he was shy around women, but also because he wanted to make a good impression on Faith. He, too, was smitten. Faith later said that what had attracted her the most to Biggie was his charm, sweetness, and quiet manner.

Faith offered to give Biggie a ride home from the photo shoot. They ended up staying together that night. From that first encounter on, they saw each other every day. But it was to be a short courtship.

Just about a week after that first meeting, Biggie announced to Faith, "I'm gonna marry you." In one of his last interviews in 1996,

Biggie explained it to *Vibe* like this: "I never, ever met no girl like my wife. She talks to me like nobody else talked to me before. When I first saw her, she was killing me with those eyes. I rolled up to her and said, 'You're the type of girl I would marry.' She said, 'Why don't you?' So I was like, fuck it, it's on."

Eight days after their first meeting, Biggie and Faith made it official. On Friday, September 8, 1995, a county clerk in Rockland County, New York, pronounced them husband and wife. A mutual friend stood up for them. They didn't tell their families, and the couple had no wedding reception or honeymoon. Most of their friends at Bad Boy didn't know right away, either, that they had married. They kept it under wraps. Biggie didn't introduce Faith to his mother until after the ceremony.

According to accounts by both Biggie and Faith, they never had an opportunity to really get to know each other. In fact, Biggie continued to live at home with his mother after the wedding. He didn't move out of his mother's apartment for two months. Faith moved in with him for a short time. Then the couple found a duplex in Clinton Hill about five blocks from Biggie's mother's home, near his neighborhood.

In June, about a month after the wedding ceremony, Biggie's maxi-single was released. Faith was working on her self-named debut album, which eventually went platinum, while Biggie focused his energies on his own career. The couple didn't spend much time together. Their relationship, as a result, suffered. Their marriage began to unravel. By the time they finally did get to know each other, they had separated. Eighteen months after the wedding, their marriage was all but over.

"He was doin' his thing as an artist, I was doin' my thing as an artist, so it was kind of hard," Faith told *People* magazine in a November 5, 1999, article. "He was a good person, but definitely not ready for marriage. I tried my best to be a good wife for as long as I could take the disrespect," she said, referring to his rumored indiscretions of infidelity.

That was when Faith changed a tattoo she had that said "Big," making it read instead, "Big Faye."

Despite their rocky start, the two would parent a son, Christopher Jordan, named after basketball star Michael Jordan. Biggie respected and looked up to Michael and had become friends with him. Biggie called his son C. J. for short. He was proud of his baby boy. Lots of snapshots were taken of him cradling his son in his arms.

Still, soon after the birth of their son, Biggie told Cheo Hodari Coker with *Vibe* magazine that he and Faith should have waited longer before marrying. "I married her after knowing her eight days," he told *Vibe*, "and I was happy. That was my baby. At the same time, with us being so spontaneous, we did it backwards. Maybe she won't admit it, but I will. We shoulda got to know each other and then got married. The relationship kinda dissolved, but we're still gonna be friends. I love her. We have a [new] baby together, and we're always gonna love our kids. Who knows? Ten years from now we might even get back together."

Before their separation, the couple had moved into Biggie's Teaneck, New Jersey, townhouse, purchased by Biggie during their on-again, off-again relationship. Biggie's friends Lil' Cease and Damien Butler moved in after Faith Evans, her daughter, and their baby boy moved out. After the separation, Biggie said he wanted to be a better father and be more involved in his children's lives. He still wanted to settle down, even though he and Faith were living apart. "I want to see my kids get old," he told *Vibe*. "I want to go to my daughter's wedding. I want to go to my son's wedding. I want to go to their sons' weddings. And you ain't gonna be able to see it wilding."

Biggie wouldn't be partying for a while. His leg was badly broken in a car accident in September 1996. Lil' Cease was driving the two of them when they crashed on the New Jersey Turnpike. Biggie's left leg was fractured in three places. A steel pin was surgically inserted to stabilize the bone. During his more than two-month stay at the Kessler Institute for Rehabilitation in New Jersey, when he wasn't in therapy, Biggie spent most of his time writing songs. At the time of his discharge, he was still in a wheelchair. He moved from the chair to crutches and, ultimately, to a cane. He was still recovering, and a hospital outpatient undergoing rehabilitation, at the time of his death; he still used a cane to walk.

Biggie's hospitalization had given him plenty of time to think. He decided he did not want to party as much as he had in the past, and planned, upon his release, to settle down. It was during one of his last interviews, done the night before he was killed, that Biggie became introspective with a *Vibe* reporter. "I think there are a lot more lessons that I need to learn," he said. "There are a lot more things I need to experience, a lot more places I need to go before I can finally say, 'Okay, I had my days.' A lot more shit have to go down, 'cause I want a lot more."

After his death, Faith described Biggie to MTV as "just a funny guy. . . . He was very loving. I guess he had the gift of gab. He had a way with words, you know?"

His way with words—often tough—carried over into his music. His storytelling was popular because people could relate to it. He once said about his own music, which some said was a cross between Barry White, Howlin' Wolf, and Dolemite, "I may be a big, black, ugly dude, but I got style."

Yet because of that tough-talking gangsta persona—he always wore a frown or scowl on his face, what people referred to as his "street-soldier stare"—there were people who felt Biggie was, at the least, standoffish and, at the worst, unkind. The ramification for Biggie was that some people feared or were intimidated by him. Faith summed it up to *Vibe* like this: "A lot of people would tell me that he seems like he's mean, but he wasn't like that at all. He actually liked to joke with the people he knew. Like if he knew somebody and thought they were approaching him and were kind of hesitant or whatever, like they were expecting him to be mean, he would actually act like that until the person was gone, and then laugh once they were gone. But, I guess that was just all a part of . . . him and all his friends. They had a really different type of humor."

Biggie remained mostly silent after Tupac Shakur in 1996, on the B side of his *Hit 'Em Up* single, called Biggie a "fat muthafucka" and claimed to have "fucked" his wife. As if that weren't enough, Tupac went further and threatened him in a song.

Biggie later explained to writer Cheo Hodari Coker in a *Vibe* article that the controversy was simply the result of a messy separation from his wife. Faith began seeing other people, and so did Biggie. The problems started, Biggie said, when their dating got played up in the press. "People was like, 'When she stopped fuckin' with Big, she started fuckin' with Tupac, and Big started fuckin' with Lil' Kim.'"

Faith denied having an affair with Tupac. After both rappers were murdered, she told *People* magazine, "People said that I'm the reason they are dead. If I wasn't as strong-minded as I am, I would probably have been somewhere trying to kill myself."

Biggie himself was not so chaste. He carried on what some said was a very public affair with Lil' Kim from his Brooklyn neighborhood, someone he had mentored along with other members of Junior M.A.F.I.A. Biggie went on to produce Lil' Kim's breakout album, *Hardcore*. Biggie's mother, Voletta, said the so-called affair between her son and Kim was embellished upon and overrated.

"He took kids from off that block," she said, "from out of the neighborhood, and formed a group, Junior M.A.F.I.A. Lil' Kim is from that crowd with Little Caesar. She exaggerated her relationship with Christopher one hundred and ten percent. She was a little girl, and Christopher made her famous. 'Oh, he was my man. He was my Big Poppa,' she would carry on. The way she was talking, a lot of people resented her. I don't resent her. She's young. I don't hold it against her. She's very grateful. She cared for him a lot. He was her boss. She was getting her paycheck through him. She was grateful because she was struggling on the street. He gave her a record deal, and this girl has made millions of dollars."

Biggie said there wasn't anything he could do about the public needling Tupac gave him in Tupac's lyrics about a relationship with Faith. Biggie told *Vibe*: "I got to make jokes about that shit. I can't be the niggah running around all serious. The shit is so funny to me because nobody will ever know the truth. They'll always believe what they want to believe. Pac says he fucked [Faith]. I asked Faith, 'You fucked him?' She said, 'No.' I can't get to ask him about it. So am I gonna hate her for the rest of her life thinking she did something, or am I gonna be a man about the situation? If she did it, she can't do it no more, so let's just get on with our lives. I hold grudges, but I can't hate nobody. That's not my nature."

Besides his relationship with Faith, Biggie was also romantically linked with rap newcomer Charli Baltimore, whose real name was Tiffany Lane, from Philadelphia. Shortly before he was killed, Biggie began dating Charli, who took her stage moniker from the Geena Davis character of the same name in the movie *The Long Kiss Goodnight*.

Charli was encouraged by Biggie to get into the hip-hop music business. "I was rapping before I met Biggie," she told MTV, "but it wasn't anything serious. It was just a bugging-out type of thing, and when I met him—not right when I met him, but a little into our relationship—I would play around and rhyme, and he was like, 'You got skills. You should keep rhyming.' "

Biggie didn't live long enough to see her become a success. In 1998, about a year after his death, her first solo album, *Ice*, was released. A single, "Money," was also featured in the soundtrack of the movie *Woo*, starring actress Jada Pinkett, who later would marry rapper/actor Will Smith.

As Biggie became more successful, and in turn more famous, Faith—herself an accomplished singer, songwriter, and arranger—saw a change in him. "I started feeling like I couldn't really tell the difference," Faith told MTV, "but that might have been because I was goin' through my personal problems in our marriage. But I always felt like in the beginning it was obvious. It was just a clear difference. He was just nothing like the raps he used to write. . . . You would get this idea of him that he cares about his money or he raps about clothes, money, and women, and that all of those things were a part of his reality, to some extent."

There was more to life, she contended, and she expressed that to her husband. "After a certain point," Faith continued, "he did express to me a couple of times that he was starting to realize that. But, of course, this is after you had your fun and you've already dabbled in and indulged yourself in all these other things. That's just a part of life. I didn't look at him any differently. I just always hoped that . . . when he got really successful he wouldn't start to change. He didn't really change, but I guess everybody else treated him differently."

People may have treated Biggie differently because by then he, next to Tupac, was one of the top hip-hop artists in the country, if not the world. He was a huge success in his own right. And he was being recognized for the authenticity of his sound and the realistic tales he wove into his songs. He once told Peter Spirer, director of the hip-hop documentary *Rhyme and Reason*, "The hardest thing I ever had to overcome is really just making the transition from being a street hustlin' niggah to, like, a star."

Before he got into the music business, Biggie, young and inexperienced, had a romantic, unrealistic notion of what it would be like to be a star. Mostly he thought it would be brothers-in-rap hanging out together, chilling. That appealed to him. But once he was actually inside the rap game and a part of that scene, and after the rap feud began, he saw what came with it: the jealousy, the backstabbing, and the threats. He was getting regular death threats on his telephone at home. He became disillusioned. He didn't like the competition that came with the business, competing with people he had once called his friends, specifically Tupac Shakur. To him, the business was turning ugly. (Ironically, in death both Tupac and Big still were competing with one another. When MTV named its top twenty-five videos for the decade, Biggie's "Hypnotize" was number 16, with Tupac's "California Love" at number 19.)

Even though he was a huge success, Biggie was beginning to tire of the rap scene and the negative hype that surrounded it. Before he was murdered, he was in a soul-searching mode and often talked seriously about getting out of the business and into something different. One thing he did like about the business, though, was the cash that came with it. "I really want to stop," he told *The Source* just weeks before his death. "If I was financially stable, I could. I figure if I was to make a cool $10 or $15 million . . . I would quit." He wanted to make enough money to one day leave it all behind.

Puffy Combs conceded there had been a time when Biggie no longer enjoyed rapping. "He wasn't really enjoying making the music as much," Puffy told MTV. "He was just trying to give you his story. On this [new] album, on *Life After Death*, he really enjoyed making the music. And then, he's had a son since then, and a daughter, and, I mean, just his family life, he enjoyed his kids a lot more. And just as a person—he was growing as a person. We all—We're in this and we're blessed to have the success that we have at a young age, but at the same time, it's like we're still just growing up. We're still making mistakes."

Just days before his death Biggie told then-*Vibe* reporter Cheo Hodari Coker: "I'm like a diamond, I got so many different cuts. Niggahs can't see me like that, not the ones that's hatin' me. But those dudes that are hatin' and disrespecting the whole baller living . . . when you get into the game and sign your record deal, do you just want to sell three hundred units and live with your mother? No. You want to sell millions of records and buy the big house with the big fence and have your daughter and all your kids playin' in the big yard. You don't want to be that broke rapper. Why are you mad at me 'cause I'm happy I got some money? I'm happy, so that's what I talk about."

What Biggie liked most about the business was the travel and camaraderie that came with it. As a rapper on tour, he was able to travel around the country, to places he'd never been before. He entered the business to do something he was good at and enjoyed doing, which was to write rap and perform, and in the process make good money—a cool $65,000 a show. He enjoyed performing in front of sell-out crowds. At the same time, Biggie felt the rap game carried with it a lot of disrespect. What he disliked most was the fierce competition.

Even though he was becoming disillusioned with the business, Biggie enjoyed making his second album. In his record-company biography that accompanied his second CD, Biggie wrote, "When I did the first album, I was in a living hell, stressed and depressed. I was more relaxed making this one, and I'm proud of what I came up with." Ironically, the *Life After Death* album unintentionally ended up being his swan song: Ads for the record depicted him, dressed all in black, leaning against a tombstone in a graveyard, attended by his own ghost. A biblical quote was written across his chest: "Whosoever believeth in Him should not perish but have eternal life." The album's cover showed Biggie, donning an undertaker's hat and overcoat, leaning against the back of a black hearse.

It was different from his first album, where he simply told his stories about living in the inner city. By the time he made *Life After Death*, more than two years after his debut CD, he had come of age, moved out of Brooklyn and away from the hustling racket on the street corners. So on the second album he made mention of the perks that went with his new life: wearing the best designer clothes (down to his underwear), such as Versace and Moschino; being chauffeured in luxury cars and stretch limos; using cell phones; drinking Cristal champagne. It meant rising above the kid-on-the-street image portrayed in his earlier music. He was moving past that life, growing, evolving into a more responsible adult from the days of being just a punk kid. "I make music about what I know, you know what I'm saying?" he told MTV shortly before his death. "If I'd a worked at McDonald's, I'd a made rhyme about Big Macs and fries and stuff like that. I'm in Brooklyn, I see hustlin', I see killin', I see gamblin', I see girls, I see cars. That's what I rap about, what's in my environment." His environment had changed.

His mother said Biggie had invented the tough-guy lyrics and look as a gimmick to sell his music. He also exaggerated his own home life. He was not raised in poverty, in a welfare home, as he alluded to in his songs.

"He sang about guns," Voletta said. "Christopher would sit here and talk about it like he lived it. His music scared the daylights out of me. He was not a violent person. If he were confronted, he would react, but does that make him a violent person? . . . I saw somewhere that Christopher said he bought me furniture and all this stuff. I said, 'Christopher, I read where you said all that.' I worked hard my whole life. I bought Christopher nice clothes. I bought him Polo-label shirts before anybody knew what they were. He never wanted for anything when he was growing up. He told me, 'Ma, that's what it's all about. It sells records.' " She emphasized that Biggie was giving the fans what he felt they wanted to hear.

The new lyrics on his *Ready to Die* album sold more than a million records. Not only that, it catapulted Biggie from a star, to superstar status.

Biggie's success also became others' success. The *Ready to Die* album marked Junior M.A.F.I.A.'s debut as backup artists, and introduced the group to the world. Junior M.A.F.I.A. was formed out of a group of undiscovered teenage rappers from Biggie's old neighborhood. Biggie had always promised them that if he made it, he would take them with him. He felt a strong sense of loyalty toward them and an obligation to share his success with his homies from the old neighborhood.

He kept his promise. After Biggie helped make them known on his debut album, Junior M.A.F.I.A. recorded their own album, *Conspiracy*. It was a commercial success.

"Junior M.A.F.I.A.'s nine people from around my way," Biggie told a *Vibe* magazine reporter. "I promised once I got on, I was gonna put them on. I got on, so they on. They about to blow, and we all gonna eat, that's all. Plenty of food. . . . We all family, we all in it for the same thing, to feed our children. It's all for the kids, that's all."

In fact, Biggie gave money to the drug dealers on the street who worked the same corner where he used to hustle. He told them not to do drugs, his childhood friend, Abraham Widdi, remembered. "He gave them clothes," Abraham recalled. "He kept a lot of gangsters from doing the wrong thing. He'd even give some of the kids who got out of jail a job."

Biggie explained it further to *Vibe* writer Laura Jamison. Relaxing in his posh Beverly Hills Le Montrosse hotel room, he told her, "That's my little heart right there," referring to Lil' Cease who was sitting in the room with them. "I was just lookin' at him, at how he was going about shit, and it was basically me in a nutshell. Kids can be so mean. They'll tease the shit out of you if your shit is anything less than what they got. You wanna be just as fly as the next muthafucka. He [Lil' Cease] wasn't going to school, so I said, 'No sense in that, just fuck with me.' Now he got a $700 leather coat, diamond rings, and a record deal. That's the whole purpose of me gettin' on. We was all doin' illegal shit, but one person out of the crew got in here, so that's my job now, to drag everybody in. They my peeps. They rollin' with me."

Biggie appeared on Junior M.A.F.I.A.'s "Player's Anthem" in 1995 and then again on "Get Money" and the "Get Money" remix in 1996.

Biggie was also appearing in more and more videos, mostly for other singers. During the fall of 1996, he appeared on the Bad Boy remix of 112's "Only You." 112 was an all-male R&B tenor quartet signed by Bad Boy. Unlike most artists on the Bad Boy label, 112's image was clean, pure, and wholesome, which helped the group cross over to a more mainstream audience. 112 wasn't as hot a commodity as Biggie. But Biggie's notoriety wasn't always positive; he was said to be a part of the bicoastal rap feud.

Biggie shrugged off the "rap war" hype. "The vibe might a felt like that, but it's all love, you know?" he said, explaining it away to *MTV News*. "I got love in L.A., Puff got love in L.A., everybody from the West Coast got love out here [on the East Coast]. Somebody just want to make a mountain out of a molehill, you know? It's not that deep. That's one of the bad things about the game, is when you get launched, even your friends will turn against you."

Two years later, in Biggie's mind, the rivalry had died down. And now, his second album, a double CD, was being released. It was highly anticipated and he was anxious to have it released. It had been more than two years in the making.

But sixteen days before it was to drop, Biggie was killed. Still, his album was released on schedule, posthumously, to critical acclaim. On Tuesday, March 25, 1997, *Life After Death* arrived in stores. It sold out immediately. Stores couldn't keep it in stock. Tower Records in New York reported that its first-day sales of seven hundred copies exceeded those for U2's *Pop* album. The national chain of stores, Best Buy, said Biggie's album had sold sixteen thousand copies the first day, more than the then just-released Aerosmith album did the entire week. According to SoundScan, Inc., the system used by the industry to track sales nationwide for *Billboard* magazine, it topped *Billboard*'s charts as the biggest first-week sales in more than a year, selling 690,000 copies during the first week. Better even than the Beatles' *Anthology 1*, which also had debuted at number one, selling 855,500 copies in November 1995. Biggie's double-CD set ultimately would go platinum *eight times*.

On the *Life After Death* album, Biggie rapped about his own death. The album begins with the pulsing sound of a heart thumping. Then Puffy and Biggie are on the telephone together. Biggie talks to him about committing suicide. The sound of a gun being fired is heard, and Biggie falls to the ground. Puffy, at Biggie's side in a hospital, says that they were supposed to rule the world, that they were "unstoppable," and had too much living to do. The sound of a heart monitor's steady, flat-line tone can be heard. The album ends with the song "You're Nobody (Til Somebody Kills You)" featuring Biggie's estranged wife, Faith Evans. Biggie told *Billboard* he favored the cut because the track "brings to mind the expression, 'You'll miss me when I'm gone.'" Indeed.

Besides singing about his own death, Biggie rapped about the death of a friend from Brooklyn, his slain friend O, who was killed on the street. In the song "Miss U," which he dedicated to O, Biggie rapped that although he was a thug, he cried for three days.

Biggie had a deep-rooted fear of dying a violent death, which could explain why his albums were centered around the topics of violence and death. He even told the *Chicago Tribune* in 1994 that he was "scared to death, scared of getting my brains blown out."

That fear manifested itself in his lyrics. He not only wrote rhymes about dying, but he talked openly to reporters about his fears. "I think about it every day," Biggie told MTV after Tupac's '96 death. "Every day it's real, that's how real it is. I think somebody's trying to kill me. I be wakin' up paranoid. I be really scared."

In one of his last interviews, given just three days before his death, while he was in Los Angeles, Biggie told a disc jockey with San Francisco's KYLD-FM radio station that he was worried about his own safety, but not because of fear of retaliation over Tupac's murder; instead, he explained, it was because he was such a high-profile celebrity, he believed it made him an easy target, just as sports figures and other well-known entertainers are easy targets.

"It's not just rappers," Biggie told KYLD. "They gonna attack anybody that's a large figure. They did it to [Michael] Jordan. They did it to [Mike] Tyson. They did it to Bill Cosby. They gonna attack you if you on top. It's your job to bob and weave. I need the security...."

Besides fearing strangers' hostilities, there were also rumors that Tupac Shakur himself sought revenge against Biggie, his former good friend. Biggie had heard those rumors and tried to ignore them. But it was a war—albeit a verbal one at that point—and Biggie, willing or not, was in the thick of it. There didn't appear to be any way out for him.

5

TUPAC AND BIGGIE: THE FEUD

BIGGIE SMALLS AND TUPAC SHAKUR were modern-day American story-tellers, but their musical careers would become ensconced in a bitter archrivalry. Blood would be shed.

Both were lauded for their ability to paint frank, realistic pictures, via their lyrics, of the plight of urban American youth. They came from the same side of the tracks. Their mix of rhythms and rhymes were a raw and vivid chronicle of the lives and times of young black men coming up in America.

The rap industry came into full bloom with Tupac's and Biggie's rhymes, taking ghetto-culture songs from childhood to adolescence. Tupac was a Panther baby, having been raised by New York Black Panther founder Afeni Shakur, one of the infamous Panther 21, while Biggie came from a working-class single-parent home. However, they both rapped about what life was like growing up in the ghetto.

Tupac came of age in a housing project on the outskirts of San Francisco, in Marin City, dubbed "the Jungle" by cops because of its inner-city crime. Brilliantly talented, Tupac escaped by writing poetry, eventually turning his poems into rap songs. Arrested eight times between 1991 and 1996, he had carved out a distinct thug image for himself: He even had "Thug Life" tattooed on his upper abdomen. Tupac's rhymes were autobiographical street hymns. Fans bought in to it.

It was those hardcore gangsta lyrics that made Tupac a huge star. His success was legendary. Before his death in September 1997, Tupac had recorded one gold and four platinum albums, giving young black America a strong, new voice. Tupac became a money machine for Death Row Records, his recording label. His 1995 album, *Me Against the*

World, sold two million copies. His solo albums produced during his lifetime—*2Pacalypse Now, Thug Life*, and *Strictly 4 My N.I.G.G.A.Z.*— were megahits. His album *Makaveli* was released posthumously by Death Row Records. It, too, became an immediate hit and ranked number one on the charts, selling more than three million copies.

Tupac was a rising star in film, as well, and appeared in such movies as *Poetic Justice*, with Janet Jackson, *Bullet* with Mickey Rourke, *Above the Rim* with Duane Martin (Dr. Dre produced the soundtrack), *Gridlock'd* with Tim Roth, and *Gang Related* with Jim Belushi. *Poetic Justice* director John Singleton praised Tupac's acting ability at the time, telling *Mr. Showbiz*, "He's what they call a natural. You know, he's a real actor." Tupac enjoyed the movie-star perks: hordes of money, luxury cars, and beautiful women.

Tupac escaped life in the ghetto, but he couldn't get the ghetto out of his system. Neither, it seemed, could Biggie Smalls.

Biggie, like Tupac, grew up on the streets, but in Brooklyn where he, too, discovered a natural affinity for rap. While Tupac fashioned himself as a full-on thug, Biggie was a street poet who modeled himself after a Chicago mobster, wearing gangsta/playa hats, matching double-breasted suits, and smoking cigars. He shared Tupac's love of the gangsta lifestyle, especially the bad-boy image. Biggie became known for his tough exterior and his steely-eyed stare. Where Tupac was outspoken, Biggie kept quiet; but though Biggie lacked assertiveness in his manner, he more than made up for that in his daunting size and seemingly hard look.

Tupac and Biggie both rose to prominence quickly by rapping about a side of life they were familiar with: sex, drugs, and violence. They were rebels who Generation X identified with. It was the only form of popular music, for them, with any true connection to real life. One conclusion, drawn shortly after Biggie's murder by Craig Kallman, president of Big Beat Records, a New York–based rap and R&B label, was this: "Biggie and Tupac were to rap what Miles Davis was to jazz and John Lennon [was] to rock. They will forever be looked at as two of hip-hop's most important artists."

Hip-hop rapper LL Cool J felt that the rap war was blown out of proportion and that their chosen careers had nothing to do with their murders. "Fate is funny," Cool J wrote in his book *I Make My Own Rules*. "And I think that's what Biggie and Tupac were—victims of a fate and the sorry violent state of this country. Rap music didn't kill either one of them."

But their celebrity may have been the death of them. Both Tupac and Biggie were looking for the same thing—fame and fortune. They both detested poverty. They both grew up rapping on the streets and were forced to balance their newfound wealth and lifestyle with their old lives, and friends from their old neighborhoods.

Once they made it, they both talked about giving back to the communities in which they'd grown up. They graduated from being young gangsta rappers wearing baggy jeans, sneakers, and baseball caps, to hip-hoppers donning expensive Versace suits and Italian leather shoes, cutting well-dressed figures.

Tupac and Biggie got to know each other when Tupac was in New York doing a show at the Ritz nightclub. Biggie had met Tupac a month earlier; so when Tupac was in New York, he invited Biggie to perform onstage with him. They became fast friends. They had met when Tupac's career was on the rise and Biggie was just beginning to make a name for himself. Tupac and his posse of backup singers, the Outlawz, invited Biggie onstage with them. They performed in front of sell-out crowds. Tupac's and the Outlawz's popularity rubbed off on Biggie.

When Tupac returned to New York to film *Above the Rim*, he did shows at night. Several times Tupac invited Biggie onstage to open for him. Tupac told people he was helping out a fellow rapper, someone he considered a friend. Tupac's generosity helped launch Biggie's career. In the 1996 movie *This Is for My Dead Homiez*, directed by Billy Wright and starring Shannon Luckey, about the Bloods street gang, there is a segment at the end of the film where Biggie and Tupac are rapping freestyle together in Tupac's hotel room. Biggie considered Tupac a brother and a friend and he was happy to work with him, whatever the venue. Tupac was generous to Biggie.

"I spoke to Tupac a lot but I never met him," Biggie's mother Voletta said. "When Christopher started his music, Tupac was his friend. He would go to clubs with him and they would hang out together. Christopher would open [shows] for Tupac. They were very, very close."

But their friendship took a major hit on November 30, 1994. Tupac was in New York City, at Manhattan's Parker Meridien Hotel, staying for the outcome of a sexual-assault trial of a twenty-one-year-old woman in November 1993. In New York for the verdict, Tupac went to Quad Studios in New York City's Times Square in Manhattan to back up a fellow rapper.

That night, someone tried to take his life. Tupac was ambushed and gunned down in the downstairs lobby. He was shot five times, including once in the head, by what police called "hold-up men," and, amazingly, survived the onslaught. Biggie and Puffy Combs were upstairs at the time, using the same studio facilities to record their own song, when the shooting went down. Tupac claimed the shooting, in which he lost $35,000 worth of jewelry, was a setup. He publicly blamed Biggie, not for shooting him, but for knowing he was going to be shot. He honestly believed that Biggie and Puffy had helped set him up for a fall. Tupac became convinced that Biggie and Puffy had been aware that Tupac was going to be shot by a would-be assassin.

But instead of dying, Tupac lived to tell about it. And he was angry—fighting mad. By some accounts, Biggie's future was fated after the New York City shooting, when Tupac Shakur declared war on him.

The day after the shooting at Quad Studios, in a wheelchair and bandaged, Tupac was ushered out of the hospital and into a courtroom. He was convicted of sexual assault and sentenced to four and a half years in a New York State prison. A few days later he was sent to prison.

While there, Tupac would accuse Biggie, Puffy, Andre Harrell, and his own close friend, Randy "Stretch" Walker, of orchestrating his New York shooting. It was also during Tupac's incarceration that Biggie's career exploded big-time onto the rap scene. Biggie was awarded the 1995 *Billboard* Rap Artist of the Year and became Bad Boy's hottest talent when his debut album, *Ready to Die*, went platinum.

By October 1995, Tupac Shakur had served eight months in prison and was desperate to get out; so he signed a handwritten record contract with Marion "Suge" Knight, CEO of Death Row Records, which at the time was the hottest rap label around. After all, Suge had come from the hard streets of Compton, California, said to be the birthplace of gangsta rap.

Suge, a six-foot-four, 330-pound former bodyguard with a violent criminal record, was the most powerful—and feared—young black man in the music business. He had built up Death Row, co-founded with Andre "Dr. Dre" Young, before he left in 1996 to start his own label, into one of the most successful rap labels in history, in its heyday grossing more than $100 million in sales of more than fifteen million records. Suge, with his megasales, proved that hardcore gangsta-rap records could sell millions to a mainstream audience. But at the height of his success, Suge was also reputed to still be connected with the Bloods, a street gang from his old neighborhood in Compton, a largely black suburb in South Central Los Angeles, and rivals of the Southside Crips. In Compton, gang territories were well delineated, and Suge grew up in Bloods turf. The horrific tales of Suge's business dealings, repeated often in the press, became so outrageous it was difficult to tell the truth from the lore. Still, the stories persisted about Suge's dealings with people and the way he did business. True or not, it became his image, a persona laced in fear. But when it came to handling his artists, Suge was said to have treated them gently, like family.

Tupac was eager to sign on with Suge and the Death Row family. In return, Suge posted Tupac's $1.4 million bond while Tupac's conviction was appealed. While awaiting the appeal process, a judge had ruled that Tupac be permitted to go free; but without Suge, he couldn't make bail. After Suge posted bail, Tupac was released from prison after serving eleven months.

Tupac, with Death Row Records, and Biggie, with Bad Boy Entertainment, were the two hottest gangsta rappers in America, represented by the two hottest and biggest hip-hop labels ever. But instead of being happy for the other's success, they were pitted against each other in a fierce rap war.

Once Tupac was released from prison, he wasn't about to let the old rivalry die. Tupac, along with Suge, repeatedly ridiculed Biggie, as well as Puffy, in public and in the press. And Tupac continued to blame Biggie for setting him up in the Manhattan shooting, while Biggie continued to deny any involvement. Tupac continued making the accusations to anyone who would listen. The remarks bothered Biggie so much that he even talked to his mother about it.

Voletta Wallace said her son initially laughed off the comments made by Tupac accusing him of being involved in the Quad Studios shooting. Biggie believed that Tupac's own weapon accidentally fired during the ensuing scuffle and that he was shot not only by someone else's gun but also by his own. But the four-year-old police reports, details of which were provided by the NYPD, say that Tupac possessed only a fifteen-round, 10-millimeter clip and was not armed that night. If he had a gun, it wasn't on him when police arrived.

"Bottom line—and this, I know, is the truth," Voletta Wallace said: "Tupac also harbored resentment because Christopher never came to see him in prison. They were hanging out together. He would get Christopher jobs. They were close friends. One thing Christopher said was, Tupac was an actor. Yes, he was a rapper, but he was more of an actor. Tupac knows the people who shot him and robbed him. To Christopher it was a joke. The reason Tupac was not saying anything, was three of those shots came from Tupac's own gun. He accidentally shot himself." Biggie never spoke to the police, she said, and, according to detectives, Biggie was never a suspect in the Quad Studios shooting.

The heat between the two rappers got even hotter, but this time it was through their music that they appeared to taunt each other. Biggie released a song called "Who Shot Ya," which seemed to be mocking Tupac, although Biggie said it wasn't aimed at him. Tupac, with confidence, braggadocio, and a certain cockiness, responded with lyrics that were shocking to some. In his "Hit 'Em Up" track, he boasted about having an affair with Biggie's wife Faith Evans.

At the time, Faith went on the radio denying she was seeing Tupac. But Tupac and Suge told writer Lynn Hirschberg, for a *New York Times* piece, that Faith had bought presents for Tupac, including an elaborately patterned gold shirt Tupac wore during an interview with the writer. "The wife of a top rapper bought this for him," Suge told Hirschberg while in Las Vegas for the Riddick Bowe–Evander Holyfield heavyweight fight. "His name is an acronym. Notorious B.I.G.'s wife, Faith Evans. She bought him this and a suit and some other stuff." Then, Hirschberg wrote, Suge turned to Tupac and asked, "And how did you thank her, Tupac?" Tupac responded, "I did enough."

Keith Murphy with *Vibe* magazine asked Biggie how he felt when he first heard the graphic lyrics where Tupac bragged about the purported affair.

"It hurt," Biggie responded, "but I kinda look at it like business. When you at the top, you gotta go for the top person's neck, you know what I'm sayin'? You just gotta get your spot, you know what I'm sayin'? That's what he wanted. I can't be mad at him for that. He just doin' what he gotta do. I couldn't be the one to do it back, though— that's not my style."

Tupac's bragging intensified even more the coastal clash for fans. In return, in Biggie's "Last Day" track, he rapped, "Beef with me is unhealthy. Fuck around and get an ulcer. Lose your pulse or collapsed lung. Look how many gats [guns] I brung." (Tupac ultimately died after doctors removed his perforated right lung.)

As Biggie and Puffy each became more famous, the rivalry only worsened. At the *Source* Awards in 1995, the feud became a public event and an open conflict. The awards show was an annual rap-world event sponsored by *The Source* magazine and held at the Paramount Theater in Manhattan. Biggie was named the Best Live Performer of the Year. The ceremony, however, would be most remembered as the night the East Coast–West Coast rivalry—between Biggie's record label, Bad Boy Entertainment, and Tupac Shakur's Death Row Records—intensified. After the awards show, there was a clash in the parking lot between the two factions. Outside, near the backstage entrance, people from the opposite camps had a heated exchange of words and squared off, threatening each other verbally. One of Biggie's bodyguards was reported to have brandished a weapon during a scuffle with a member of Tupac's entourage, who was also armed. Word quickly spread on the street that the verbal altercation had been peppered with threats.

A month later, on Sunday, September 24, 1995, at a birthday party in

Atlanta for R&B producer Jermaine Dupri, the two sides—East Coast versus West Coast—met up. Late into the evening, at an after-party at the nightclub Platinum House, Jake Robles, a Death Row employee and close friend of Suge, got into an argument with a fellow guest. Puffy was waiting outside for his limousine when some patrons, including Suge, began pouring out amid shouting and arguing. Suddenly shots rang out and Jake was down. He was paralyzed and in critical condition for a week before he died. Almost immediately, Suge blamed Puffy. No arrests were ever made, but several witnesses maintained that the gunman was a personal bodyguard of Puffy Combs. Suge blamed Puffy for his friend's murder, while Tupac blamed Biggie for the assault against him at Quad Studios.

Then, at the Tenth Annual *Soul Train* Music Awards, held on March 29, 1996, Death Row was heavily nominated, and appeared with Snoop Doggy Dogg, Dr. Dre, Suge Knight, and Tupac. Biggie performed onstage, but Tupac won Best Rap Album for *Me Against the World*. When Suge went onstage at the Shrine Auditorium to accept the award with Tupac, he made a comment aimed at Puffy Combs, who at the time was known for his flamboyant appearances in his artists' videos. Without naming names, Suge announced from the podium, "If you don't want the owner of your label on your album or in your video or on your tour, come sign with Death Row." Everyone knew he meant "Puff Daddy" Combs, with Bad Boy Entertainment.

Puffy was shocked. Even so, when he took the stage to hand out an award to Snoop Doggy Dogg, formerly with Death Row, he made a speech about unity, then threw his arms around Snoop.

Biggie and Tupac were hyped by the media as the figureheads of two feuding entities, identified in several ways: Bad Boy Entertainment versus Death Row Records; East Coast versus West Coast; the Crips street gang versus the Bloods street gang; a bicoastal rap war. Whatever the name for it, it was known coast to coast.

Voletta Wallace has said her son laughed at comments made by Tupac accusing him of being involved in the Quad Studios shooting: "He would laugh about it, because he knew that Tupac was just acting like he was angry, and Tupac wouldn't say who really shot him."

After Tupac was killed, Biggie stopped laughing.

In search of answers to Tupac's murder, speculation again focused on Biggie. "My son had nothing to do with Tupac's murder," his mother said. "He was shocked and upset when Tupac died."

Biggie knew he was as high-profile a rapper as Tupac. Unlike Tupac, however, he didn't thrive on trouble. But trouble slammed him head-on when he was cut down in the same manner as Tupac had been.

Within months of each other, both rap stars were murdered in near-identical gang-style killings. Tupac's and Biggie's murders, said Walter Leaphart, a music agent for veteran rapper Chuck D, were the product of young black rappers "being raised in a world which has no structure. You're talking about a whole generation of guys who weren't taught any values. From our standpoint [in the music industry], these guys made some money and stayed in the old environment."

Biggie and Tupac appeared to be casualties of the very vision they portrayed in their rap songs. Each career paralleled the other, but the similar circumstances surrounding the rappers' deaths were eerie: Both were killed after attending high-profile events, and both were killed in what police termed "professional hits," while sitting in the passenger seats of cars, when unknown gunmen drove up, ambushed them, opened fire, and fled. Both murders went unsolved.

Biggie's murder thrust the so-called "rap war" into the national spotlight and created a call for peace from both sides. Rappers from opposite coasts, including Snoop Doggy Dogg, Chuck D, and Doug E. Fresh, attended a rap summit in Chicago held, just a few days after Biggie's death, by The Nation of Islam's Louis Farrakhan, pledging their support for a unity pact that would include a joint peace tour and an album. Puffy Combs didn't attend but sent his support, as did rappers Ice-T and Ice Cube.

"Isn't that tripped-out that they still haven't found the killers in either case?" Chuck D, leader of Public Enemy, asked *Playboy* magazine. "If somebody had killed the CEO of a major label, they would have found the killer within a week."

After Biggie's death, Chuck D released a statement, saying, "We have to be careful about hysteria and overhyping of the terms of East

Coast and West Coast confrontation that is being projected in the media." Referring to the deaths of Tupac, Yafeu "Yak" Fula, and Biggie, Chuck D said, "It's a terrible fact that we've had three casualties connected to this concocted situation that's much bigger than rap and hip-hop. It shows how the problems of the black community, black-on-black crime, that has been in dialogue in the art form for so long, has floated to the top and is out of control."

Sway, a DJ with KMEL radio in San Francisco, was one of the last to interview Biggie. He also was the last radio disc jockey to interview Tupac. Sway said the hype about a rap war was just that: hype. "It's individuals," he said, "who happened to be friends at one point who had a conflict. Friends have conflicts. Brothers have conflict. I knew both of them personally. People are killed every day. These two happened to be artists . . . I have no idea who killed Biggie. [But] I don't believe in the East Coast–West Coast thing."

After Biggie was murdered, Chaka Zulu, Tupac's cousin, told The Associated Press: "I think, to some extent, this was a retaliation for 'Pac's death. I don't think it came out of 'Pac's camp though. I think it came from people who are caught up in the hype of the East Coast–West Coast thing."

There were some who believed that gang-member fans of Tupac, buying in to the rap turf-war hype, independently went after Biggie, thinking he had something to do with Tupac's demise. West Coast rapper Ice-T, in New York following Biggie's murder, announced to a radio station, "This is the first time I ever felt unsafe."

Following Biggie's murder, Suge Knight, who was jailed for charges arising from a scuffle the night Tupac was killed, issued a news release from prison. "The entire Death Row Records family are shocked and saddened by the death of Mr. Christopher Wallace, aka Notorious B.I.G.," the statement read. "We would like to take this time to express our deepest condolences to the family and friends of B.I.G. Having just had the untimely death of one of our own, Tupac Shakur, by way of the same senseless violence, we do sympathize with those closest to Mr. Wallace. A gifted rapper, we are sure that Mr. Wallace's passing will affect many and it is certain that he will be missed throughout the music industry by his peers and fans."

Like Biggie, Puffy also attempted to distance himself from the East Coast–West Coast hype. But it wasn't until early November 1996, after Tupac's murder, that Puffy spoke out. "I think people have a misconception that first of all we were in a feud," he told *USA Today*. "I don't think you can be in a feud with somebody if there's not two people arguing. I mean, I've never had a problem with Tupac or a problem with Suge Knight or a problem with Death Row, a problem with anybody in the industry, for that matter. The only thing I've heard is the records that you've heard. I've never been approached on any other level besides that. So it was more hype than anything."

Ironically, "Stop the Gunfight," a single recorded when Tupac and Biggie were still friends, featured them both. It was released soon after Biggie's death.

Many in the music industry hoped the tragedy of Biggie's murder would put a halt to the rap war, real or perceived. "I think that it's time that the authorities got serious about recognizing that the East Coast–West Coast thing is dangerous, and it's legitimate," said Don Cornelius, creator and executive producer of *Soul Train*.

Russell Simmons, CEO of Def Jam Records, said in a *Spin* magazine article that he was concerned about the lives of rappers. "I'm concerned that [West Coast rapper] Warren G doesn't want to go to New York," he said, "and New York artists don't want to go to L.A. There wasn't any East-West war. There was a Bad Boy–Death Row beef, but it didn't have anything to do with anybody else. The war was created and fueled by our own radio stations and our own [black] magazines."

Rapper Chris France, better known as Thrust, who was a promoter for black artists at Virgin Music Canada, told the *Toronto Sunday Sun* that he respected Biggie as an artist "but there wasn't anything positive in [Biggie's] music. The image he presented, it seemed inevitable he'd be tested sometime. People are looking at it as an issue of violence as opposed to music. What happened reflects what's happening every day in the black community."

Since the first rap record hit the charts in 1979, with "Rapper's Delight" by Henry "Big Banle" Hanle under the first hip-hop label, the Sugarhill Gang's Sugar Hill Records, the music has found a huge audience—and not only among blacks, but also in the white teen world. Rap has left an indelible mark on North American pop culture.

Sacha Jenkins, music editor for *Vibe* magazine, said in a telephone interview in February of 1999 that rap music has come into its own, for good reason. "I don't think the music itself has changed," he explained. "I think what has happened, like rock and roll and all the other genres that have come up in [this] country, initially there is resistance from the masses, resistance from the keepers or those who document pop culture, the outlets that expose the sound and sight of pop culture. But since we now have a generation of kids around the world and around this country who have grown up listening to rap music, it was only a matter of time that the demand for the music would grow. . . . Hip-hop is here to stay.

"Lauryn Hill hasn't toned down her lyrics. And I don't know that everyone fully understands what Lauryn Hill is talking about in her music. If they did, then people wouldn't necessarily feel that she is this very wholesome artist. I don't think that's discussed much. She's on the cover of *Time* magazine and everyone loves her. I don't hear much discourse on her lyrics. I think at times she can be raw. She talks about a lot of things that are relevant to hip-hop and to young people coming up in black America, from love to education, to drugs, to sex, to growth and change.

"These young people become old people and old people run things in this world. There's always a changing of the guard. Every little kid will one day have his or her day. And that's what hip-hop is today. Not every single Tupac song was about guns or violence. You can have Will Smith or Biggie Smalls, just like you can have the Rolling Stones and you can have the Beach Boys. Hip-hop is here now. It's their time."

Following Biggie's murder, a *Newsweek* cover story, dated March 24, 1997, called hip-hop music the Vietnam dividing American blacks in the 1990s. "Three decades after the heyday of the civil rights movement," the story said, "black America is facing a generation gap similar to the one that divided white America in the 1960s. This time the wedge is hip-hop, not rock and roll."

Some believed—as Biggie once stated about Tupac's death—that their own celebrity may have contributed to their demise. "The reality of the so-called gangsta life or thug life is that notoriety can kill you," journalist and cultural critic Justin Onyeka in 1997 told *Ethnic News Watch*. "For all the financial benefits that notoriety can bring you, it's no good being the richest man in the graveyard."

Hip-hop magazines had milked the Biggie-Tupac feud with provocative stories, and fans had lapped them up, following the coverage of the feud like they would have watched a boxing match.

Heavy D, a rapper and producer and a friend to Puffy, suggested that the feud eventually could have been handled privately. "I believe the whole thing would have been resolved," he told *Playboy*. "Tupac and Biggie would have made records together. It got so out of hand, and then the public got involved. It became another example of what is really going on in urban black America. I spent a lot of time with both of these brothers. It may be hard for someone who didn't know them to understand how nice these guys were. Their lyrics came from what they saw in a certain environment. Hip-hop is based on the essence of it all, but you get these kids looking at it like it's real. When you talk about killing people and shooting people, they take it like, 'Oh, yeah, that's the new flava,' like they're talking about a pair of sneakers. That's the thing that really scares me."

Writer and author Kevin Powell, who once covered the rap scene for *Vibe* and *Rolling Stone* magazines, said in a college newspaper article published a week after Biggie's death that the feud between Biggie and Tupac, two former good friends, was fueled by the media who wrote about it. "I could not help thinking about the fact that I, as a *Vibe* staff writer, had been in the middle of a storm that began in late 1994 when Tupac Shakur was shot five times in a New York City recording studio's lobby area," Powell said in the *Daily Bruin*, UCLA's student paper. "Tupac would, via *Vibe*, brazenly implicate Biggie and his mentor Sean 'Puffy' Combs. From there things would escalate out of control, and Tupac, then Biggie, would be killed. By whom, I do not know, and if I did know, I would not say in this space. Yeah, it is like that."

It was more than that, though. The rappers, in a sense, were egged on by comments they made that were printed in the media. "What I do know," Powell continued, "is that a certain guilt has followed me: a guilt born of the knowledge that we in the media—*Vibe, The Source*, MTV, BET, and any and everyone else you can think of—helped to shape, due to haste, poor judgment, and a greed for magazine sales and TV ratings, the tension between Tupac and Biggie, which became the tension between Bad Boy Entertainment and Death Row Records, which became the East Coast versus West Coast 'beef.' "

Powell noted that the media, along with the killers, had blood on their hands. "When the nineties end," he wrote, "I think many of us are going to have to really look at ourselves, and ask ourselves as journalists, music fans, and thinking human beings, 'How did I contribute to the turmoil?' . . . One day, journalists will face the reality that they can provoke deaths of stars."

6

NEW YORK CITY INVESTIGATION

On November 30, 1994, Tupac Shakur was ambushed, shot, and robbed inside the lobby of Quad Studios in Manhattan's Times Square. At the time, Tupac's attorneys, who were in New York with Tupac awaiting sentencing on a sexual-assault conviction against the rapper, said the shooting "looked like a setup and smells like a setup." Tupac publicly blamed Biggie Smalls, who was upstairs in a recording session at the time, for helping to set up the shooting.

The shooting happened like this (which is based on statements made to police by witnesses to the shooting): Just after midnight, Tupac was on his way to meet Little Shawn, an East Coast rapper, for a recording session. The session had been arranged by a man named Booker and was to take place at Quad Studios, at 723 Seventh Avenue between Forty-eighth and Forty-ninth Streets in Times Square.

Earlier that night Tupac had been paged by Booker, asking Tupac to record with Little Shawn. Tupac agreed to do it only if they paid him $7,000. Booker and his people said yes. The calls and pages went back and forth all night. Booker, according to Tupac's claims afterward to reporters, kept calling him, asking what time would he be showing up for the session.

Finally, at 12:16 A.M., according to Detective George Nagy with the NYPD's Midtown North Eighteenth Precinct, Tupac and his entourage—his manager Freddie Moore, his common-law brother-in-law, Zayd Turner, and his cousin, Randy "Stretch" Walker—arrived. They left their car in a parking garage at 148 West Forty-eighth Street. Then they walked the short distance, around the corner, to the studio on Seventh Avenue.

Tupac and his friends arrived at Quad Studios nine minutes later, the police report stated. Standing on a small terrace overlooking Forty-eighth Street, smoking, were a couple of teenage members of Junior M.A.F.I.A., the group Biggie Smalls sponsored. They hollered down to Tupac to say hello, then went back inside to tell everyone Tupac had arrived.

Upstairs, there was a party atmosphere. It was a large studio and a lot of people in the business were in there that night. Word spread that Tupac would be arriving. People were excited, anticipating the popular rapper's arrival. Also recording, but on a different floor from where Tupac was scheduled to record, were Biggie Smalls and Puffy Combs. They were working on Biggie's "Warning" video. The group Junior M.A.F.I.A. was upstairs too recording with Biggie and Puffy. At the time, Quad had recording studios and equipment on five different floors.

Back on the street, on Seventh Avenue, as Tupac and the others approached, there was a black man dressed in an army fatigue jacket standing just outside the lobby door. Inside the lobby, Tupac could see two black men a few feet inside, near the elevator. One was standing. The other was sitting down reading a newspaper. Tupac and his group didn't think anything of it.

Tupac pressed the intercom button and asked to be let in. The four were buzzed in. As Tupac and his crew walked toward the elevator, Tupac was ambushed by the three men, the police report stated. Two of the three men displayed guns, NYPD detective Nagy said.

The men grabbed jewelry from Tupac, and Tupac in turn lunged at one of the gunmen. They fought and that's when the gunman leveled his gun, squeezed the trigger and a staccato round of at least five shots went off. The men also snatched jewelry from Freddie Moore as they continued holding guns on the others, the police report said.

Tupac was shot five times—twice in his head, twice in his groin area, and once in his left hand. Freddie Moore was shot once in his abdomen. Both survived.

Tupac had $35,000 worth of gold taken from him. Stolen was a diamond-and-gold ring, a gold bracelet, and several heavy gold chains. Freddie had $5,000 worth of jewelry stolen, which consisted of a gold bracelet and several gold chains, according to the police report.

After they finished robbing Tupac, then Freddie, the would-be assassins stepped out of the lobby, still pointing their guns at the four, and, backing away so they could watch Tupac and the others, walked out the door. When they were gone, Tupac said to Stretch, "Yo, I'm hit."

The four, with Tupac stumbling and bleeding from his wounds, stepped outside and yelled, "Police!" Then they walked back inside. Just then, they saw an NYPD squad car pull up. The door to the elevator in the lobby opened, so Tupac got in even though the police had arrived. Zayd and Stretch followed him. Freddie, who was also bleeding from a gunshot wound, stayed downstairs and waited for the police.

The three took the elevator to the eighth floor. Upstairs at the eighth floor reception area, Booker was waiting for Tupac when the door opened. "Call the police, call the police," Tupac yelled at him. Biggie and Puffy were on a different floor recording. Tupac, pacing back and forth, was by that time hysterical. He looked at Booker and said, "You the only one who knew that I was coming. You must a set me up." Booker was astonished and told him, "Yo, you buggin', Tupac. C'mon. Talk to me." But Tupac kept repeating, "Call the police." Reporters, as well as the police, eventually showed up at the scene. Tupac was interviewed by newspaper reporters who quoted him as saying it was a setup. Tupac also accused those with him of "dropping like a sack of potatoes" and not coming to his aid.

A lot of people were in and out of the studio that night, Tupac pointed out, many of whom were as bejeweled with gold as he was, but were not robbed like he and Freddie were.

Included in those present that night was record producer Andre Harrell.

"Everybody was all excited about 'Pac comin' in," Harrell told a *Vibe* reporter, in April 1999, "but we were starting to get antsy because he was supposed to get there at a certain time, and we wanted to see how this song with Little Shawn was going to set off."

When Tupac got off the elevator, "we were all standing in the hall," Harrell said. "Tupac was just bopping back and forth saying, 'I was set up.' At first I didn't realize he had been shot, because he wasn't bleeding heavily from the head. It looked like he had a fight. He said, 'It's not goin' down like that.' I was like, 'Yo, you shot. You need to sit down.' He told Stretch to roll him up a spliff [marijuana cigarette]. He was in movie mode at this point. He did the whole James Cagney thing."

Harrell directed people inside the studio at the time to call for an ambulance and for the police. He also told Stretch to ride with Tupac to the hospital so Tupac wouldn't be alone. He didn't want anything more to happen to him, like on the way to the hospital.

Officers with NYPD's Midtown North Eighteenth Precinct in Manhattan wrote in their police report that Tupac was unarmed and carried only a 10-millimeter clip. Freddie had a 10-millimeter live round in his pocket. No mention was made in the police report that Tupac was carrying a gun. A security guard was on duty at the time of the shooting, but he wasn't mentioned in the police report. It wasn't clear if the security guard was in the lobby or in another part of the building at the time of the attack. Later, a security guard working in the lobby said a camera was pointed at the door at the time of the shooting and showed the studio personnel upstairs who was outside the lobby. "It's pointed at the door so they can see who's there," the guard said. "Then they're buzzed in." That news was an integral piece of the investigation because it meant that whoever shot Tupac was also let in by someone upstairs. But an employee later said that police did not confiscate videotape from the studio's surveillance cameras. Instead, the investigation was abruptly halted.

Stretch, before he was shot to death in Queens exactly a year later, told *Vibe* magazine that Tupac was armed that night. "Tupac got shot trying to go for his shit," he said. "He tried to go for his gun, and he made a mistake on his own. But I'll let him tell the world that. I ain't even going to get into it all like that. . . . He tried to turn around and pull the joint out real quick, but niggahs caught him, grabbed his hand when it was by his waist." The gun, according to accounts posted on the Internet, went off when the attacker tried to grab it from Tupac. Some say Tupac was shot with his own gun. There was no mention of that charge, however, in the police report.

Stretch, in his account, said that Zayd took Tupac's gun before the police arrived on the scene so Tupac wouldn't be in possession of a firearm.

After the shooting, videotape shot from outside Quad Studios by a TV cameraman showed Puffy inside the downstairs lobby in a baseball cap with a straw hanging from his mouth, staring at the camera while talking to several men. Film footage also showed Biggie walking out of the lobby, followed by Puffy.

Tupac underwent surgery that night at Bellevue Hospital. The next morning, Biggie visited him. At that point, Tupac didn't accuse Biggie of being involved in the shooting.

Tupac, still recovering from his wounds and surgery, checked himself out of the hospital so he could be in court for his sentencing in the earlier sexual-assault trial. Rather than convalesce in a hospital, he stayed temporarily at actress and friend Jasmine Guy's New York apartment. A few days later, Tupac went to prison in upstate New York to serve out his sentence for the sexual-assault conviction.

Before his sentencing, Tupac told *MTV News:* "If God sees it fit for me to spend some time in a cell, if he's brought me so far from hell, to put me here and now he wants me to go to jail, I'll go. When I come out I'll be reborn. My mind will be sharper. The venom will be more potent. They shouldn't send me there. You don't throw more gasoline on a fire to put it out."

During Tupac's incarceration, Death Row released his album *All Eyez on Me*. For the first time ever, a jailed man had the country's number one best-selling album.

While in prison, Tupac obsessed in his isolation, and became convinced that Biggie and Puffy had helped set up the Quad Studios ambush. The case would never be solved.

Just a month after the shooting, the New York Police Department closed its investigation into the shooting. No one would ever learn what really went down that night. The NYPD ended its investigation when, they say, Tupac opted not to cooperate.

"Calls were made to Shakur's lawyer, but they never responded,"

NYPD detective Nagy said. "His lawyer never called back. No one ever called back. Therefore, the case was closed."

The police contended that because Tupac refused to cooperate, it meant the end of their case. "They were totally uncooperative. . . . They more or less handled it their own way," Nagy emphasized. The officer—clearly frustrated—then went on to outline the police's attitude in a bold admission of the way things really are: "Why would a guy go out of his way to investigate a case when the guy who was shot didn't even care?" he asked. "Why are you going to try hard when you have a million other cases?" That was the attitude he said investigators on the case had at the time. He noted that, to close a case, "you really need a valid reason. The boss has to sign off on it. This was a high-profile case. There had to be a valid reason to close it."

Once Tupac was killed in Las Vegas, Nagy said, the Quad Studio's case was not reopened. He explained, "You can reopen a case if somebody walks in and says, 'I shot Tupac.'" Without a willing eyewitness, there would be no one to testify against a suspected shooter, and therefore, no case, Nagy said.

Gregg Howard, Suge Knight's publicist, said the shootings were nothing more than the result of jealousy by immature rappers. Combs's attorney, Kenny Meiselas, on the other hand, said the record companies did not engage in petty jealousies among rappers and that Puffy was not involved in any way in the shooting.

When Tupac was killed in Vegas, Nagy said, Las Vegas police did not contact the NYPD to see if the murder might be connected to the Quad Studios shooting. But Las Vegas police had a different story. They said they did contact New York detectives but were unable to learn who was handling the case. "Of course we'd work closely with another [police] department," Nagy said. "You give them a call and see what they've got. You see what you can dig up. I'd say every effort was made to solve this case."

Robert Norris, an operations manager, had worked for Quad Studios for twelve years when the shooting occurred. He, too, said he believed the attempt on Tupac's life was a sign of jealousy and envy acted out in a violent way. "It was nothing more than rivalry," Norris said. "I think it was nothing but gang-related. Nothing less. It's because they were selling records. They've got friendly competition going on. What's a little gunfire amid friendly competition, among friends?"

Norris stopped short of pointing fingers at specific individuals, saying, "I don't want to name names. I'm more afraid of these people than I am of a mafioso in a nightclub. They're gang members, and the shooting was gang-related. It was two bands who were selling a lot of records."

Because of the shooting in the lobby, Quad Studios made a business decision to cater less to young rap singers and more to other groups. "We're tired of dealing with these yahoos," Norris said. "They all pack weapons. They're young, and they don't know the difference between wrong and right. We're cynical here [at Quad Studios]. Just because we're here in a recording studio doesn't mean we're embracing what comes through the door. This is a recording studio. There comes a point when you have to ask yourself, 'Is it worth it for one client to screw it up for everyone else?' You have to draw the line. We don't want to be a police station. We don't want to have to police people, but we have to be very, very selective."

Quad Studios was a success in its own right. For years Quad racked up an enviable list of credits that included such names as Madonna, Aerosmith, the Rolling Stones, Whitney Houston, Toni Braxton, and longtime client Yoko Ono. Dozens of hit albums, including Madonna's *Erotica*, Marc Cohn's Grammy-winning self-titled debut, and Metallica's *Load*, have been recorded or mixed at Quad's Seventh Avenue studios. Some of the tape transfers for the Beatles' *Anthology* series were done at Quad.

Norris described R&B (the category under which rap music falls) as "the bread and butter of recording studios in Manhattan." Nevertheless, Quad Studio officials, Norris said, didn't appreciate the negative publicity they got after Tupac was shot there. "After that shooting, we cut down on that kind of music," he said. "We had a lot of groups canceling for weeks after that incident. At some point you have to be responsible to the other groups and performers and the people who work here, and say, 'No more.' These are not a savory bunch of people. They're all packing guns."

Walter Leaphart, a music agent for rapper/author/talk-show host

Chuck D, agreed, saying, "They're just some ignorant shits—that's just some ignorant niggah. That was just some ignorant niggah [who] shot some fool." As for Tupac, "He started believing he was Bishop [a street-smart thug role from the movie *Juice*]. When he didn't talk the shit, he didn't sell records. He wanted to sell records, so he started acting like Bishop. And it worked. He sold records. Lots of them."

In October 1995, Suge Knight put up the bail money to get Tupac out of prison pending an appeal of his conviction. In exchange, Tupac signed a three-year record deal with Death Row Records. Suge also signed the Outlawz, as a group, to the Death Row label.

After he was released from prison, Tupac publicly blamed Biggie for helping to set him up in the Manhattan shooting. And he became more security-conscious. He began wearing a bullet-resistant vest and tried, like the police have historically done, to always sit in public places with his back to a wall.

"I'm just mad at my little brother when he don't respect me," Tupac said in a videotaped interview with MTV after he was freed. "Now, when you don't respect me, I'm going to spank your ass. I don't give a fuck how rich you got. On the block I'm your big brother and I'm gonna break your big ass down. Study why I would be mad. Study why I wouldn't be whooping mad when half of New York, half of the major New York rappers, or their agents, or their somebody was there when I got shot and nobody could give me no information."

Biggie, for his part, responded, "The rumor that's spreading is all this shit like we set him up—you know what I'm saying?—and that's crazy."

Biggie wanted an apology from Tupac. "It's real niggahs in the streets thinking, 'That's fucked up, what B.I.G. did to Tupac.' I think that should be erased. . . . As far as with me, he always gonna be my man. . . . But he need to just check himself. And I want an apology. 'Cause I don't get down like that."

The rumors continued to fly and the story "just completely got switched around," Biggie told an *MTV News* reporter, "niggahs saying I set him up, and I'm the one that got him shot. They're saying that my record 'Who Shot Ya' is about him. That shit is crazy. That song was finished way before Tupac got shot. Niggahs was taking little pieces of the song and trying to add it to the story, and that shit is crazy."

Biggie said the police thought everyone in the Quad Studios building was on the same floor when Tupac got out of the elevator upstairs. "But when he actually came out from the elevator, I wasn't even there," Biggie said. He didn't see Tupac until he saw him being wheeled away on a stretcher by paramedics and taken by ambulance to the hospital.

Puffy Combs later talked about the feud between Tupac and Biggie during an MTV interview, saying: "We knew we were in a situation where it was unfair to be involved in something as stupid as the East Coast–West Coast, whatever the media called the feud, or whatever, for, like, two years. We never did nothing. We felt unsafe just walking the streets. We never even said one thing about anybody disrespecting anybody. We've never had anybody robbed or set up or shot or nothing even like that. It didn't even get down like that. And so we felt the whole point about having a talk about safety or any of that would hurt our feelings. It was like, we didn't get into rap for that. We didn't get into music for that."

Despite Biggie and Puffy's repeated denials, Tupac was still fighting mad. "The prodigal son has returned. I'm alive. The ghost is walking around," he said on MTV. Just before Tupac was killed, Biggie told people he didn't know what happened to his friendship with Tupac or where it had gone wrong. "I can't really call that one," he told *Vibe*, "because I don't know what happened in that camp. But the way I looked at it, it was like an ongoing role, a character he [Tupac] couldn't get out of."

"We used to ball out in Cali in the days," Biggie said. "We still goin' out there. But the first thing [people] gonna think about is that situation, which has been blown up to much more than it was. They done made a personal beef between me and [Tupac and Death Row] into a coastal beef, East against West. And that's crazy. I never did nothin' wrong to Tupac, to Faith, to [Lil'] Kim, to nobody."

Just before his death, Biggie told a San Francisco radio disc jockey: "It just happened to be a coincidence that he [Tupac] was in the studio. He just—He couldn't really say who really had something to do with it at the time. So he just kinda leaned the blame on me."

On Thursday, November 30, 1995, a year to the day after the attempt in New York on Tupac's life, Randy "Stretch" Walker, Tupac's cousin who toured with him and witnessed the Quad Studios shooting, was shot to death. He was killed by three assailants during a high-speed chase in Queens. His murder was never solved, and police said there was no link to the shooting at Quad Studios and Stretch's murder.

In 1996, two months after Tupac's murder and two years after the Quad Studios shooting, a man was arrested and charged on multiple counts related to three armed robberies in Brooklyn. The *New York Daily News* reported that investigators had identified him as a suspect in the Quad Studios robbery and shooting. He, however, was never charged with that crime.

Speculation erupted that the murders of Stretch Walker and Jake Robles were connected to the New York shooting. Even so, the investigation remained closed. And after Tupac's death, NYPD's investigation into the 1994 Quad Studios shootings and robberies of Tupac and Freddie Moore remained closed. Las Vegas and New York police said there was no link.

The assaults didn't stop with the New York shooting. Another attempt would be made on Tupac's life. This one would be successful.

7

VEGAS INVESTIGATION

On Saturday, September 7, 1996, twenty-five-year-old Tupac Shakur attended the Mike Tyson–Bruce Seldon heavyweight boxing match in Las Vegas. A few hours later, Tupac was on his way to a post-fight party at Club 662, where Tyson was to appear and Tupac and Run-D.M.C. were to perform.

Marion "Suge" Knight, CEO of Death Row Records, for whom Tupac recorded, was behind the wheel of a black BMW 750 sedan. Tupac was in the passenger seat, sitting shotgun.

At a stoplight at the gridlocked intersection of Flamingo Road and Koval Lane, about two blocks off the Las Vegas Strip, a late-model white Cadillac with four men inside drove up to the right of Suge's BMW and stopped. The BMW was second in line in a caravan on its way to a party. Strangers had recognized the celebrity group of rappers and joined in the motorcade. When the Cadillac came to a stop, the BMW was boxed in.

Suddenly a gunman, identified by witnesses as a black man sitting in the backseat of the Cadillac, stuck his arm out of the window and— aiming for the passenger side of the BMW—opened fire. The shooter sprayed the passenger door and side of the BMW. Frank Alexander, a bodyguard driving in the car behind Tupac, saw a man's arm with a gun in his hand reach out of the Cadillac's left rear passenger window and shoot. Then, *bam!*—thirteen times. The gunman emptied a fully loaded magazine clip into the side of the BMW. Five bullets pierced the metal door and frame. Tupac's window was rolled down.

The back of Suge's head just above his neck was grazed by a bullet. Tupac wasn't as lucky.

As the gunman continued firing, Tupac frantically tried to climb into the backseat to avoid the onslaught of bullets. But he was hit four times. He never made it to the rear of the car.

The driver of the Cadillac, with the shooter and accomplices inside, fled the scene. No one—at least no who will admit it—saw the car or the shooter again.

The worst of Tupac's injuries was a gunshot wound to his chest. Doctors had to remove his right lung in an effort to stop him from bleeding to death internally. Despite their efforts, Tupac never regained consciousness. He died six days later, on Friday the thirteenth, at University Medical Center. He was twenty-five years old. Tupac had been executed in cold blood, gangland style.

Frank Alexander was the only bodyguard in Tupac and Suge's caravan when they were shot. The rest of the bodyguards—more than a dozen—were waiting two miles away at Club 662, a special-events club operated by Suge, where Tupac, Suge, and their crew were headed. Alexander was sitting in the driver's seat in a Lexus owned by Kidada Jones, behind Suge and Tupac's BMW 750. Kidada, Quincy Jones's daughter and Tupac's girlfriend, had stayed behind at the Luxor hotel-casino, where the couple had a suite. At the last minute, Frank decided to drive Kidada's car. His gun was in his own car, in a parking garage. That left Frank unarmed.

Alexander and the other bodyguards, all former or off-duty cops, including Las Vegas police who were moonlighting that night, had been hired to guard Tupac and his entourage while they were in Las Vegas. Nevada law requires that in order for security officers to carry guns while in the state, they have to obtain temporary concealed weapons permits in advance. But, according to Frank Alexander's account of the events that night in his book *Got Your Back*, that advance permitting had not been done.

After Tupac and the bodyguards arrived in Las Vegas, they were disappointed to learn that the proper permits allowing them to carry firearms had not been requested by Wrightway Security, a firm used by Death Row Records that, according to Frank Alexander, hired nothing but off-duty cops. A Las Vegas attorney for Death Row informed the bodyguards before the Tyson fight that they would not be legally allowed to arm themselves while guarding the Death Row entourage across the Nevada state line. That left them as little more than unarmed rent-a-cops.

If they were caught packing weapons without permits, the police could charge them and they could face stiff penalties. The majority of the security guards were accustomed to carrying Colt .45s. But not that night: At the advice of Suge's attorney, all of the bodyguards had left their guns behind that night. Frank Alexander had left his in his car.

When Tupac, Suge, Frank, and a friend of Suge's walked into the MGM Grand Garden Arena for the Tyson fight, they headed ringside, with Tupac sitting in section 4, row E, seat 2. It was a $1,000 ticket. Even though Death Row had earlier purchased twelve tickets, which included seats for the bodyguards, only four tickets were used by Suge's crew that night.

Sitting near Tupac were other celebrities, including actors Charlie Sheen and Louis Gossett Jr., former star baseball player Reggie Jackson, and the Reverend Jesse Jackson.

It was later rumored that Tupac and Suge Knight had gotten into an argument, as they went to sit down, with several people who were sitting in the seats reserved for Death Row. But witnesses and security officers at the fight said no such argument occurred.

What did happen, however, was a scuffle after the fight, between Tupac's entourage and a man named Orlando Anderson. The scuffle would prove to be a monumental moment in the evening's unfolding events.

The boxing match lasted just 109 minutes, ending with Tyson knocking out Seldon. Immediately following the match, Tupac and Suge tried to go backstage to see their friend Tyson. But they couldn't get past security. That was okay with them, though. They were supposed to hook up with Tyson in just a few hours at Death Row's after-party at Club 662. Tupac, walking ahead of the others, stopped for a quick TV interview—the last he would ever grant—with cameraman Cornell Wade, who was working for BET that night.

After the interview, the four—Tupac and his entourage—headed out of the MGM Grand Arena where they found the rest of their group, which included Suge's Death Row associates and members of Tupac's backup group, the Outlawz.

Now together, they all walked past the hotel's restaurants and shops toward the casino, which led to the hotel's main lobby. The hotel, the second-largest in the world, is a sprawling array of rooms, a casino, shops, a food court, and restaurants. It's a long walk from the MGM Grand Arena to the hotel's main lobby. Just before reaching the lobby, near a circular bank of elevators, the Death Row group encountered Orlando Anderson, who at the time was a twenty-two-year-old known member of the Crips L.A. street gang. Orlando was standing there, looking like he was waiting for someone, when Tupac and his entourage encountered him.

Tupac, according to the Compton Police Department's account, looked at Orlando and said, "You from the South?" Then Tupac lunged at Orlando, dropping him. Others in Tupac's group joined in. Once they had Orlando down on the ground, they kicked and stomped on him. A few minutes later, hotel security guards broke it up.

Las Vegas police were called by the security officers for backup, but Orlando declined to file a complaint. No one from Tupac's group was stopped or questioned by security or police. Tupac and his group, visible on surveillance cameras, simply walked away. No police or incident report was written or filed by the Las Vegas officers, according to police at the time. After the scuffle, Orlando was seen on videotape talking to LVMPD and security officers. He was standing up and was not visibly injured. Security guards offered to provide first aid to him. He declined. They also asked him to go downstairs to the security office with them to file a complaint. He declined.

The question that begged to be answered was this: If police felt a crime had been committed against Orlando Anderson that night, why didn't they file a crime report and try to arrest Tupac and his entourage? In the state of Nevada, victims don't have to press charges or file complaints. The police do that for them if there are witnesses present, which there were, and if there's probable cause. The scuffle caused a crowd to gather and caused a large commotion at the casino. But no attempts to arrest Tupac and his group were made. At the time, officers said they declined to file a police report because Orlando Anderson did not want to file charges. One man eventually would be arrested because of that scuffle—Suge Knight, for a parole violation.

Not until after Tupac was shot, and during the first few days following the shooting, did the significance of the MGM incident come to light. Investigators had the entire scuffle on film, captured on the hotel's surveillance video cameras. The cameras are programmed to record the date and time by hours, minutes, and seconds. The incident was there, blow by blow, as it occurred.

The LVMPD confiscated the hotel's videotape as evidence. When hotel security and Las Vegas police recalled the victim's name only as "Orlando," Los Angeles–area police were contacted and given a copy of the tape. Police there were extremely helpful. They recognized the victim as Orlando Anderson, an unemployed Crips gang member from Lakewood, California.

In search of answers to Tupac's murder, speculation once again focused on Biggie Smalls. Voletta Wallace, Biggie's mother, insisted that that hypothesis was simply wrong. "My son had nothing to do with Tupac's murder," she said.

Optimism that the case would be solved came in October 1996 when authorities with the Las Vegas Metropolitan Police Department said they had a possible suspect: Orlando Anderson, the target of the scuffle at the MGM Grand. An affidavit signed by Compton police detective Tim Brennan, dated September 25, 1996 (but not unsealed until February 1997 in Los Angeles Superior Court), stated: "Informants have told police that Southside Crips were responsible for the Las Vegas shooting. There is also an ongoing feud between Tupac Shakur and the Bloods-related Death Row Records with rapper Biggie Smalls and the East Coast's Bad Boy Entertainment, which employed Southside Crips gang members as security."

Compton Police subsequently obtained a warrant and arrested Orlando Anderson in Compton. Las Vegas police were there to interview him. The day after Orlando's arrest, a New York radio station reported that Orlando had told police Suge Knight was the intended target of the shooting on September 7.

But Las Vegas detectives said they were unable to directly link

Orlando Anderson to Tupac's slaying. They could place him in Las Vegas at the time of the murder, and they had in their possession surveillance videotape showing Orlando being kicked and stomped on by Tupac and some members of his entourage. But they said that wasn't motive enough for Orlando to kill Tupac. If Tupac's murder was connected somehow to Orlando, a known Southside Crip, the motive seemed clear: Orlando was a member of the rival gang of the Crips, whom police said was a rival of Death Row and Suge Knight. Tupac's association with Suge Knight and the Bloods was well known; Tupac had even appeared in photographs wearing a red scarf—the gang color of choice for the Bloods.

Could Orlando have had another, more obvious motive for the killing? Could it have been out of revenge for the assault on him at the MGM Grand?

Frank Alexander, the lone bodyguard watching out for Tupac the night he was fatally wounded, contended in his book, *Got Your Back: The Life of a Bodyguard in the Hardcore World of Gangsta Rap*, that it was more complicated than that.

Alexander wrote that as the Death Row entourage approached Orlando inside the hotel, Suge's friend, Travon Lane, had whispered in Tupac's ear just before Tupac took off after Orlando, decking him. Alexander said he learned a few days later that Orlando was one of about six Compton Crips whom Tupac's entourage believed had snatched from Travon's neck an expensive solid-gold Death Row medallion two months earlier in a Foot Locker store in a Lakewood, California, mall. That event was eventually laid out in a Compton police affidavit. Had Travon Lane pointed out Orlando Anderson to Tupac as one of those who had stolen his necklace, giving Tupac reason to attack Orlando at the MGM Grand?

That scenario has never been substantiated; however, circumstantial evidence of that showed up during a search of a house in which Orlando lived. In October 1996, a Death Row pendant was confiscated during a gang raid on a Compton house belonging to Orlando Anderson's uncle. Police said Orlando lived in the house, but Orlando claimed he didn't. Las Vegas police continued to say they had no evidence or motive linking Orlando to Tupac Shakur's murder. During that search, Orlando was detained on an unrelated warrant for the April 1996 murder of Edward Webb. An eyewitness had fingered Orlando as the trigger man in that homicide. Around the same time, a Compton police affidavit stated that an informant told a police officer that Orlando Anderson had been spotted with a .40-caliber Glock handgun. This was a potentially significant tip, since it was rumored that a .40-caliber Glock had been used in the attack on Tupac. The Glock, however, did not surface during the search.

It needs to be pointed out that the twenty-nine-page Compton police affidavit was largely based on Compton police informants. It does not legally prove who killed Tupac, nor does it legally prove that his death was a gang murder. Captain Danny Sneed with the Compton Police Department would say as much.

The affidavit lays out a startling account of the events that led to Tupac's murder, and a shot-by-shot account of a five-day bloodbath in Compton that his killing allegedly prompted. The gang war left three men dead and ten wounded. It also identified—based upon those statements from informants—Orlando Anderson as the man who shot Tupac Shakur in Las Vegas.

Included in the "bloodbath" laid out in the affidavit was the September 9, 1996, shooting of Darnell Brim, identified by police as "one of the leaders of the Southside Crips." He was shot several times, suffering injuries to his back, at 2430 East Alondra. Darnell was alleged to be one of the men in the Cadillac from which Tupac was shot. During the Alondra Street drive-by, a ten-year-old bystander, Lakezia McNeese, was shot and critically injured. She survived. On September 10, George Mack, identified as a "Leuders Park Piru," and Johnnie Burgie, were shot in front of 713 North Bradfield Street, a known hangout for Pirus. They both survived. Again on September 10, Gary Williams, brother of former Death Row Records security employee George Williams, was shot while on the corner of Pino and Bradfield Streets. He, too, survived his wounds.

On September 11, Bobby Finch was shot to death while standing outside a house on South Mayo. Compton Police told Las Vegas detectives that Finch was believed to be connected to Tupac's shooting. Finch, not a gang member himself, was a bodyguard who grew up in the same neighborhood as the Southside Crips, Compton police captain Sneed said.

On September 13, Tyrone Lipscomb and David McKulin were shot at while in front of 802 South Ward. They both survived. The suspects in this case, Compton police said, were believed to be members of the Bloods. Also on September 13, Timothy Flanagan and Marcus Childs were both shot to death during a drive-by at 100 North Burris Street, allegedly by gang members.

Then, on September 14, Mitchell Lewis, Apryle Murph, and Frederick Boykin, were shot while in front of 121 North Chester. All three survived. Three Bloods members were alleged to have done the shooting, on foot.

All of the shootings, as outlined in the Compton PD's affidavit, were believed to be retaliatory acts following the shooting of Tupac in Las Vegas. Gang member Marcos, who declined to give his last name, made a telling statement while standing outside the University Medical Center in Las Vegas the day Tupac passed away: "We know who did it. . . . I'm just saying that whoever did this is going to get found. The people who find him, I don't know what they'll do, but they'll take care of it in their own way. I mean, the payback, it's already started." He didn't name names.

About two weeks later, Orlando Anderson claimed that police, during the search of his uncle's house, had told him that he was the prime suspect in Tupac's murder. "Before he put the cuffs on me, the officer picked up the CD jacket with Tupac's photo on it and he asked me if I knew who it was," Orlando, after the October raid, told reporter Chuck Philipps with the *Los Angeles Times*. "I said, 'Man, everybody knows who *that* is.' " Orlando said that police told him that he was a suspect. They told him this, Orlando said, as they put him in a squad car and took him to the station. Orlando was detained for two days. He was released after Los Angeles prosecutors declined to charge him in an earlier L.A. slaying, and Las Vegas police opted not to file charges against him in the Las Vegas murder. Compton police told *MTV News* that Orlando was still the prime suspect in the April 1996 homicide, and that charges were expected to be formally filed "imminently." Ultimately, no charges were ever filed against Orlando Anderson.

"When the Las Vegas police got done interviewing me in October, they told me I was no longer considered a suspect in the murder of Tupac," Orlando told Phillips. "No one has ever contacted me or asked me a single question about it since. If they have all this evidence against me, then why haven't they arrested me? It's obvious that I'm innocent."

On September 8, 1998, exactly a year and two days after Tupac was shot in Las Vegas, Orlando Anderson filed suit against Tupac's estate for the assault on him by Tupac and his entourage at the MGM Grand. The action would have a domino effect and prompt three more suits.

Four days later, Tupac's mother, Afeni, filed a countersuit in California Superior Court in Los Angeles. In that suit, she claimed that Orlando was the triggerman in her son's fatal shooting. She sought money to cover her son's medical and cremation costs, as well as money for her pain and suffering. She alleged that Orlando's cousin Jerry "Monk" Bonds was the driver of the car used in the slaying. The suit stated that she had "reason to believe . . . that Bonds was the driver of that Cadillac and Anderson was a passenger in the Cadillac," referring to the car that pulled alongside the BMW in which Tupac and Suge Knight were riding. The suit then painted a scene in which Orlando exited the Cadillac, pulled a gun, and sprayed the BMW with gunfire. Orlando filed suit against Tupac's estate, Death Row, and Suge, based on mental and physical injuries he said he suffered in the attack. However, that the gunman got out of the car and shot Tupac from the street was later found to be inaccurate by investigators and witnesses. Instead, they said the gunman, sitting in the Cadillac, had fired from the backseat on the driver's side.

The MGM Grand Hotel's surveillance tape was what eventually sent Suge to prison on a nine-year sentence. Involvement in the scuffle, Superior Court judge J. Stephen Czuleger ruled, was grounds for revocation of Suge's probation in December 1995, when he had pleaded no contest to assaulting two rappers at a recording studio in 1992.

Orlando Anderson had claimed earlier that both Tupac and Suge joined in on his beating at the MGM Grand. But Orlando later changed his story when he appeared at Suge's hearing, claiming Suge had not been involved. In fact, Orlando testified under oath that Suge was the only one in Tupac's entourage that night who tried to come to his rescue. (It was rumored that Suge had purchased a sport-utility vehicle for Orlando in exchange for his positive testimony, but those rumors were never substantiated and investigators were never able to link the car back to Suge. When Orlando was later shot to death in an unrelated gunfight, he was in a late-model sport-utility vehicle registered in his name.)

David Chesnoff, Suge's Las Vegas attorney who had represented him in the federal investigation of Death Row, and David Kenner, Suge's longtime counsel, met with Orlando Anderson. Chesnoff was partners with Oscar Goodman, once a self-proclaimed "mouthpiece for the mob" who for years represented members of the mafia and who was elected mayor of Las Vegas in 1999. A former assistant U.S. attorney, Chesnoff has also made a national name for himself with appearances on the *Charlie Rose* PBS talk show and others.

"We met with [Orlando Anderson] in his lawyer's office," Chesnoff explained. "We told him we wanted the truth."

At one point, Orlando had told the police that he had purchased a ticket for the prizefight the day of the match. Fight fans knew, of course, that the fight was a sellout and that tickets, except for the remote possibility of pricey scalped ones, were not available on fight day. Later, however, Orlando changed his story and told reporters he had not attended the Tyson fight and that he had gone to Las Vegas with his girlfriend to gamble. He said he had stayed for free at the Excalibur hotel-casino, next door to the Luxor, where Tupac was staying. It was never learned where Orlando, who was unemployed, got gambling money.

Then, at the hearing for Suge Knight where prosecutors were seeking to revoke his probation because of the scuffle with Orlando Anderson, Orlando again changed significant accounts of his trip to Las Vegas. It was after the meeting with Suge's attorneys that Orlando changed his story. During that hearing, he admitted to lying earlier under oath; he had been deposed as part of a wrongful-death civil suit filed against him by Tupac's estate. Tupac was seen administering blows on a videotape of the scuffle, and Suge Knight was returned to prison on a parole violation as a result of his participation in that incident. At Suge's parole hearing, Orlando testified that Suge did not harm him and was only trying to stop the fight. But in his earlier deposed testimony, Orlando had said he was punched and kicked by Suge.

Donald David, the lawyer for Tupac's estate who took the deposition, had this to say about Orlando's testimony: "One thing that's been accomplished is that we've shown that [Orlando] Anderson has lied under oath," he told the *New York Times* after the hearing. "That's a critical accomplishment. And we now have Anderson's side of the story for the first time. And once you have that, you can start verifying or disputing it."

Lawyers for Orlando minimized their client's contradictions. They said that he had lied previously because he had been threatened by Suge Knight's associates and that the wrongful-death lawsuit was simply retaliation against the personal-injury suit Orlando had filed as a result of the hotel beating. Lawyers for Tupac's estate, however, pointed to other contradictions. In previous sworn statements, Orlando had pleaded his Fifth Amendment right against self-incrimination when asked whether he and members of his family were members of the Crips. This time, Orlando answered no to both of those questions.

And there was Orlando's previous testimony that the Excalibur had given him a free room because he was a big gambler. But in the new deposition, he said that he had had no income for the past five years, had not filed any tax returns for that period, had spent less than $100 gambling, and had paid for his room in cash.

Afeni Shakur's attorneys were attempting to establish a motive for her son's killing. Tying Orlando to the Crips, with Suge's longtime known association with the Bloods, could possibly provide a motive: an ongoing gang feud between the Crips and the Bloods.

The second defendant in the wrongful-death suit, Jerry "Monk" Bonds, accused by Tupac's estate of being the driver of the white Cadillac used in the killing, was also said to be a Crip. Bonds turned up missing after the filing of the suit. Under oath, Orlando denied knowing Bonds. Typically, a wrongful-death suit would follow a completed police investigation, but Richard Fischbein, a lawyer for Tupac's estate, said he was forced to step in. "We would end the civil trial in a second if they [the police] would take a very serious look at this issue," he told the *New York Times* at the time. "But I've called and pushed and prodded them, and these guys aren't doing anything. So that leaves us with the mother forced into a position of having to deal with this situation on her own, and that's an outrage. I have my own theory. And that is that they're trying to create the Disneyland of the Far West in Las Vegas and the last thing in the world that they want is a story about black-gang drive-by shootings taking place in their town. So this is not something they're going to bring to a big trial that will be covered by the national press."

LVMPD have denied dragging their feet in the Tupac investigation.

Suge, meanwhile, maintained his innocence in the rumble with Orlando Anderson, and claimed he was trying to break it up, not take part in it. In the end, Superior Court Justice J. Stephen Czuleger didn't believe him, and instead believed a hotel security guard who testified seeing Suge kick Orlando at least three times. The hotel's black-and-white videotape was hazy and unfocused and it was difficult to make out exactly who was involved.

Judge Czuleger, relying on testimony from the police and hotel security, revoked Suge's probation for joining in on the scuffle. The judge said he was inclined to issue a prison sentence because Suge "has a history of violence." He did. He ultimately sentenced Suge to nine years in prison. After a stint in the Los Angeles County Jail during his hearings, Suge was remanded to the California Men's Colony East in San Luis Obispo. His attorneys appealed the judge's decision. "I think if the court does what it should do, he'll be released. He's been punished enough," said attorney David Chesnoff, noting that he believed Suge looked at himself as a political prisoner.

In September 1998, a state appeals court overturned Judge Czuleger's decision. But as Suge's attorneys were preparing to have him released from prison, the state challenged the higher court's decision. Suge's attorneys asked that he be released from prison pending the outcome. Their request was denied. The outcome of the case was under review and pending at the time of this writing, but David Chesnoff was optimistic Suge would be released. By 2000, Suge was still imprisoned.

Suge, in the meantime, "is fine," Chesnoff said. "He has a very good perspective. He'd rather not be there [in prison]." But Suge's release was ultimately denied. "What happened is the court withdrew the opinion and is reviewing it," Chesnoff explained. "I still think his chances are good that he'll get out. It will probably be just after the first of the year." The first of the year 2000 came and went and Suge remained in custody.

Suge's life has gone on in prison. He was rumored to have married while at the Men's Colony, to R&B singer Michel'le (pronounced Mish-a-LAY), after divorcing his first wife, Sharitha. (A prison official in northern California, however, said there was no marriage certificate on file for Suge. A prison officer in central California said, if he was married while in prison, that would be confidential inmate information. There was no marriage on file with the county of San Luis Obispo for Suge, but a county clerk said the marriage, at the bride and groom's request, could have been made confidential and sealed from the public.)

Chesnoff described better days for Suge and Death Row, when Chesnoff would accompany Suge to sporting events and dinners, along with Tupac and other rappers and Death Row associates.

In the midst of the Tupac investigation, rumors surfaced that newspaper tabloids were offering $100,000 for a photo of Tupac either in the hospital or dead. One rumor was that word had spread at the hospital that the *National Enquirer* would pay for a photo of Tupac in the intensive-care unit. At that point, I indirectly became involved. A source had slipped me a photo of Tupac's body lying on a gurney in the Clark County Coroner's Office. Rather than sell it to the tabloids, which was against government policy and possibly prosecutable, the source gave it to me, at the time a crime-beat reporter for the *Las Vegas Sun*. I, in turn, published it in my book *The Killing of Tupac Shakur*. Once the book with the autopsy photo was released, reporters began flooding the coroner's office and homicide detectives with inquiries. Stories were written and moved on The Associated Press wire. An investigation was launched by the LVMPD into who had leaked me the photo. As a journalist, I protected my source and did not reveal the name.

Ron Flud, the coroner, confirmed for reporters that the photo was in fact an authentic one, taken after the autopsy was done on Tupac the evening he died. I was told by Coroner Flud, "I will never speak to you again," if I did not reveal who leaked me the photo, or, at the least, have a story published in the *Las Vegas Sun* saying that the photo was not leaked by one of his employees. Police investigators asked the same of me: that I issue a statement saying that they did not leak me the photo. I told both offices that I would not discuss the photo with them or anyone else, nor would I narrow their search by eliminating one or the other.

Lieutenant John Alamshaw, then with the LVMPD's internal affairs bureau (IAB), called me, asking to set up an appointment in his office for an interview with his detectives. I, of course, declined to be interviewed and did not schedule an appointment. Later I learned that a report was written by IAB saying that I had been interviewed by detectives and supposedly told them that I had solicited several officers and offered them $10,000 if they would slip me a photo of Tupac. As a result, a criminal investigation of me was about to be launched. The notion, of course, was preposterous, especially in light of the fact that detectives had never interviewed me. Once I learned about their bogus report, I telephoned Undersheriff Richard Winget. The undersheriff told me he would have the IAB report destroyed because it wasn't true.

The police investigation into who leaked me the autopsy photo ended thirty days later without success. To this day, Coroner Ron Flud will not take my calls. The photo, as difficult as it is for some to see, quelled news reports that Tupac had faked his own death and that he was still alive.

Meantime, Suge's earliest release date from prison would be June 10, 2002, according to prison spokeswoman Terri Knight (no relationship to Suge). During his incarceration at the central California prison, Suge did not participate in a work program, which was optional and not mandatory. He was housed along with the general population. As of December 1998, he had one disciplinary action in his folder that had been placed there after he refused in October 1997 to take an evaluation examination, Terri Knight said. His behavior was considered "failure to follow an order," the prison report stated. Suge did not, however, lose any good time for that refusal, according to the prison records. Suge also was given credit for time already served in the L.A. County Jail. But Suge would eventually be moved to another prison and his release date pushed up.

While Suge languished in prison and fought his legal battles, the investigation into Tupac's killing continued. Whatever the motive in Tupac's murder, his mother believed it was Orlando Anderson who was the one responsible.

Afeni, an original member of the Black Panther Party in the 1960s, became an anathema for Las Vegas police, often publicly criticizing them for not trying harder to solve her son's murder. Dealing with the police and the law was nothing new to Afeni. She had successfully represented herself in the 1960s after being indicted as one of "the Panther 21" in a murder case in which she was later acquitted of all charges.

For her son's case, Afeni Shakur hired New York attorney Richard Fischbein, who was also handling the estate and for whom Afeni had worked as a legal assistant. After filing the wrongful-death suit against Orlando, Fischbein announced that two crimes had been committed against Tupac: one by Anderson and the other by an incompetent police investigation. "It's a shame that the mother of the murder victim is put in a position to have to do the work of the Las Vegas Police Department," Fischbein said. He noted that he and his team of attorneys had spent more time questioning Orlando than did the Las Vegas police investigators.

Afeni's attorneys were confident that depositions from Orlando would reveal information about the case she insisted was never sought by the police.

The case against Orlando was scheduled to go to trial September 1998. Orlando himself, however, was murdered in May 1998. Ironically, it appeared as if retaliation for Tupac's murder had nothing to do with Orlando's death. In June 1998, following Orlando's murder, Afeni Shakur's attorney said that even though Orlando was dead, the lawsuit would continue against Orlando Anderson's estate. Afeni Shakur's civil suit against Orlando, however, had been precipitated by Orlando filing suit against Tupac's estate for the beating at the MGM Grand hotel-casino. Both suits would continue.

After Orlando was killed during an unrelated driveby in 1998, attorneys for Orlando's estate then filed suit against Tupac Shakur's estate, its administrators, three law firms, and four attorneys for breach of oral contract and malicious prosecution. Orlando had sought $1 million for damage to his reputation. The suit, filed in March 1999 in California Superior Court in L.A., charged that Tupac's estate declined to complete a May 1998 agreement to dismiss a 1997 wrongful-death suit against Orlando. A settlement of $78,000 was allegedly agreed upon before Orlando was shot to death May 29, 1998. In return, Orlando had agreed to dismiss a 1997 suit he filed against Tupac's estate, alleging he had suffered physical injury and emotional distress from the 1996 attack at the MGM Grand hotel-casino in Las Vegas hours before Tupac was shot. The action alleged that Tupac's administrators—his mother Afeni, and her attorney, Richard Fischbein—and the other lawyers filed the wrongful-death suit with malice and "without probable cause."

After Orlando was killed, Afeni told *MTV News* that she felt compassion for his family and four children because the question of Anderson's innocence or guilt would always hang over them. When asked whether she believed Orlando killed Tupac, she said she believed he was responsible but that he didn't act alone.

Before his death, Orlando Anderson had been questioned by Afeni Shakur's attorneys about Tupac's death. The declarations made by Orlando, however, didn't shed any new light on the case, and Afeni Shakur would be disappointed once again.

Instead, Orlando's statements offered little more than a new set of contradictions. Afeni's lawyers interviewed Orlando for six hours on Thursday, February 26, 1998. Afterward, they said the details offered up by Orlando at that time differed from accounts he previously had given the authorities, including the role of Suge Knight in the hotel altercation.

The lawyers had said as they prepared for the September 1998 wrongful-death court case that they intended to subpoena documents previously ignored by police, including cellular-phone, hotel, and car-rental records, and to interview a number of witnesses, including Suge

Knight, who had been held since November 1996 for a parole violation related to the assault on Orlando.

In an affidavit filed by Afeni Shakur's attorneys, the suit claimed that the altercation at the MGM Grand came as a result of Tupac's entourage accusing Orlando of stealing the gold Death Row medallion from Travon a month earlier at the Lakewood Mall. The lawsuit contended that Orlando was riding in the white Cadillac later that night when it pulled up beside the car carrying Tupac and Suge and a gunman opened fire, fatally wounding Tupac. Before he himself was also killed, Orlando adamantly denied the allegations.

While Afeni Shakur blamed police for a lack of a thorough investigation into her son's murder case, LVMPD detectives blamed witnesses for not providing them with enough information to make any arrests.

But there was one witness, Yafeu "Yak" Fula, also known as "Kadafi," one of Tupac's backup singers in the Outlawz, who said he could possibly identify Tupac's killer. Fula was riding in the car behind Suge's on the night Tupac was mortally wounded. But the police let him go home to New Jersey without interviewing him in depth about what he saw that night. Also sitting in the backseat of the car with Fula, was Malcolm Greenridge, who was also a member of the backup group the Outlawz and who rapped under the moniker E.D.I. Mean. Fula and Greenridge sat on the curb at the scene for several hours, waiting to be questioned. Greenridge told the police he didn't see anything. Fula told them, "Maybe." David Kenner later served as the mediator between Fula and detectives, who tried to schedule an interview with the witness. However, Fula was soon ambushed and killed, rendering forever mute the only witness willing to talk to investigators.

On Sunday, November 10, 1996, two months after Tupac died, Fula was visiting his girlfriend at a housing project in Orange, New Jersey. In the middle of the night, gunfire erupted inside a dark hallway. When the police arrived, they found the nineteen-year-old Fula slumped against a wall near a third-floor stairwell. The bulletproof vest he was wearing didn't save him. He died hours later. He had been shot in the face at point-blank range. "Execution style," was how Orange police captain Richard Conte described it to me.

Fula was the witness the LVMPD had been looking for for two months. The day after Fula's murder, LVMPD Homicide Unit sergeant Kevin Manning said, "I don't know how you pronounce his name. I don't even know how you spell it. We had a hard time finding him. We didn't know where he was until he showed up in New Jersey on Sunday, dead."

"He was the only guy who ever said he saw anything, and we were ready to set up a lineup for him before he really disappeared," said Lieutenant Larry Spinosa, who was heading the investigation at the time.

Lieutenant Wayne Petersen, who later replaced Spinosa in the Homicide Unit, said the same thing: "Yafeu Fula was the only one who gave us any indication in the interview [at the scene] [that] he could identify the gunman. His statement was, 'Yeah, I might be able to recognize him.' "

Orange and Las Vegas police insisted that Fula's death was unrelated to the Tupac investigation and that it was not the result of trying to silence a witness. The day after Fula's murder, Sergeant Manning said that Fula's death was simply one more young black man gunned down—"the odds were against him" because of his race, not because he was a witness to Tupac's murder. It was a case, police said, of Fula being in the wrong place at the wrong time. No conspiracy there, they said. Yafeu Fula, who performed with the Outlawz as Kadafi, was the son of Yaasman Fula, Tupac's office manager, and Sekou Odinga, a self-proclaimed "New African" and "political prisoner of war" and a member of the Black Liberation Party now imprisoned in a federal penitentiary in Lompoc, California, for racketeering and attempted murder of police.

Biggie Smalls was once asked where he had been that fateful September day when Tupac was shot in Las Vegas. "I got home and it was on the news, and I couldn't believe it," he told *Vibe*. "I knew so many niggahs like him, so many rough, tough muthafuckas gettin' shot. I said, 'He'll be out in the morning, smoking some weed, drinking some Hennessy, just hangin' out.' You ain't thinkin' it's gonna happen to him. . . . You be thinking that when a niggah is making so much money that his lifestyle will protect him, that a drive-by shooting ain't supposed to happen. . . .

"I'm just realizing that nothing protects you from the inevitable. If something's gonna happen, it's gonna happen, no matter what you do. It's crazy for me to even think that a rapper can't get killed just because he raps. That shit can happen. Even if you clean your life up, it comes back at you. What goes around comes around, 'cause karma is a muthafucka." Then he added, "I'm gonna deal the cards of my own fate."

Critics of both Los Angeles and Las Vegas police have opined that if Tupac Shakur and Biggie Smalls were white men, both cases would have gotten more attention from investigators. These were two mega-stars, tops in their field, each with double-platinum albums.

Three-and-a-half years later, Biggie's murder remained unsolved; four years later, Tupac's case was still unsolved. Detectives have explained that the cases were difficult to work from the beginning because witnesses had been uncooperative. However, in the Ennis Cosby L.A. freeway murder case, to which Los Angeles police initially assigned every available investigator from the force, the lone witness, a female acquaintance of Cosby's, originally said she didn't see anything. Still, the case—high-profile because the victim was the son of comedian Bill Cosby—was quickly solved by police, and the killer has since been convicted. But Tupac and Biggie were not protected by their notoriety or their fame. Both were shot during professional, ambush-style hits on the streets.

"Thousands have been murdered," Afeni Shakur told a reporter. "It is not a priority to find out why they were killed. That's what I'm left with, the sorrow that our children are expendable."

For his part, Tupac's stepfather, Mutula Shakur, whose real name is Jeral Wayne Williams, issued a statement from prison, where he is serving a 60-year sentence for a Bronx murder/robbery. It read: "Afeni and I have never supported a Crip versus Blood feud as presented by the Las Vegas police concerning our son's assassination. . . . Our family has not come to any final conclusion as to who killed our son, Tupac. Nor, why he was killed. His murder and the death of [backup singer] Yafeu 'Kadafi' Fula . . . a month after Tupac . . . has our family and extended family in constant grief as well as searching for the truth in all matters. It has always been our position that with no investigation, [there's] no right to speak or act."

Four years later, however, Afeni Shakur's critical stance toward the Las Vegas police softened.

"I'm sure the truth is not as simple as who pulled the trigger," Afeni told *Vibe*. "It's too easy to blame the police or to talk about black and white. That messes up the real issue, which is that we help to make ourselves expendable by not valuing the lives that come before us, whether that is Tupac or Biggie or any other mother's son."

On the first anniversary of Tupac's death, Afeni Shakur said: "As long as you keep Tupac's vision, his music . . . his music will not die. I believe in my heart you can kill a revolutionary, but you cannot kill a revolution."

After Afeni Shakur settled Tupac's affairs with Death Row in 1997, via an out-of-court agreement, she launched Amaru Records. She released a double CD of Tupac's music, titled *Are You Still Down?* The CD sold three million copies. However, in 1998, Afeni told *MTV News*: "Currently, we have an agreement that Death Row is very, very, very, very sluggish on keeping. We have an agreement, and they actually have not, as of yet, kept their agreement . . . I'm sorry to say this, but it's like the slimeball method."

Death Row has always been identified as a producer of gangsta-rap releases. The label has been trying to break out of that mold, however, especially with the 1999 release of an R&B album by Michel'le, who eventually became Suge's girlfriend and, it's rumored, his wife. Bad Boy, since it was formed in the early 1990s, has produced mainstream albums for top artists such as Mariah Carey in Combs's studio, dubbed "Daddy's House." On the other hand, Death Row, so named because most everyone there was an ex-con or parolee, historically has been strictly a gangsta-rap label. Death Row's sound was considered by many to be the epitome of West Coast rap; and the name became synonymous with the term "gangsta-rap."

"We've always been known as gangsta-rap, but that's not what Suge Knight ever intended," Suge's then publicist, Gregg Howard, said in 1999 in defense of Death Row's choice of rappers and style. Suge wanted to diversify the field of artists. But he was jailed while in the process of trying to accomplish that, Howard said.

Tupac and Suge had become inseparable after Tupac signed with Death Row. Tupac had signed a five-page handwritten contract, penned by Suge's attorney David Kenner, in return for Suge posting a $1.4 million bond releasing Tupac from prison pending an appeal of his sexual-assault conviction. Tupac had left the Clinton Correctional Facility in upstate New York, flew to California, and went straight into Can-Am Studios, on Oxnard Boulevard in Tarzana, to record.

Critics accused Suge of controlling Tupac and other rappers at Death Row. Suge was sued and arrested several times for using heavy-handed tactics in some of his business dealings. His critics, including Tupac's mother in her civil lawsuit, said signing Tupac had been another strong-arm tactic by Suge, a former football first-team defensive lineman and rookie of the year for the University of Nevada, Las Vegas, Rebels. Many in the industry said they feared Suge even while he was imprisoned in the California Men's Colony in San Luis Obispo.

By the time Tupac joined Death Row, Snoop Doggy Dogg, whose real name is Calvin Broadus, had also signed to the same label. Snoop and Tupac ultimately became close friends. "Me and Tupac," Snoop told MTV in 1995, "I look at him like he's a relationship I've been seekin' in rap—as far as a companion, someone I can look up to, like a brother, and he can look up to me. We're equals." Suge Knight posted $1 million bail when Snoop was charged with murder. (He was later acquitted.)

" 'Pac is in heaven. This is hell where we're living at," Snoop said, after Tupac was murdered. Tupac's death had fueled fears of a plot to kill the nation's rappers. After Biggie's death, Snoop said: "I'm not trying to be no Martin Luther King. I'm just sayin', 'Let's be real.' We could have more fun just chillin' instead of stressin' and worryin' who's behind you, and paranoid. A lot of things happened that shouldn't a happened. As I get older, I don't want to go that route." After Biggie's murder, Snoop took measures to protect himself and his family from violence. First, he postponed his thirty-eight-concert tour, called the

"Doggfather East-West Fresh Fest 1997 World Tour." The postponement was done, Snoop's PR group said, "out of respect for the late Notorious B.I.G." For his 1997 Lollapalooza tour, he traveled in a $140,000 bulletproof vehicle. Dubbed the "gangster tank," it was an aquamarine Chevy van custom-built by Royal Motors in Beverly Hills, complete with gun slits. Instead of off-duty police officers, though, Snoop reportedly hired bodyguards belonging to a security force connected to the Nation of Islam, a Muslim group affiliated with the minister Louis Farrakhan.

Suge Knight and Sean "Puffy" Combs, while their labels have been rightly or wrongly compared, come from opposite sides of the track. Suge grew up in the ghetto in Compton and has never hidden his street-gang ties to the Bloods, painting his homes, offices, and cars blood red. After high school, he received a full football scholarship to the University of Nevada, Las Vegas, where he played for the Rebels for two years. Knight, because of his large size, later became a personal bodyguard for singer Bobby Brown, who later married singer Whitney Houston. He broke into the music business after meeting people in the industry through that job. Combs, on the other hand, grew up in a middle-class household and attended a Manhattan prep school, then Howard University in Washington, D.C., where he was a business-administration student. Still, Puffy seemed less interested in academics and more interested in the social scene. While at Howard, he began promoting house parties and small campus concerts, one of which ended in a deadly stampede and landed him in hot water. He also allegedly sold term papers and old exams. He entered the music industry as an intern at nineteen and was quickly promoted. He became the youngest CEO ever of a record label.

Attorney Kenny Meiselas explained: "Even the police who sat with Puffy during the [homicide] investigation came to know he is just a professional entrepreneur. He's a young black entrepreneur in the same way a David Geffen is a white entrepreneur. Puffy's not a thug. Once he got into the business, he was very successful and became the hottest record guy in the business."

An investigation by the U.S. Justice Department into where Suge

Knight got the money to finance Death Row continued for several years with no charges being filed. Although it has been heavily reported, using unnamed sources, that Bad Boy was also under investigation by the feds, there is no evidence that there was an inquiry. In fact, neither Combs, his attorney, nor anyone at Bad Boy has ever been contacted about such an investigation. LAPD Robbery-Homicide Division lieutenant Pat Conman responded with, "I have no idea what the feds are doing. To my knowledge, that's not true [that Biggie was under surveillance]. I have no knowledge of that. I believe detectives have had some conversations with the FBI, but just in the normal course of business."

Nevertheless, Puffy Combs complained to the *Los Angeles Times* in an April 23, 1997, article that he and Biggie frequently observed what appeared to be undercover officers monitoring their movements for weeks before Biggie's shooting. "We had no idea why," Puffy said. "We figured, hey, if the government wants to waste taxpayers' money following artists and entertainers like us around, well, at least we might get a little free security out of it." The *Los Angeles Times*, citing unidentified sources, wrote that undercover officers from New York were also in the L.A. vicinity during the shooting, as part of a federal investigation of criminals allegedly affiliated with Bad Boy Entertainment. Also, Biggie, on his second album, wrote about being monitored by the feds.

It has been widely publicized that Tupac, as well, was under surveillance by the FBI at the time of his shooting, leading to speculation that federal agents may have been watching when the two were alternately murdered.

If Biggie was under surveillance, it was because of something he was doing that had nothing to do with Bad Boy, said Meiselas, Puffy Combs's attorney. The company had gotten a bad rap because of the federal investigation into Death Row, he says. The feds, meantime, weren't talking.

But Lil' Kim, who was a friend of Biggie's from Brooklyn, and eventually recorded under the Bad Boy label, told *Sister Sister* magazine that Puffy had hired police officers and federal agents as security guards at the Impact Music Convention.

"They were federal agents and stuff like that," Lil' Kim said. "They're still watching because people were still saying nasty things after Biggie died and nasty things was happening, so we had to just be really careful. Puffy assigned a few of them [federal agents]."

Puffy's attorney, however, adamantly denied the notion.

Death Row has said its money came from Interscope Records. Suge, however, approached Interscope with CDs and albums already cut, which took money to produce; it's the seed money it took to produce those CDs and albums that the Department of Justice may have been curious about.

David Chesnoff, Suge's attorney in the federal case, confirmed that a grand jury had convened to look into Death Row and Suge Knight. Chesnoff noted that he had not been privy to the findings of that grand jury. The grand jury was looking into whether convicted drug kingpin Michael O. Harris had contributed $1.5 million in seed money to the Death Row label. The federal grand jury convened shortly after Suge was jailed for a parole violation (stemming from a 1992 assault) that had occurred during the beating of Orlando Anderson at the MGM Grand the night Tupac was fatally wounded. Suge was sentenced to nine years in a California state prison for his involvement in that beating. About five employees of Death Row Records—once dubbed the Motown of the nineties—were running the company during Suge's incarceration. Reggie Wright, who ran Wrightway Security, was one of those at the helm, according to Death Row publicist Gregg Howard.

"Unlike the President Clinton grand-jury investigations, we don't get to read in the newspapers about what they [federal investigators] are doing," Chesnoff said. "Apparently there's a grand-jury investigation. There's been document production and I know they've interviewed witnesses. But that's all I know."

Suge has repeatedly denied that any money from illegal activity financed Death Row. He has also suggested that the federal probe was racially motivated. Besides investigating Suge and Death Row, the feds were looking into whether Suge's attorney, David Kenner, was involved with Death Row extending beyond his role as counsel. Kenner, a former Los Angeles County prosecutor, has acquired a fortune defending rappers, including Death Row co-founder Andre "Dr. Dre" Young, Snoop Doggy Dogg, and Tupac Shakur. Kenner has denied any wrongdoing.

Chesnoff said Suge, like Puffy, has been given a bad rap. He referred to his client as "a political prisoner"—a successful African-American man by whom people felt intimidated and threatened. "Suge is a very exceptionally smart and talented person who got tainted with a bad image that's really undeserved. He's one of the few entrepreneurs who has made significant contributions to the community from which he came. Suge is a dynamic person.

"I predict that, like a phoenix, he is going to rise from the ashes. We're confident things are going to turn out well for him. I know that Suge is anxious to either have his present sentence reversed by the appellate court, or finish his sentence and get out and go back to work."

Death Row released an album in October 1998 with three songs by Tupac. "Tupac's records have done well since he passed," Gregg Howard, publicist for Death Row Records, said. Unfortunately for Tupac's estate, bootlegged copies of Tupac's music were at one point selling more than the commercial units. Still, all told, Tupac's albums grossed more than $70 million.

As for Death Row's status without Suge Knight, Howard said, "Our job at the company is to put out the records." A group of employees has been running the business, he said, since Suge was incarcerated in November 1996. Although Sharitha Knight, Suge's ex-wife, was earlier said to be running the company, "She never did," Howard said. "Sharitha managed some of the artists—Snoop, Tha Dogg Pound—but that was the extent of it. She never ran Death Row."

Meantime, Jimmy Iovine, head of Interscope Records, Death Row's record distributor, dropped the controversial label. Then, in early 1998, Snoop Doggy Dogg left Death Row. Before that, Dr. Dre, who co-founded Death Row, left the label. Snoop explained to the *Long Beach Press-Telegram* that he left Death Row because he was concerned about his career and his personal safety. Iovine and Interscope quickly swooped up Dr. Dre with a multimillion-dollar contract on one of its labels, Aftermath Entertainment.

Even so, Suge said to the *L.A. Times*, "The future looks positive."

"We understand now that the things we do affect people's lives," he told the *L.A. Times* during a jailhouse interview in 1998, "and it's up to us to try and make people's lives as positive and strong as possible. Even with all these setbacks, Death Row will survive."

Suge also told the *Times* that Interscope's decision to drop Death Row's distribution deal with the rap label came directly from the head of that label's parent company, the Seagram Company.

"Seagram, which makes most of its money manufacturing alcohol, says they don't want to put out hard rap music because of the effect it might have on kids," Suge said. "But let me ask you this: What kills more kids each year? Is it rap music or is it alcohol?"

But even from prison, another distribution deal, this one with Priority Records, came through for Suge.

Suge also said that prison made him stronger. "My mind is free. My heart is free. I'm stronger. I'm smarter. I'm more focused. . . . It's strange, but this might be the best thing that ever happened to me."

And in February 2000, Death Row Records teamed with LoadTV, an Internet media company, to feature uncensored music videos at deathrowtv.com, according to the *Hollywood Reporter*. The site hosted videos deemed to be "too hot" for MTV and BET, drawn from the full-length video *Death Row: Uncut*, which featured banned videos from Dr. Dre, Ice Cube, and Tupac Shakur. *Death Row: Uncut* was number 4 on *Billboard*'s Top Music Videos chart and number 21 on its Top Video Sales chart the week of February 11, 2000.

Even though Suge's business savvy seemed to carry him along, some felt his tough reputation as head of Death Row had caused Tupac's death. While the East-West rivalry was an initial plausible theory for the murder, *Vibe* editor-in-chief Alan Light said he "wouldn't be surprised if it didn't have anything to do with Tupac, but was more related to Suge. There have been up to three contracts on Suge's life at any given time. He's very public . . . about his gang affiliation. There are a lot of people with a lot of issues about him."

But Suge, in the September 1996 issue of *The Source*, said, "Ain't no East Coast–West Coast thang. That ain't it." Puffy said essentially the same thing, only to the *New York Daily News*: "I really don't know who killed him. I would be just like the media if I speculated. The honest answer is that I have no idea. I can't go on rumors and speculation." He said the feud, which he noted was "fictionalized," could have been a random act of violence.

If not a feud, what then? And if their claims were true, then why weren't they telling the police?

Suge's friends defended his silence about Tupac's murder. According to them, he wanted to tell Las Vegas Metropolitan Police investigators the story behind Tupac's death. But detectives posed only ancillary questions to him, they claimed, that didn't even scratch the surface. According to both LVMPD sergeant Kevin Manning and attorney David Chesnoff, Suge's interview with the sergeant and two detectives lasted between fifteen and thirty minutes. Was that enough time to give a rundown on the events of that fateful evening? One person in the police interview room that evening answered no.

While Las Vegas police say they did not get a break in the case because witnesses were unwilling to come forward, Suge's interview session appeared to be cursory at best. "They didn't ask him in-depth questions," David Chesnoff noted. "It was like they didn't want to know details."

Suge Knight, along with attorneys David Kenner, Steve Steiner, and David Chesnoff, went to LVPMD's Homicide headquarters on West Charleston Boulevard about four miles west of the hospital where Tupac Shakur was still listed in grave condition, his chances for survival were fifty-fifty. Not more than a half-hour later, Suge and his attorneys left the Homicide headquarters. The sergeant and two detectives, the lead investigative team, would never speak to him again.

Suge Knight's interview at six P.M. Wednesday, September 11, 1996—four days after the shooting—lasted thirty minutes. Investigators afterward said Suge was not helpful during their interrogation of him and that he gave them little information. That information, they told reporters, was not beneficial in helping to solve the case. What they had hoped for was that Suge would finger the assailant by giving them the name of the gunman. It wasn't to be.

In a news release, the LVMPD stated, "Knight made himself available for the interview but was unable to give the investigators any information that would help in determining a motive, nor was he able to help identify possible suspects."

Suge, his attorney, David Chesnoff, said, *was* willing to talk, which was why he went to Homicide headquarters to begin with. The detectives didn't ask Suge specific questions, he said. And Suge didn't volunteer any information. Suge didn't consider it an interrogation, but rather, a short and simple question-and-answer session. Sergeant Manning afterward said that what Suge gave them was "very little" information. And what minute information he did provide was inconsequential in their quest to solve the crime.

The purpose of a police interrogation is to gather the facts. Officers are trained at the police academy that an effective interrogator forces witnesses and suspects to give specific details and to repeat those details, with the interrogator prodding them, to see if the story stays the same or if there are holes in it. It's also an opportunity for investigators, who usually aren't present when crimes go down, to glean the facts from as many people as possible so they can piece together the puzzle of the crime to learn exactly what occurred.

When Tupac died on Friday, September 13, 1996, the case immediately went from an attempted-murder to a homicide investigation.

The following Monday, September 16, 1996, Compton detectives Paul Fournier and Mike Caouette met in Las Vegas with Sergeant Manning and detectives Brent Becker and Mike Franks, a Compton police affidavit stated. The Compton officers viewed a videotape of the MGM Grand scuffle and identified the victim for the LVMPD as Orlando Anderson, a member of the Southside Crips. The out-of-town officers told Las Vegas detectives that they had received several tips accusing Orlando of Tupac's murder, according to the affidavit.

LVMPD police have said that the Tupac investigation, which from the start was investigated by two detectives and one sergeant who worked on other cases at the same time, was "ongoing." More than three years later, the investigation was still stalled. Police, however, said they continue to follow up on leads as they receive them. In Las Vegas, unsolved homicide investigations are not closed. They're either in active or inactive status. They remain open until they're solved.

Suge, then thirty-one years old, was driving the BMW on East Flamingo Road when he and Tupac were shot and was an eyewitness to the murder. He has maintained from the beginning that he would be happy to answer any questions, but that he was not going to make it easy and do the Las Vegas police investigators' work for them. He stated so on a national television news program. His stance was that he would cooperate but they would have to be the ones to track down the shooter.

Conversely, the police felt Suge, if he had any idea who the shooter was, should have freely given up the identity to them. The LVMPD Homicide team went into the interview room hopeful that Suge Knight would finger the shooter. They were disappointed. "He didn't give us anything beneficial," Sergeant Manning said the day after the interview. "I would consider him telling us who shot him beneficial. Nothing he said helped us." Because Suge did not point a finger and name a suspect, the police didn't press him further for details.

The day after their short interview with Suge, investigators said they would have no reason to ever reinterview Suge. They also noted that Suge was never considered a suspect and that he was, instead, a victim and a witness.

In November 1998, Lieutenant Wayne Petersen, who headed the LVMPD's Homicide Division, said it had been some time since any new information had been discovered in the Tupac case. "We haven't gotten anything of consequence in a while," Petersen said. "Information still continues to trickle in, but nothing that's been of any value. There hasn't been any significant progress in quite some time."

The day Tupac Shakur died, Friday, September 13, 1996, six days after he and Suge had been shot, the scene inside the waiting room at University Medical Center's trauma unit was more than somber. Patricia Cunningham, a radio reporter and correspondent for Sheridan Broadcasting Networks, sat down inside the hospital and talked with Billy Garland, Tupac's father, and Kidada Jones, Tupac's girlfriend. Patricia had been introduced on Monday, September 9, to Billy Garland by a black minister in the community. Patricia wanted to interview Garland for a radio piece she was working on. She visited with Billy for a bit, then left. She returned the next day. She met with Billy Garland again. While she was sitting in the trauma center's waiting room with Tupac's father, Kidada Jones walked up to them. She had just been to Tupac's room in the intensive-care unit. She was excited, Patricia said, because Tupac was showing improvement.

"Doesn't he look a lot better today?" she asked Billy.

Billy responded, "He does."

Kidada declined to be interviewed by Patricia on the radio. "We're not speaking to the media," she told her.

Patricia ended up driving Kidada and a bodyguard to a hair salon that day.

"Kidada asked me if I knew where to buy hair products for black people," Patricia said. "I told her, yes, there were a couple of places." Kidada asked if the shops were within walking distance from the hospital or if she should take a taxi there. Patricia offered to drive Kidada to the shop in West Las Vegas, a predominantly African-American neighborhood, for the hair products. Kidada told her she also wanted to buy a CD player so she could play Tupac's music for him in his room. Billy Garland told a bodyguard he needed to go with Kidada.

Kidada, a bodyguard, Patricia, and Tupac's cousin headed for the west side of Las Vegas. Paricia took them to a beauty supply shop and an indoor swap meet. "As I sat in my van and waited for Kidada and her bodyguard to come outside from the store," Patricia said, "I thought to myself, 'No wonder Tupac got shot.' The people around him were too trusting. They weren't careful. They knew I was a radio talk-show host and a radio reporter, but they only knew what I told them. It occurred to me that they didn't know anything about me. I could have been anybody. They didn't know me from Adam."

Earlier in the week, throughout the six days that Tupac was in the hospital in a coma, one by one, celebrities, including Suge Knight, visited Tupac: Diana Ross, the Reverend Al Sharpton, the Reverend Jesse Jackson, MC Hammer, Mike Tyson, Jasmine Guy. Hammer sat down next to Patricia Cunningham in the waiting room. "He looked scared and vulnerable. He was a rapper, too," she said.

Visitors filed in, past the security guards, to his room in the intensive-care unit. Once Tupac was gone, except his parents, no one, including Suge and Kidada, was allowed in.

One person Patricia didn't see during the week at the hospital was Tupac's mother, Afeni Shakur.

"I never saw Afeni Shakur. I was at the hospital all day for several days. I never saw her come into the hospital. I don't know when she came to see him. But it wasn't when I was there."

According to the coroner's report, it was Tupac's mother, Afeni Shakur, who made the decision to not revive Tupac, who was on a respirator. His heart kept failing and doctors kept reviving him. The decision was made that if Tupac's heart failed again, doctors would not try to bring him back, according to the report.

Patricia was at the hospital the day Tupac succumbed to his injuries. When she pulled up to the hospital, Kidada was outside, sitting on the curb, talking to Tupac's aunt. "I had my son with me. He said, 'Mom, that's Kidada Jones. Quincy Jones's daughter.' I didn't know who she was till then. We went inside and I asked someone where Billy Garland was. I was told he was in Tupac's room." A little while later, Kidada went back into the waiting room. Kidada was sitting next to Tupac's aunt. "I said, 'Hi, Kidada. How're you doing?' She said, 'Okay,' but she looked angry, upset. I said, 'How is he doing today? There's not been a change, has there?' She said, 'I don't know. I'm not allowed to say. You'll have to speak to the family about that.' She sounded like someone had pulled rank and said, 'You're just the girlfriend. You're not family.'" Kidada, and later Suge, was out of the loop.

Kidada, after Tupac passed, ran outside, in tears, to the parking lot. "It was so sad," Patricia Cunningham said. "It broke my heart to see her like that."

When Suge was told that Tupac had died that afternoon at 4:03, he went to the hospital. "Suge found out," Patricia Cunningham said. "He walked up to the security desk and he said he was Marion Knight and asked to go back [to Tupac's room]. They turned him away. Then he said, 'I'm Suge Knight.' They looked at him like, 'Who's that?' They didn't know who he was. He looked so hurt and devastated. He left."

That afternoon, at 4:03 P.M., Tupac was pronounced dead. No public funeral service was held.

In the aftermath of his death, Tupac's music has sold more than ever before, both commercially and underground. The November 24, 1998, release of *2Pac: Greatest Hits*, a double CD, was a commercial success. During its first week, it debuted at number one on the *Billboard* charts.

For those who had refused to accept Tupac's death, claiming he faked his own death, each time a new song or video was released, they asserted that this was proof of his existence. They couldn't comprehend that he had recorded the music *before* his death. That the music was released after his death was "proof" to them: If it was released after the shooting, then it had to have been *recorded* after the shooting. Therefore, to their way of thinking, he was alive and well. An autopsy photo would prove otherwise.

A track titled "God Bless the Dead," begins with Tupac shouting out, "Rest in peace . . . Biggie Smalls." The song features Tupac and Randy "Stretch" Walker. All three rappers on that track—first Stretch, then Tupac, and, ultimately, Biggie—were later shot to death. (However, the Biggie Smalls mentioned in that song was a lesser-known California rapper, an old friend of Tupac who had died.)

Also fueling the persistent rumor that Tupac was still alive was the fact that there had been no public funeral and, therefore, no closure to his death for some of his fans. Then there was the supposed numerological significance surrounding the time of his death, 4:03 P.M.—the digits of which add up to seven—and the numbers in his age—25—which also add up to seven. And one of the three albums released since his death, his fifth solo album, was titled *Don Killuminati: The 7 Day Theory* under the pseudonym Makaveli. The use of that alias also provided "evidence" for those who bought into the notion that Tupac had somehow tricked the public. His die-hard fans believed he was sending them clues that he was still alive. Machiavelli, the sixteenth-century Florentine writer and political philosopher, best-known for his book *The Prince*, also became known for his deception and cunning, and for advocating staging one's own death to gain political advantage. Tupac had taken the moniker "Makaveli" when he formed the Outlawz; each member had taken on a new handle—Sadat, Kadafi, Edi, etc.

Sergeant Manning, the lead investigator in Tupac's murder, said the notion that Tupac faked his own death was ridiculous. "I was at the autopsy," Manning said. "He's definitely dead. I saw the body."

Tupac sang about coming back after his death. On his single "Only Fear of Death," he rapped, "Remember when I die, I'll be back/Reincarnated as a muthafucka mack." Additionally, videos for songs like "I Ain't Mad at Ya," which were released shortly after his death, and featured an ethereal Tupac watching from Heaven after being gunned down in front of friends, seemed to foretell actual events.

Danyel Smith, former editor-in-chief of *Vibe* magazine and former editorial director of *Blaze*, said part of the mythology stemmed from a romantic notion of Tupac. "He was just a rebel—defiant—on top of that he was very good looking and very smart," Smith told the *Washington Post*. "He comes from rebel stock, being that his mother was involved in the Black Panther Party. On many occasions, he cheated death, which seemed to make him more than just a man . . . [People] loved him . . . Can you imagine if I'm seventeen and listen to radio all day? I'm living my life with an adult sensibility, but I still have an emotional intensity about who that man was. These kids—it was a turning point in their lives. They'll be at a dinner party when they are fifty talking about where they were when Tupac was murdered."

Poet Nikki Giovanni, who honored Tupac in a book of love poems published in 1997, also heard the rumors. "People just don't want to believe a gifted young man like Tupac is dead. When people don't let people die, it is because of need," she said.

Tupac wanted to be remembered. "I want to be a hero," he had declared to MTV months before he died, "not just for the black world, but the whole world. That's what I want to do." He once told *Vibe* magazine, "There's two niggahs inside me. One wants to live in peace, and the other won't die unless he's free."

Tupac was a prolific writer and performer, and left hundreds of tracks of unreleased music at the time of his death. His *Greatest Hits* album debuted at number 5 on *Billboard*'s album chart.

Besides the commercial release of that album, bootlegged material was also selling like crazy underground. The talk on the street was that Death Row released the bootlegged units so that Afeni Shakur, Tupac's mother and heir to his estate, couldn't reap the financial benefits. Those accusations, however, have not been substantiated.

Afeni Shakur tried very hard to control the sale of merchandise relating to her son. Afeni filed suit against Death Row Records on December 13, 1996, after noticing that the record label was selling T-shirts, hats, and sweatshirts through an insert ad in Tupac's *All Eyez on Me* album. On Tuesday, January 21, 1997, federal judge William Matthew Byrne ordered Death Row to halt all sales of Tupac Shakur merchandise without first obtaining the consent of his estate. Death Row was also ordered to pay the estate total back revenue, estimated at as high as $500,000. Judge Byrne also ruled that Death Row and its merchandise manufacturer, Cronies, and its distributor, Globex, must get permission from Tupac's estate before marketing any more Tupac merchandise. The judge said that Afeni Shakur was entitled to eighteen percent of all the money made in the last quarter of 1996 from Tupac merchandise.

Chris Elliott, an independent rapper who performs as Cflo, said the bootlegged material was watering-down Tupac's commercial music. By December 1998, more than fifteen bootlegged albums of Tupac's material had been released. The bootlegged CDs included about fifty songs. "The songs are just recycled in a different order than the last bootleg, with maybe one or two new songs," Cflo noted. "Tupac would be outraged if he knew this. And, also, his mother has been getting jerked around for Tupac's unreleased musical legacy. I hope Amaru [Records] and Death Row can find a way to get the wheels of distribution turning on Tupac's music. I hope if I ever blow up with my rhymes, that my music doesn't get bootlegged like that. Tupac had a lot to say to the world, but it all needs to be released legally."

Cflo also noted that Tupac's fans would be surprised to hear the caliber of Tupac's soon-to-be released tracks. His *R U Still Down?* CD, released after Tupac's death, was of the same lesser quality, he said. "I think that the *R U Still Down?* album disappointed a lot of Tupac's fans and turned them away from his music simply because the music was recorded between the years 1991 and 1994 and was not brought up to current musical standards."

Before his death, Tupac Shakur recorded some three hundred unreleased songs. By some predictions, around two hundred would be out of record companies' vaults and in fans' bootlegged collections by the year 2000. Besides his own titles, Tupac made an untold number of guest appearances on albums and in videos. It was predicted that new Tupac songs would be released indefinitely, via legitimate commercial, as well as illegal bootlegged, routes.

Both Biggie Smalls and Tupac Shakur were worth more dead than alive. Upon their deaths, their music sales took off. Neither one left wills or legal documents. Their mothers were forced to fight in the courts to gain control of a piece of their sons' music.

8

THE STREETS

IF RUMORS SURROUNDING BIGGIE SMALLS'S MURDER were to be believed, there should have been reason for Biggie to be fearful that hanging out on the streets with gang members might not be in his best interests. Nine months into the investigation, law-enforcement sources said the investigation was focusing on the likelihood that Smalls was gunned down over a financial dispute with a member of the Southside Crips. The group, a notorious Los Angeles street gang, was said to be involved in a violent long-standing rivalry with the Bloods, the street gang Compton police said Suge Knight was associated with. The financial dispute Biggie was allegedly tangled up in, was reportedly the result of an unpaid security bill with Crips bodyguards.

Biggie was rumored to have gone into a gang-turf area in Compton, a park where gang members hung out, just days before his death. There were also rumors that he owed money to a former bodyguard— a known Southside Crips gang member—and that he had refused to give it to him. The story, according to the lore, was that the man came looking for him. After he found him, he killed him, or so the story goes. The same Compton gang is believed by some to be connected to the Las Vegas slaying of Tupac Shakur six months earlier.

Puffy Combs, in an interview with the *Los Angeles Times* in his New York City office, insisted that Biggie had not visited a Compton park nor had he visited Compton on any of his previous trips to California.

According to the Compton Police Department's Web site, "Gang members are criminals whose actions range from drug dealing to drive-by shootings to murder. Gangs thrive on intimidation and notoriety. They find violence not only glamorous but necessary in establishing their gang as a gang to be feared."

Biggie talked the talk, but he wasn't a gang-banger, and he wasn't known to hang out with members of a street gang. The streets of Brooklyn, as rough as they were for him when he was growing up, were nothing compared with the streets of L.A. Biggie apparently either didn't see the signs of potential violence or didn't take the warnings seriously enough to stay away from Tupac's California turf.

Despite the warnings to stay away, Biggie told reporters he planned to continue traveling to Cali, where "they got the women, the weed, and the weather." Amidst the negative turf-war hype, Biggie said he intended to go to L.A. anyway. But if he had better understood the world of crime on the streets of L.A., perhaps he would have stayed away.

In February 1997, Biggie went to L.A. with a group from Bad Boy Entertainment. He told *Vibe* magazine he wasn't concerned about the negative hype. "I'm getting ready to buy a house out in L.A.," he said during an interview in L.A. with writer Cheo Hadari Coker. "I get love out here. And if they don't love me, they are going to learn to love me. If I'm scared, I'll get a dog. Go out every night. It's all love. . . . I don't care if people hate Christopher Wallace. As long as you like Biggie, that's what it's all about."

Frank Alexander, Tupac's personal bodyguard and a former Orange County Sheriff's Department corrections officer, said it was a dangerous move for Biggie to be hanging out in Tupac's home turf, especially on the heels of Tupac's death. "No one's joking about gangstas on the West Coast," Alexander said in his book, *Got Your Back: The Life of a Bodyguard in the Hardcore World of Gangsta Rap.* "People get murdered all the time over beefs, and if Biggie's hanging out with the bad boys, he can't just walk away when it gets too deep. These dudes don't care if he's famous. To them, it's another day at the office.

"Since Tupac's death," Alexander continued, "Puffy and Biggie have come out on the West Coast as if they live here, and they have an open range of coming out here without any fear. Tupac's dead and Suge's in prison, so that right there always made me think there was someone who—just out of love for Tupac, someone who wouldn't shed a tear over Biggie's death—may have had his hand in it."

That didn't make it an East Coast–West Coast beef, he said; that made it a personal beef. Alexander also said in his book that when he heard Biggie had been killed in L.A., he thought to himself, "Ah-hah! That's what them muthafuckas get for thinking they had free range of the West Coast." If Tupac were still alive, he lamented, "Biggie and Puffy wouldn't have been out there."

Biggie himself wrote in his song "Going Back to Cali" from *Life After Death* that if he had to choose a coast, it would be the East because that is where he was from. But that didn't mean that a "nigga" can't "rest in the West."

In the frenzied days after Tupac Shakur was gunned down in Las Vegas, word circulated that one of Compton's Southside Crips had fired the shots at Tupac. The Southside Crips, a subset of the Compton-based Crips, were rivals to the Mob Piru Bloods from Lueders Park in Compton, where Death Row's Suge Knight had grown up. Rumors began to circulate that a bloody order—"A Crip a day"—had been issued. By mid-September, a gang war had erupted from the roughest and toughest streets of Compton. Crips and Bloods aligned themselves in preparation for battle. Southside joined forces with Kelly Park, Atlantic Drive, and neighborhood Crips. Mob Pirus joined up with Lueders Park and Elm Lane Pirus.

Despite their differences, both Biggie Smalls and Tupac Shakur delivered similar messages. In their lyrics, they glorified the gangsta street life of endless battles, gun toting, drug dealing, easy women (with their lyrics, both rappers came across as misogynists). Their described lifestyles, spawned by inner-city poverty, were provocative and dramatic, but it may have inevitably proved suicidal for them both. In the worlds they described, violence begat violence.

The term "gangsta rap" was first used by N.W.A. (Niggaz With Attitude) in the song "Gangsta Gangsta." The lyrics dealt with reflections of gang life in L.A. straight from the street. Gangsta rap speaks about life on the street. "Angry black voices. That's rap music," Chuck D explained in his book *Fight the Power*. Rap has been around for some twenty-odd years, but it was Arsenio Hall, during his talk-show stint, who first helped make rap groups famous by allowing them on his show. At the time, it was the only vehicle a rap artist had to be seen by a national TV audience. Today, of course, rappers' videos, which have crossed over, are regularly shown on cable-TV music stations.

Because street gangs in L.A. are so prevalent, black rappers who go there have to be careful to dress in all-black clothing—no red or blue— so they're not wrongly associated as members from a rival gang. For the Bloods, it's red clothing. For the Crips, it's blue.

Life on the streets in L.A. is different from life on the streets of Brooklyn. In New York, kids mostly get around by using the subway. In L.A. they have cars. For a drive-by, they simply drive in, shoot, and drive away. They can take care of business and, nine times out of ten, not get caught.

But an Anti-Gang and Youth Crime Control Act of 1996 made it easier for police to charge youth who commit violent acts and sentence them as adults. President Bill Clinton, when he signed the bill into law, issued a strong statement against gang-bangers: "The message today to the Bloods, the Crips, to every criminal gang preying on the innocent is clear," he said. "We mean to put you out of business, to break the backs of your organization, to stop you from terrorizing our neighborhoods and our children, to put you away for a very long time. We have just begun the job and we do not intend to stop until we have finished." With the ratification of the bill, prosecutors were armed with a law to hit hard at black organized street crime. Still, as of 2000, the gangs were alive and well in South Central Los Angeles. There may be more teenagers serving longer prison sentences, but the new law has not stopped the violence. Even Tupac acknowledged the black-on-black gang violence. On his *Makaveli* album, he stated, on the "White Man'z World" track, "Use your brain. It's not them that's killing us, it's us that's killing us."

DJ Theo, host of a hip-hop show on L.A.'s 92.3 *The Beat*, commented that "if you live on the West Coast, you know that this type of violence is an everyday occurrence. It's just a way of life out here."

Could the chorus of boos in Los Angeles, on Tupac's home turf, aimed at Biggie Smalls at the *Soul Train* Awards the night before he was murdered, have been a sign of Biggie's fate? Phil Casey, an industry insider, believed so. "Puffy thought it was all calmed down out here," Casey told *Vibe* magazine. "But at *Soul Train* there were boos, and they were throwin' up Westside from the balcony. That should have been a sign right there."

But Biggie mistakenly thought the hype had calmed down. On Wednesday, March 5, just before he was murdered, he told San Francisco's Wild 107 Doghouse KYLD radio: "I'm just getting over—you know what I'm sayin'—this whole situation with this East Coast–West Coast thing, you know, and they was going through their thing and we was going through our thing and I just came over, you know what I'm saying? Try to like basically squash it. My album's about to drop March twenty-fifth. I need to be all up in the Bay, Oakland, all over. So I'm here, so I gotta grind. I just want to let everybody know that, I'm here. . . . I ain't going nowhere. Bad Boy ain't going nowhere. . . . I'm going to continue to keep making those songs, though, make you dance, and make you groove and have kids and all kinds of things. I'm here, me and my man Caesar Leo . . . just gonna do our thing forever. Forever and ever."

Three-and-a-half years after Biggie's murder, and four years after Tupac's, there have been no arrests. No indictments. No convictions. The slayings raise many questions but provide few answers. Does the police's failure to clear up the murders simply reflect the apparent randomness of the violence, or is it the result of a troubling reluctance to solve murders in which the victims are black? Or have the investigators failed because some facts are being concealed? Some people in the African-American community believe that a dark pattern links the murders. And many see a conspiracy to cover up the real facts of the cases.

It's perhaps no big surprise that conspiracy theories are alive and well in the African-American community. Such theories are the refuge of the disaffected and the disenfranchised. Those who already perceive themselves to be disempowered find it easy to believe in obscure forces. The assassinations of Malcolm X and Dr. Martin Luther King Jr. continue to be questioned. And it took thirty-one years to bring the murderer of civil-rights leader Medgar Evers to justice after all-white juries twice before had acquitted the killer (a third jury, in 1994, finally convicted the murderer).

The theory that the CIA helped flood the black neighborhoods of

Los Angeles with crack cocaine has been debated from the streets of South Central Los Angeles all the way to Capitol Hill in Washington, D.C. There were shrieks of horror when movie producer Spike Lee announced in a magazine advertisement that "AIDS is a government-engineered disease." But the fact is, as far-fetched as it may sound, many blacks believe that theory to be true. A 1990 poll of New York City's African-American community showed that 29 percent of the people believed that AIDS may have been "deliberately created" in a laboratory in order to infect black people, and 60 percent thought the government could have "deliberately" made drugs available to poor black people.

It's common, of course, for rumors of conspiracy and cover-up to proliferate around icons like Tupac and Biggie, especially when there's been a stone wall of silence surrounding their deaths. It would appear these drive-by shootings were crimes that few wanted to help solve. But not solving the street murders of Tupac Shakur, gunned down on a Las Vegas street, and Biggie Smalls, shot on an L.A. street, just might be the biggest crimes of all. Both symbolize the obstacles detectives confront every day as they try to solve gang-related shootings where fearful witnesses often restrain their efforts. The unsolved slayings also underscore the wide gulf and mistrust between the police and potential witnesses.

Los Angeles police were still nervous two and a half years after Biggie's death. They were out in force for the *The Source* Hip-Hop Music Awards show at the Pantages Theatre in Hollywood in August of 1999. Authorities were called in to break up an after-party. About forty-five officers in riot gear disbursed some of the twelve hundred partygoers at the Hollywood Athletic Club on Sunset Boulevard about midnight August 19 following the taping of the awards show. Lieutenant Howard Silverstein, with LAPD's Hollywood Station, told reporters that the size of the crowd created an "unsafe situation."

"There had been a few fights and a few drunks," he said. "We assisted the fire department. It was their decision. It was to protect the public." The lieutenant also told reporters that officers were already monitoring the *Source* Awards because of the history of violence associated with the rap world. Officers first used a loudspeaker, asking the two to three hundred people milling outside the club to leave. After the crowd outside was dispersed, officers spent about ninety minutes thinning out the masses inside the party. No arrests were made. One of those seen leaving the club was Lakers basketball star Shaquille O'Neal. He had been honored earlier that night at the awards presentation as Athlete of the Year.

The LAPD didn't want another rap-related murder on their hands, not in their backyard, anyway. And, of course, they had reason to be nervous. The two highest-profile murders in the rap industry had been associated with parties: Biggie while leaving a music-industry party in Los Angeles; and, six months earlier, Tupac on the way to a post–boxing match party in Las Vegas. The LAPD already had enough to handle, what with the twenty-odd detectives they had assigned to the Biggie Smalls homicide investigation.

9

L.A. INVESTIGATION

TWENTY-FOUR-YEAR-OLD BIGGIE SMALLS was pronounced dead at 1:15 A.M. on Sunday, March 9, 1997. He was cut down in a fashion eerily similar to that of Tupac Shakur: on a crowded street during a drive-by shooting in a bold attack in front of hundreds of potential witnesses, attending an out-of-town party. Biggie's body was taken that same morning to the Los Angeles County Coroner's Office at 1104 North Mission Road, ten miles from the hospital where he died. An autopsy—standard procedure in homicide cases—was performed.

Faith Evans, Biggie's estranged wife, and Voletta Wallace, his mother, went to the Coroner's Office on the afternoon of March 9 and identified his body at the morgue.

The day after Biggie's murder, before findings could be released from the coroner's examination the day before, LAPD Wilshire District detective Kelly Cooper placed a security hold on Biggie's autopsy file. Once such a hold is put on a file, information may not be released to the media or the public, per California Evidence Code 1040. That code states a public entity has the right to withhold the information against the public's interest because disclosing that information could interfere with an investigation.

"This is an exclusionary rule," said C. Scott Carrier, a spokesman for the L.A. Coroner's Office. "The police department has the right to withhold information."

No details about Biggie's death—case number 97-01812—would be released to the news media by the Coroner's Office. All requests for information were referred to LAPD's Robbery-Homicide Division at Parker Center.

The Notorious B.I.G. clutches his awards at the podium during the annual *Billboard* Music Awards in New York City on December 6, 1995.
MARK LENNIHAN AP

Biggie Smalls walks to a waiting police car outside the NYPD's Sixth Police Precinct in Manhattan on March 23, 1996. He and a friend were accused of using a baseball bat to attack fans. ADAM NADEL AP

Sidewalk view of Brother Mike's Barber Shop at 932 Fulton Street, a few blocks from Biggie's house, where Biggie hung out as a teenager. CATHY SCOTT

The brownstone apartment, at 226 Saint James Place in Clinton Hill, Brooklyn, where Biggie Smalls (Christopher Wallace) lived with his mother from his birth until he moved out in 1994.
CATHY SCOTT

First composite sketch of suspect released by the LAPD a few days after Biggie's death.

A second composite sketch of the suspect that wasn't released to the media until December 1999, two years, nine months after the murder.

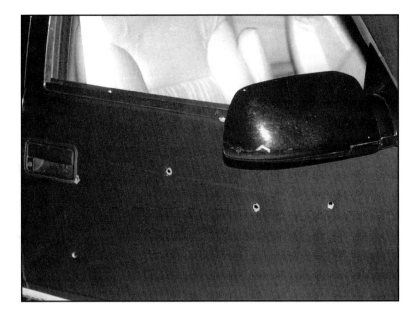

The passenger door of the GMC Suburban in which Biggie was shot outside the Peterson Automotive Museum. MIKE MEADOW AP

Suge Knight poses for a Californian state prison mug shot taken March 12, 1997. USED WITH PERMISSION BY THE CALIFORNIA DEPARTMENT OF PRISONS

Puff Daddy and the Bad Boy Family pose, following the *Billboard* Music Awards in Las Vegas on December 8, 1997. USED WITH PERMISSION BY THE LAS VEGAS CONVENTION AND VISITORS AUTHORITY'S NEWS BUREAU

Rapper Mace, left, Puffy Combs and fellow rappers at the *Billboard* Music Awards in Las Vegas on December 8, 1997. USED WITH PERMISSION BY THE LAS VEGAS CONVENTION AND VISITORS AUTHORITY'S NEWS BUREAU

Voletta Wallace, Biggie Smalls's mother, accepts a posthumous Best Rap Video award, with Puffy Combs, right, and other Bad Boy Entertainment members, at the MTV Video Music Awards at New York's Radio City Music Hall on September 4, 1997. ADAM NADEL AP

From the get-go, the Biggie Smalls murder case and the ensuing investigation were sealed from the public.

"A lot of people are naturally curious about a high profile case," said Detective Kelly Cooper with the Robbery-Homicide Division, "so we placed a security hold on it so no information could get out."

A standard drug toxicology test on Biggie's body was taken, Scott Carrier said. Those results, too, were not to be released from the forensics lab to the public, he said, per the same code.

What the police and Coroner's Office did release early on to reporters were brief details about the shooting. They included confirmation of Biggie's death, the time he was pronounced dead, and his weight of 315 pounds, an item that turned out to be wrong. In fact, Biggie weighed 395 pounds. The writing on the original copy of the autopsy report did not go through to the carbon copies underneath, according to coroner's office spokesman Carrier. Biggie's weight was initially reported as 315 pounds and was erroneously and inadvertently repeated in later reports. "The number 9 didn't show through completely," Carrier said, "and it looked like 3-1-5. But the 1 on the original was really a 9. Christopher Wallace weighed 395 pounds."

Theories abounded about the motive behind Biggie's slaying, the most popular of which was that it was a result of the East Coast–West Coast feud between rappers. Biggie's murder, some said, was payback for the earlier killing of Tupac Shakur.

A rumor was buzzing around L.A. that the local rap community was unhappy with the high-profile presence Biggie and the Bad Boy group had demonstrated while on the West Coast. Some considered it their turf, not Biggie's, and a personal affront to the memory of Tupac for Biggie to even be in L.A.

Biggie's appearance at the *Soul Train* Music Awards, where people in the audience had showed their distaste by booing him for several minutes, was the final straw, or so the theory went.

Another theory that gained prominence was that the murder was the act of a Southside L.A. street gang that Biggie and Puffy had allegedly hired to protect them during their West Coast stay. The gang had asked for an exorbitant amount of money, as the story went, so

Puffy hired Inglewood off-duty cops instead, replacing the gang members. That's when the members allegedly tried to collect their debt through Biggie, who met up with some of them in a Compton park. But Biggie refused to pay up, the story says. In return for nonpayment, Biggie was shot.

The official police crime report stated that Biggie's shooting was a drive-by. One witness account said a man on foot approached the SUV, and as Biggie rolled down the window to talk to him, a gunman in a nearby car opened fire on Biggie. Although several off-duty police officers were working security for Biggie at the time, none could provide any concrete evidence of the crime, its perpetrator, or exactly what went down that night.

The most startling theory to emerge, which has since been discredited, came from the LAPD when it was revealed that they suspected one of their own in coordinating a professional hit on Biggie with Death Row founder Suge Knight. One irrefutable fact was that Suge clearly was not at the scene that night and could not have been the trigger man. He was in jail in California when the murder was committed. In the early hours of March 9, 1997, Suge was still being housed at Los Angeles County's downtown central jail. On March 12, Suge was driven in a prison bus to Delano, California, where he was incarcerated at the North Kern State Prison near Bakersfield awaiting permanent housing. On May 21, Suge was transferred to the California Men's Colony East in San Luis Obispo.

In February 1999, police appeared to still be puzzled over a possible motive in Biggie's murder. "I don't think it was a regular drive-by by some inexperienced gang-bangers; otherwise we would have found them a long time ago," LAPD detective Russell Poole said. "It's more complicated than people think."

Then, a few months later, the LAPD named one of its own as a possible suspect in a murder-for-hire plot against Biggie. The year before David Mack's name surfaced in the investigation, LAPD homicide detectives had served search warrants on several locations linked to Death Row Records. Investigators accused former police officer David A. Mack and Suge Knight. Suge's incarceration didn't stop police from naming him as a prime suspect, along with the ex–LAPD cop.

"He [Suge] was in custody at the time so he didn't pull the trigger," said LAPD Homicide-Robbery Division lieutenant Al Michelena. "We are investigating the possibility of him being implicated in this. We would certainly consider him a possible suspect."

Mack, who was serving a fourteen-year prison sentence for heisting $722,000 from a bank in November 1997, was suspected of hiring a former University of Oregon classmate, Amir Muhammad, known as Harry Billups in college, to execute the hit on Biggie. Investigators were told by informants that the alleged gunman was Muhammad. However, authorities had been unable to locate Muhammad ever since a prison visit with Mack the day after Christmas 1997. Police documents indicated that an eyewitness placed Mack at the scene of the March 1997 shooting. Mack was said to drive a car similar to the dark-colored Chevrolet Impala that was seen leaving the shooting. The case was circumstantial, at best.

On Tuesday, April 20, 1999, LAPD investigators searched three locations linked to Suge Knight, including his twelfth-floor Death Row offices at 10900 Wilshire Boulevard in Beverly Hills. They also went to the prison and interviewed Suge.

Suge Knight, CEO of one of the hottest hip-hop labels in music history, was officially under investigation by LAPD homicide detectives in connection with the Biggie Smalls murder. If the accusations were true, it would mean that the East Coast–West Coast rap war was more than just hype to sell records. It would mean it was a feud that had turned deadly.

The searches of Death Row's offices marked a significant turn in the investigation.

Homicide lieutenant Al Michelena, reached at his office in LAPD's Parker Center headquarters, said the warrants were a result of "a lead we're following, a relatively new lead, and the search warrants are a big step in that part of the investigation. But by no means is it the last. This is a search warrant to gain evidence."

His words were very telling.

If the investigators' theory was to be believed, it would be a textbook case of a contract murder assignment, commonly known as a professional hit. Once a contract is ordered, the person ordering it—in this case, allegedly Suge—is protected. He is intentionally distanced and disconnected from the trigger man. The contract is passed to a second party, who, in this case, allegedly would be Mack. This party then assigns the hit man, who, according to the police scenario, would be Amir Muhammad. The actual trigger man is given nothing more than the identity of the victim, background information about his habits, and a place where he most likely can be found. Sometimes the trigger man is given a spotter, or fingerman, who points out the victim for the assassin. Once the murder is completed, the assailant vanishes, often in a vehicle, which is called a "hitmobile" (so dubbed years ago by the media who covered the mob). What detectives are left with in a contract hit, according to the *Mafia Encyclopedia*'s explanation, is a killing with no clues and no likely suspects because very often the killer doesn't even know who the victim is. Thus, the conviction rate in contract murders runs about one-tenth of 1 percent.

Amir Muhammad, a southern California mortgage broker, the supposed shooter in the Biggie case—coincidentally or not—did vanish. At least, police couldn't locate him. And that posed a big problem for detectives who were eager to question him. Police had no direct or solid proof for probable cause necessary for an indictment to be handed down.

Michelena had this to say about the searches of Death Row offices: "That was just a tool and another part in an ongoing investigation, a very long, two-year-old investigation. A lot of times when we do search warrants, it's usually a signal that, 'Okay, we got it. Let's go get 'em.' That's not the case in this situation."

Police seized business records and a metallic-purple Chevrolet Impala that matched witnesses' descriptions of the vehicle used in the Biggie Smalls shooting. They also searched the apartment in which the grandmother of Suge's girlfriend, singer Michel'le, lived. LAPD detective Fred Miller said Death Row employees were surprised by the warrants served at Suge's studios. "No one knew about the search warrants," Miller said. "His attorneys didn't know they were coming down." Affidavits filed to obtain the search warrants, like Biggie's autopsy results, were sealed. Detective Miller noted that findings from the Biggie Smalls investigation "will be sealed until there's an indictment. We feel we can keep that baby sealed until we go to court."

Lieutenant Michelena said the documents from Death Row were returned after police made copies of business records and materials found in the search. The car was also analyzed and returned and not held as evidence for a potential trial.

After the searches, the lieutenant noted, "We are in the very boring part of detective work, going over records we got from our search warrants, talking to people, and moving along at our slow and deliberate pace."

Then, in March 2000, in a revelation that had not been made public, a spokeswoman for the district attorney's public information office, when asked if a case against Suge Knight and David Mack had been handed over to her office for prosecution, said, "I don't believe they're suspects any longer." Robbery-Homicide Division detective Steve Katz, when pressed, responded, "The case is obviously open and unsolved right now." Are they still suspects? he was asked. "No comment," he said, adding, "I can't elaborate further than that."

Suge and Mack did not make the investigation any easier for Homicide detectives. They held their ground and refused to cooperate with investigators.

Even while investigating the theory that Mack and Suge orchestrated a contract killing, according to sources and confidential LAPD documents obtained by the *Los Angeles Times*, at the same time police did not rule out the gang-dispute theory. They continued pursuing that possibility.

But the Suge-Mack focus coincided with a corruption probe of officers within the Rampart station of the LAPD. This latest scenario was reported by the *Los Angeles Times*, quoting a former detective on the case. Mack was convicted of the November 1997 bank heist. He was sentenced to fourteen years in prison. In the wake of his arrest, detectives received tips that he drove a black Chevy Impala similar to the car witnesses reported seeing leaving the scene of Biggie's murder. Detectives tried for two years to nail down hard evidence and build a case that Mack allegedly arranged, at Suge's order, for his former college buddy to carry out the ambush on Biggie.

Detective Miller had this to say about the Suge Knight connection: "We plan to keep going in that direction [toward Suge] to see where it leads us. We're not in a hurry. We know he's not going anywhere."

As of June 2000, no arrests had been made and no charges filed in the Biggie Smalls murder. If police had undisputable, concrete evidence, then an indictment certainly would have been filed in court naming both Mack and Suge as suspects. But that didn't happen. And if the case against the pair was solid, would police leak the story to the *L.A. Times?* Historically, investigators and prosecutors tend to keep tight-lipped about solid cases until indictments are handed down.

A composite sketch of the Biggie Smalls shooter was drawn the day after the murder. But that sketch never made it into the hands of the media until it was slipped to the *L.A. Times* thirty-six months later, an omission that would later come under attack by witnesses. Because the murder was committed with such precision and ease, an easy deduction was that it had involved a professional, perhaps even a cop. Detectives had begun looking at one of their own. Not until the *L.A. Times* wrote a story breaking the fact that ex–police officer Mack and Suge were under investigation and suspected by police of orchestrating the hit, was the composite sketch released to the public. The sketch drawn a day after the slaying was withheld from the public and differs dramatically from the one provided to the media eighteen days after the shooting. Neither composite looked like Mack. But police contend his friend, Amir Mohammad, matched the second composite.

A driver's-license photo of Muhammad obtained by detectives allegedly resembled the first composite sketch of Biggie's killer. Detectives searched for Muhammad, but were unsuccessful. Damien Butler, who was in the same vehicle as Wallace, identified David Mack as a man he saw at the scene of the Biggie Smalls murder. Damien, police told the *L.A. Times*, picked Mack out of a photo lineup of six men during an April 15, 1998, meeting with LAPD Homicide detectives in New York. "I'm sure this guy was standing just outside the door to the museum as we were entering into the party," Damien told police, according to notes of the interview obtained by the *Times*.

If Muhammad was missing and police were looking for him, why wasn't the first sketch that resembled him released to the media? When asked eighteen months after Biggie's murder for a copy of a composite drawing of the suspect, media-relations officer Lieutenant Anthony Alba said his office didn't keep a copy of it. Homicide detective Fred Miller said the same thing. "We didn't keep it on file," he said. How about the artist? Did he keep it? "No," a spokeswoman in the LAPD's public information office said after checking their files. The police had released information about one suspect, not two; yet there had been two composite drawings—for the same suspect? They wouldn't say nor explain. On the LAPD's Web site (www.lapdonline.org) was a page of composite sketches of wanted suspects. The sketches of the suspected murderer in Biggie's case were not included.

Eyewitnesses had described the lone gunman in the car as an African-American wearing a suit and bow tie, similar, police said, to the attire favored by Nation of Islam members. Witnesses had told police that the assailant was driving a dark-colored Chevrolet Impala. Police also knew that the gunman was right-handed, as reported by Lil' Cease, who witnessed the gunman squeezing the trigger.

Donald M. Re, Mack's L.A. attorney, rejected the notion that his client was involved in Biggie's murder, telling reporters that the allegation was "absolutely ridiculous."

As for Suge, his attorney, Robin J. Yanes, also dismissed the theory. "A year ago it came up and now they're recycling it to cover their butts," Yanes complained to the *Los Angeles Times*. Suge, he noted, didn't know Mack. Mack, who, like Suge, grew up in a Compton neighborhood, was a former partner and close friend of Rafael Perez, the now disgraced officer at the center of the LAPD's 1999 Rampart scandal, who himself would land in prison. It was Perez, after his own arrest, who fed investigators information about Mack and the alleged Biggie Smalls connection.

When detectives searched Mack's house in connection with the bank robbery, they found what police termed "a shrine" to Tupac Shakur. As detectives delved further into Mack's possible involvement, they noted similarities between his work schedule and the Biggie Smalls killing. Mack had taken days off before and after the crime.

According to the *Times*, detectives seized at least one gun belonging to Mack and test-fired it to determine whether the weapon matched the gun used in Biggie's slaying. It didn't.

Rumors lingered for years in law-enforcement circles that Mack and other former LAPD officers had ties to Suge Knight and Death Row Records. In fact, Kevin Gaines, an officer who attended Death Row parties with Mack, lived with Suge's then estranged wife, Sharitha Knight. Gaines was under investigation by the LAPD's Internal Affairs Division in March of 1997 when he was shot to death during a traffic dispute with fellow officer Frank Lyga, who was working undercover. An investigation determined that Gaines had been hostile toward the other officer, Lyga, and threatened to "cap" him. When Gaines drew his gun, the other officer fired. It was eventually determined that Lyga was justified in the shooting, and no charges were filed against him.

Because Suge was implicated in Biggie's murder while still incarcerated, prison officials said they immediately moved him to more restrictive quarters for his own protection pending the outcome of the LAPD's investigation. Also, prison officials didn't want him communicating with the general-population inmates. Suge repeatedly refused to assist police in their ongoing investigation.

Suge's former business partner at Death Row, Dr. Dre, defended Suge, even though they had split on less-than-friendly terms. "I got to step to his defense on that one because I don't think he had anything to do with it," Dre told *Blaze* magazine. "Suge was coming up for his appeal and the law decided to fuck with him. That's foul. I don't wish that on nobody."

At the time the LAPD implicated Suge in its investigation of Biggie's murder, Suge was working a yard detail job at the prison. According to a guard inside that facility, "The 'gardening jobs' are pretty much a farce. The guys walk around and pick up trash for seven hours. We have no 'gardens.' We do have lots of grass, so a few of the guys in those jobs cut the grass once or twice a month in the summer, but I haven't seen Suge doing that. In actuality, the guys in those jobs work for about half an hour a day. They check in with their supervisor a couple of times a day, then get lost for most of their work shift. There are usually two shifts of eight or ten yard crew workers each day. Typically, there are maybe twenty or thirty hours worth of real work each day to share among those sixteen or twenty workers. The workers are very loosely supervised if they are supervised at all, because their supervisor is responsible for lots of other custodial duties that make it impossible for him or her to actually spend much time with the yard crew."

All that became history for Suge after the LAPD said he was under investigation for helping with Biggie Smalls's murder. Suge was moved to Administrative Segregation, or "ad seg." "He only leaves his cell for showers, exercise, or to go to non-contact visits, which take place in a small room with both participants behind glass," the prison guard said. "He is fed in his cell. They justified it as a protective custody precaution since he is now a suspect in Biggie's death."

In an interesting aside, the prison guard said that officials hung on a wall in Suge's prison module an LAPD "wanted" poster for the suspect in the Biggie Smalls murder.

On May 13, 1999, Suge Knight, prisoner number K43480, was moved from the California Men's Colony East in San Luis Obispo to Mule Creek State Prison, a medium- to high-security facility in Ione, in Amador County, in the Sacramento Central Valley.

At Mule Creek, Suge was housed in the general population with a cellmate. "He's programming well with no discipline problems," prison spokesman Sean McCray said. Suge was adjusting so well that on February 17, 2000, his release date was moved up to April 25, 2001. "He's received some good-time credits," McCray said. Also, because Suge had no disciplinary problems, he was given more privileges at the four thousand-inmate prison. "He had his custody reduced from closed-custody to disciplinary-clear, giving him more privileges," McCray said. "They did an assessment. He met the criteria for custody reduction. That allows Mr. Knight to go out into the evening yards in the after-daylight hours. He has visiting rights in the evenings as well as family visits."

Night visits were Thursdays and Fridays until seven-thirty P.M. Just as they did at the San Luis Obispo prison, Suge's visitors sometimes arrived in limos at the Ione prison.

"We have several limousines showing up now and then to see

Knight," McCray said. Included on his visitors list was singer Michel'le, whom he reportedly married while incarcerated in the San Luis Obispo prison. Michel'le, a petite R&B singer who has a squeaky, Betty Boop–like speaking voice, and surprised many with her rich, throaty singing style, was once the fiancé of Suge's Death Row Records co-founder Dr. Dre. Guards at the prison entrance allowed Michel'le to sometimes bypass the lengthy processing of visitors because she visited so often. At the Ione prison, family visits include conjugal ones, McCray said. "But he has to request them and show proof of marriage." As of March 2000, "He has not had a family visit," McCray said. Also, the prison had no marriage certificate on file for Suge.

Suge, McCray noted, did not ask to be taken out of general population despite earlier being named a suspect in the Biggie Smalls murder. "He has not asked for protective custody," McCray said. "There's been an indication that he wants to be where he's at in general population. He didn't want to be in protective custody at the Men's Colony. The safe thing to do is to put him in protective custody so nobody can get to him. But he's fine here. We have a very low violence rate here. The inmates like it here and the staff likes it. We're very fortunate. The inmates don't like to transfer out." A fellow inmate of Suge's was "Tex" Watson, a convicted member of the Charles Manson family.

Ione, founded as a gold mining town, supply center, and stage and rail stop, is 280 miles north of San Luis Obispo and forty-three miles southwest of Sacramento on California State Highway 104. The population of the city of Ione is just 2,667, not including the nearby inmate population. The training- and work-oriented institution, which had a female warden at the time of Suge's incarceration, is primarily a high- to medium-custody prison. To accommodate overcrowding, Mule Creek converted its gymnasiums into dormitories to house low- to medium-custody inmates. There are also academic, vocational, and industrial programs available for inmates.

The only known breakout was around 1988, when a trustee simply walked away. "He was gone about a week when they finally found him," said Alan Bengyel, a city administrator for Ione. "It's a lot of wide-open country with lots of snakes and other things. There's a lot of wide-open space between here and Sacramento."

Immediately after Biggie's death, investigators with the LAPD interviewed more than two hundred people about the drive-by shooting. Then they went to New York and interviewed more. Jack Webb's character Sergeant Joe Friday in the TV series *Dragnet*, which was fashioned after the LAPD, described the role of a detective like this: "For every crime that's committed, you've got three million suspects to choose from. And most of the time, you'll have few facts and a lot of hunches. You'll run down leads that dead-end on you. You'll work all-night stakeouts that could last a week. You'll do legwork until you're sure you've talked to everybody in the state of California."

With hundreds of people on the street that March 9 night, finding Biggie's shooter was like that: few facts and a lot of hunches. Detectives were looking for a needle in a haystack. All the investigators had to go on were sketchy descriptions from witnesses. At that point, they didn't have a suspect. Biggie's assailant drove in, fired, and drove out—the same scenario used by gang members over and over on the streets of L.A. And the same one used in the killing of Tupac Shakur.

Kevin Kim, who was standing with Biggie's wife at the time of his shooting and witnessed it with her, told The Associated Press, "Someone just rolled by and started shooting."

Robert Payne, a security guard working at a high-rise bank building directly across the street from the shooting said the sound of gunfire was unmistakable. "All of a sudden," Payne told The Associated Press, "I heard about five or six shots. *Pow, pow, pow, pow, pow.*" He told reporters he heard people screaming and saw some passengers in a dark-green vehicle jump out and then jump back in before speeding away. The same driver of that car was seen driving erratically right before the shooting, he said. (Investigators, however, have contended that no one got in or out of the shooter's car and that the gunman was the only person in the car.)

One of the first questions trained detectives ask themselves at a crime scene is, Why? And, in this case, Why Biggie Smalls? They would later gather information leading them to believe that it wasn't necessarily Biggie who was the intended target that night. Instead, Puffy Combs may have been the planned victim. That would have meant the gunman shot the wrong man. It would also mean that Puffy Combs's life was still in danger. Bad Boy's previous hiring of security guards, some of whom were reported, using unnamed sources, to be Crips gang members by the *Los Angeles Times*, may have contributed to the ill will toward Puffy, Biggie, or both of them, about money the gang members felt was owed them.

"We haven't ruled out that scenario," LAPD detective Fred Miller said eighteen months into the murder investigation.

Voletta Wallace was adamant that her son's murder had nothing to do with Tupac Shakur or Death Row Records. "I don't think my son's death was connected to Tupac. And I don't think Christopher had anything to do with Tupac's death," said Voletta, who said she was told that by Biggie's friends. "The other thing I heard was the shot was not meant for my son. The shot was meant for Puffy. My son was supposed to leave for London the same day he was killed. Puffy asked him to stay. He didn't want to stay. He had to go to a party he didn't want to go to. The only reason he was in L.A. was to help Puffy finish an album."

But before police could look at possible motives, they first had to first look to the scene of the crime for clues. When detectives arrived at the Petersen Automotive Museum shortly after the drive-by, the GMC Suburban shot up during the crime was already on its way to Cedars-Sinai Hospital, with the mortally wounded Biggie Smalls inside and Puffy Combs close behind. The assailant, too, had left the scene.

Officers were immediately dispatched to the hospital. They cordoned off Biggie's Suburban in the parking lot.

Back at the scene of the crime, detectives were interviewing witnesses and getting a description of the shooter and his car. Like the Tupac Shakur murder, there were now two crime scenes: the museum, where the shooting had occurred, and the hospital, where Biggie and the Suburban were taken.

At the first crime scene, there was no smoking gun—just smoke and lots of people. A steady stream of officers converged on the murder scene at 6060 Wilshire Boulevard. Officers cordoned off the area and set up yellow crime-scene tape to keep the people off the street and away from the crime-scene analysts. Detectives arrived on the scene. As they began interviewing witnesses, the theories as to why the shooting occurred began to emerge. The theory about an accomplice standing on the street came from one witness claiming a man was talking on a cellular phone—on the street but in view of the entrance to the museum—when he saw Biggie and Puffy emerge from the Petersen Automotive Museum. According to what the witness told police, that man then spoke into the cell phone and said, "Here he comes."

That witness's account led to speculation that someone at the party had been keeping an eye on Biggie and Puffy, perhaps alerting the shooter and setting up the drive-by shooting on the street. That would explain how the shooter in the car, who may have been sitting in wait, was able to quickly catch up to Biggie's car.

LAPD investigators confiscated surveillance videotape from the museum's security department. After reviewing it, police found that the security cameras did not show the intersection, at Wilshire and Fairfax, where the shooting took place outside the museum; the cameras were out of range. Five cameras were aimed at different areas of the museum, including outside in the parking garage. The cameras alternately switched, recording on a single videotape.

The camera aimed at the parking garage clearly showed Biggie, Puffy, and their entourage walking out of the parking garage and turning onto the sidewalk. That was the last time they were picked up by the camera's lens, according to the museum's dispatcher on duty that night. Seen on the videotape walking alongside Biggie and Puffy were the off-duty Inglewood police officers.

Detective Fred Miller, the onetime lead investigator in the murder case, talked openly about the investigation, but when asked a question about the off-duty Inglewood officers guarding Biggie that night, Miller clammed up, saying, "I have no comment about the Inglewood cops." Lieutenant Dan Milchovich, an adjunct to the Inglewood chief of police, reacted in like fashion. "Let me put it this way," Milchovich said. "The policy that we have [regarding off-duty work] is public information. Any questions concerning the case, any questions concerning the activities of officers off-duty, or any internal investigations that may have taken place and are over, are, 'No comment.' "

But the *Los Angeles Times* reported that one off-duty police officer who worked security detail for Biggie on the night of his murder was recommended for a twenty-four-day suspension because of his activities that night. It was also reported that all were reprimanded for failing to obtain pre-authorization to work as bodyguards, including five who received written reprimands.

Inglewood police chief Alex Perez told The Associated Press at the time, "The violations ranged, on the low end, from failure to obtain a permit to work off-duty, ranging all the way up to conduct unbecoming an officer." The Associated Press also reported that one officer violated another rule forbidding employment by a person with a criminal record, which stemmed from Biggie's previous violations of drug, weapons, and assault charges. Six other Inglewood police officers, according to the *Los Angeles Times*, received either recommendations for lesser suspensions, or written letters of reprimand for working security for Biggie. "We don't have a policy that spells it out," Perez was quoted as saying by The Associated Press. "That's kind of a given thing. The way it should have worked is the officers should have requested a permit. In their permit process, they would say who they're guarding. We would have said, 'Who is this person?' done some checking, and said, Absolutely not.' "

Effective July 1998, a new policy was put into place laying out in detail specifically what work officers may and may not perform when off-duty. The one-page policy addresses "security work."

Questions also arose as to why the trained police officers kept quiet about the murder and what they may have seen.

It was reported that as many as six or seven off-duty officers were working for Biggie and Puffy that night. They left in the Blazer, following the shooter's sedan. They later escorted some of Biggie's friends to the hospital.

Friends of Biggie's who were with him the night of the shooting told the *Los Angeles Times* that LAPD investigators showed them a stack of police surveillance photos snapped as late as ten minutes before Biggie was shot to death. That confirmed, for them, that Biggie was indeed under surveillance the night he was killed.

Biggie's road manager, Damien Butler, told the *Times*: "If they were

there all that time before, it just seems impossible to me that they didn't
see the incident. Where did they go? They had to see it." Damien, who
was sitting in the backseat of Biggie's Suburban when Biggie was shot,
helped describe the suspect for the police artist who drew LAPD's
composite sketch of the suspect.

Previously, Los Angeles police confirmed to reporters that at least
one off-duty officer from Inglewood had been working security for
Biggie the night he was gunned down. After that came to light, Ingle-
wood's chief of police made a statement to reporters, responding to an
April 23, 1997, *Los Angeles Times* second report about the bodyguards.
The article, quoting sources, said the Inglewood officer driving the
Blazer may have fled the scene without reporting his observations
about the shooting to investigators.

"If an officer of ours was a witness to something like this and didn't
immediately report it," Inglewood police chief Alex Perez said in his
statement, "we would consider it a very serious matter."

The Inglewood cops hired by Bad Boy Entertainment were all black
officers, Inglewood police spokeswoman Linda Collegian said. Inglewood is an affluent, middle-class, predominantly black neighborhood,
located next door to the poorer Compton, and not far from the Los
Angeles International Airport. It used to be an all-white neighborhood
until the 1970s when middle-class blacks moved there. Twenty percent
of the officers on the Inglewood police force are black, according to sta-
tistics provided by Collegian.

The *Los Angeles Times* also reported, quoting unnamed sources, that
undercover detectives from New York had trailed Biggie, Puffy, and
members of the entourage to L.A. as part of a federal investigation of
criminals allegedly affiliated with the Bad Boy record label.

Puffy has said if such an investigation existed, it would be a waste of
taxpayers' money. Kenny Meiselas, Puffy's attorney, said he has never
been contacted by officers or agents with the NYPD, FBI, or Department of Justice about an investigation of Puffy, Biggie, or Bad Boy
Entertainment. "To our knowledge there has been no such investigation," Meiselas said.

That rumor may have started because Death Row was under investigation by the feds. "Death Row is so different from Bad Boy," Meise-

las said. "The music is so different. They're nothing alike. If you look into Death Row, to my knowledge, they funded themselves, so the FBI can say, 'Where'd these guys get the money to fund themselves?' " Bad Boy was funded by Arista Records, he said. Bad Boy was half-owned by Arista, which is a subsidiary of BMG. Death Row Records was originally distributed by Interscope, which was half-owned by Universal, formerly MCA.

Oscar Goodman, a colorful, flamboyant criminal defense attorney who for years acted as the consigliere for wise guys in his fight to keep them out of jail, represented Suge with law partner David Chesnoff. In 1999 Goodman was elected mayor of Las Vegas, a town that for years has been, ironically, trying to dress itself up as a family playland and cover its past as a mafia money machine. (Oscar played himself in Martin Scorsese's movie *Casino*, arguing before a Nevada gaming panel why Robert De Niro's character should get a gambling license. Coincidentally, Suge Knight's 5,200-square-foot Las Vegas mansion was also used in the same film for scenes of mobster Frank "Lefty" Rosenthal's home.)

In real life, Oscar Goodman is used to having famous clients. He became famous himself for defending some of organized crime's most notorious figures, who nicknamed him "Big O." He bristles at being called a mob attorney. "I don't apologize for one day in my life," he said. "I'm proud of what I've done. I'm not ashamed of anything. I've made America a better place by making sure the Constitution is upheld. If you can assure an unpopular person's rights are protected, the average person gets the spillover effect of that." He was used to fighting the feds, so his firm's handling of the federal investigation into Death Row's finances was nothing new for him. About the federal investigation of Death Row, Goodman said, simply: "From my perspective, it's in a non-status. It's a non-issue." That's because, two years into the investigation, his office had received no word from the feds as to the status of their investigation.

The fact that off-duty police officers were present and in the Blazer behind Biggie's vehicle at the shooting scene and apparently have not been able to help in the investigation has left some wondering.

Police in Biggie's investigation stated the drive-by shooting appeared to be a planned hit. Hit men were defined by Martin Roth in his book *Strictly Murder* as "cold-blooded killers who have no feelings or compunctions as to whom they kill as long as they are paid to do the job. They are most often used by organized crime or street gangs. . . ." The mark, or victim, is "usually one who has been disloyal, has screwed up, or is a threat to the gang that issued the contract."

Roth noted that "a hit can take place most anywhere: in a restaurant, a mall, a parking lot, or on the street, as in a drive-by shooting." Street gangs such as the Bloods, the Crips, and the 18th Street Gang are considered by law enforcement to be prominent crime organizations. Members of organized-crime operations "will kill at the drop of a hat as long as it is profitable, gives them more power, rids them of competition, or merely throws fear into those they prey upon," Roth wrote.

Biggie's murder, according to LAPD's initial report, was a hit. Detectives, after their crime-scene investigations at both the hospital and the museum, released this press release, dated Sunday, March 9, from LAPD's Wilshire District:

On March 9, 1997, at approximately 12:35 A.M., Los Angeles City Fire Department personnel closed an overcrowded event that was held at the Petersen Automotive Museum, 6060 Wilshire Boulevard. As the crowd was disbursing, a shooting occurred on the Fairfax Avenue side of the building. Unknown suspects drove alongside a Chevrolet Suburban occupied by Christopher Wallace, twenty-four years of age, also known as Big-E-Small [*sic*], a music industry rap artist. The suspects fired multiple rounds at the victim who was transported to Cedars-Sinai Medical Center via private party. Christopher Wallace was pronounced deceased at the hospital as a result of gunshot wounds. There were hundreds of people in the area when the shooting occurred. Los Angeles Police Department, Wilshire Area detectives are conducting the investigation. The Los Angeles Police Department requests anyone with information about this shooting to contact Wilshire detectives at (213) 847-5932 or (213) 485-2504.

The next day, the LAPD issued a second press release, which read:

On March 9, 1997, at 0049 hours, Christopher Wallace (aka Notorious B.I.G. and Biggie Small), a twenty-four-year-old rapper, was shot and killed during a drive-by shooting as he exited the Petersen Museum at Fairfax Ave. and Wilshire Blvd. The victim was in his 1997 green GMC Suburban northbound on Fairfax Avenue approaching Wilshire Blvd. when the suspect in a dark vehicle pulled alongside him and began shooting. The victim was transported to Cedars-Sinai Medical Center in his vehicle. Victim sustained multiple gunshot wounds and he was pronounced in the emergency room.

Although detectives have interviewed numerous witnesses, they have not been able to provide detailed descriptions of the suspect or their vehicle. Witnesses have stated that there were hundreds of people standing outside the museum when the shooting occurred. Wilshire detectives are requesting that anyone with any information regarding this incident to [sic] contact Wilshire Homicide at (213) 847-3990.

Additional: During the crime scene investigation at Wilshire and Fairfax, officers arrested Don Harrell, a thirty-year-old male Black, for 246.3 P.C. (Negligent Discharge of Firearm). The suspect had fired a shot in the vicinity of the museum at about 0005 hours. It does not appear that this incident was related to the murder. On 3-10-97, [LAPD Detective] DDA Savitt filed (1)count 246.3 P.C.

Then, handwritten at the bottom of the press release, "Susps: M/B. Early 20's/Poss. more in veh. Dark Sedan. Working on a composit [sic] drawing."

On Thursday, March 27, eighteen days after Biggie was killed, police said they knew what the man who gunned down Biggie looked like, and all but guaranteed that an arrest was imminent. During a news conference at Parker Center, LAPD's headquarters in downtown Los Angeles, police released a composite sketch of the man they believed may have killed Biggie Smalls. They also revealed that, thanks to Fox TV's *America's Most Wanted* show, they were tracking down a videotape recorded by fans outside the Petersen Automotive Museum. The camera may have captured the shooting, police told reporters. That story also broke that same day in the *Houston Chronicle*.

The tip initially was believed to be a huge break in the case. LAPD officers flew to Texas, and on Tuesday, March 18, the tape was seized at a north Harris County apartment complex by detectives with the LAPD and officers with the Texas Department of Public Safety.

"Call me an incurable optimist," said the lead investigator at the time, Lieutenant Ross Moen, "but I can tell you we're going to make an arrest."

Initially Moen told reporters, "We're not overlooking any possibilities of a payback or gang-related type shooting. We're not overlooking the fact that this was possibly a hit, a direct target, coming out of possibly New York. It could come out of L.A. It could come out of Atlanta."

Lieutenant Moen gave an update on the progress of the investigation to reporters, saying: "We believe the vehicle [the gunman] was driving was a late-model dark car. That has not changed. And it's still described as a drive-by shooting with one suspect in the vehicle and that was the driver of the vehicle who did the shooting, firing numerous shots into the Suburban containing Notorious B.I.G. or Biggie Smalls. We believe he may be part of more than one ·individual involved in the shooting although there was only one shooter in the vehicle. I can tell you that we are going to make an arrest, but I cannot tell you when we're going to make that arrest. We have to—there's a lot left to be done yet in this investigation."

When he released the composite drawing, Lieutenant Moen also told reporters, "We believe it was gang-related. We believe that it was premeditated, [that Biggie] was targeted for the purpose of killing him." As for a connection to the East Coast–West Coast rap feud, Moen told reporters, "The East Coast–West Coast rivalry is just something I've read about in the papers." Then Moen added, "The suspect knew what he wanted."

Homicide cases often intertwine with others—shooting, retaliation, then another shooting and another retaliation, or a domino effect of sorts—but in the Tupac and Biggie murder cases, police didn't see a link. LAPD detective Raymond Futami, one of the original detectives assigned to the case, added, "We don't have any evidence to show that there's a connection."

When pressed, Moen refused to say precisely how close police were to capturing the suspect. He did, however, say that "we expect the tape to give us some key information. We're hoping the tape is going to assist in having people come forward to identify the shooter for us."

The video was made by one of a group of nineteen young women from the Houston, Texas, area who were in Los Angeles trying to get videotape of their favorite rap stars. One of the women saw an *America's Most Wanted* segment about Biggie's murder and called the show's tip line. The show, in turn, notified LAPD detectives.

"We believe the videotape is going to be very instrumental in us solving the case," Moen said during the news conference at Parker Center. The tape was recorded just before, during, and after the shooting outside the museum, where hundreds had lingered when the party was disbursed. The footage was one of thirty-five videotapes collected, according to police, including hours of videotape from the museum's security surveillance cameras.

While the lieutenant refused to talk about the contents of the videotape, he said investigators checked their composite drawing against the tape and didn't make any changes to the drawing. The sketch released to reporters depicted the image of a clean-cut black man in his early twenties with a slight mustache, close-cropped black hair with a possible receding hairline, who was wearing a small black bow tie. The drawing was based on the descriptions of two of the men in the Suburban with Biggie at the time of the shooting, who, Moen told reporters, "had a face-to-face confrontation with the shooter." Reporters were not told that there were two composite sketches. The media were given the second sketch.

Moen was deliberately vague on the specifics of the investigation, offering few details about the contents of the tape or if they had the identity of the man depicted in the composite sketch.

The police emphasized that the suspect was the only person in the dark-colored sedan, acting as both the driver and the shooter. The police also said a 9-millimeter handgun was used as the murder weapon.

Lieutenant Moen was asked if the bow tie worn by the shooter indicated that the suspected gunman may have been affiliated with Minister Louis Farrakhan's Nation of Islam—well-known for donning such neckwear and suits—or if the gunman was simply wearing evening attire. "We are drawing no conclusions about the bow tie," the lieutenant responded.

Moen described for reporters the scene of the shooting: "Now, Mr. B.I.G. is sitting here, in the right front passenger seat of his Suburban," as Moen hand-drew on an easel a rough map for reporters. "The other vehicle pulls up alongside—excuse my graphic-artist skills—and the driver shoots numerous times into the vehicle."

The same morning the composite sketch was released, the *Los Angeles Times* reported that Biggie "had been warned during recent weeks that his life would be in danger if he did not pay the alleged killer." Compton police that week filed a twenty-nine-page court document saying a subset of the Los Angeles Crips had been hired to provide security for Biggie Smalls during past West Coast visits, and the alleged killer reportedly felt he had been shortchanged by the rapper in an unspecified transaction that took place months earlier.

On Sunday, April 27, LAPD returned Biggie's 1997 GMC Suburban to Budget Rent a Car of Beverly Hills. At the time police told co-owner Corky Rice that they were finished with their analysis of the Suburban. A story was released and run across The Associated Press wire that the bullet-riddled door from the Suburban's front passenger side was about to be offered on the auction block to raise money for charity. "We haven't decided when or where to auction the door," Rice told reporters at the time. "We don't want to be tacky. We want to be in good taste. We don't want to make any profit at all.

"Everybody's telling me the door must have some value. We'd like to somehow find a way to sell the door to the highest bidder and then donate the money to charity. So many people say it has value. I'm trying to figure out how to turn this terrible incident into something good. If you put the money to good use, I don't think it's in bad taste."

Bad taste or not, the police intervened before the door hit the auction block.

After the story broke about the planned sale, and while Rice was making arrangements for the auction, LAPD detectives returned on Wednesday, April 30, and confiscated the door. "They said it was needed for evidence," Rice told The Associated Press. Budget had rented the Suburban to the Los Angeles production company FM Rocks. The passenger door was the only part of the vehicle that was damaged during the drive-by shooting.

On Tuesday, April 29, 1997, the Los Angeles City Council voted to offer a $25,000 reward for information leading to the arrest and conviction of Biggie's killer. Arrangements were being made to formally announce the donation at a later date.

There was no breaking news in the case from when police released the composite sketch until Friday, June 13, 1997, when it was revealed that investigators had impounded a Chevrolet Impala that they said matched the description of the car used during Biggie's murder.

At one point in the investigation, detectives interviewed Dwayne Keith "Keefee D" Davis, a Crips member and Orlando Anderson's uncle. Davis, too, owned a Chevy Impala, bringing the investigation back to the theory that Biggie's slaying was tied to the Southside Crips street gang. LAPD's Detective Miller, however, was quick to defend Davis, emphasizing that he was not suspected in the murder. "We haven't named him as a suspect," Miller said. "We don't think he had anything to do with it."

That would bring the tally of people owning dark-colored Impalas who were questioned by police to three: Suge Knight, David Mack, and now Dwayne Davis.

The car had been seized during a raid in Compton on Thursday, May 29. It was registered to Dwayne Keith "Keefee D" Davis, who turned out to be the uncle of Orlando Anderson, the now deceased Crips gang member who once had been purported to be connected to Tupac Shakur's murder. While Davis owned the car, his lawyer, Edi M. O. Faal, also Orlando's initial attorney, said his client did not resemble the suspect in the police sketch. "Mr. Davis intends to make it absolutely clear that he had nothing to do with the death of the Notorious B.I.G.," Faal told reporters. Moreover, Davis had an alibi, Detective Fred Miller said during an interview at his office.

Several weeks into that portion of the investigation, detectives returned the car to Davis after they learned he could not have been the driver. Davis was not charged with a crime. "We know where he was [the night of the murder]," Miller said. "He was out of town. We don't think he had anything to do with it. There was no physical evidence in the car." It was one scenario police investigators could rule out, Miller said. But unnamed sources told the *Los Angeles Times* that detectives had chased new leads indicating that a Compton gang member had stolen or borrowed the Impala to kill Biggie. Faal, however, said that was impossible because Davis's Impala was in his garage and had not been driven in more than six months.

Police, as reported by the *Los Angeles Times*, continued to believe that an unpaid debt could possibly be at the center of the murder. Sources close to Biggie told the *Los Angeles Times* that he had refused to pay a branch of the Crips $100,000 for security they claimed the street gang had provided him and his entourage during an earlier visit to Los Angeles. Police were trying to locate and question—with much difficulty—a Harlem man known as "Zip," who allegedly may have introduced Biggie to the Crips, and who was seen the night before his murder talking with a man in the same vehicle believed to have been used in the shooting. The angle of the unpaid debt being the motive for Biggie's death was the same one broached by the Compton police in their affidavit seeking a search warrant for a gang raid. Biggie's friend Damien Butler, who witnessed the shooting, disputed that account, saying Biggie never mentioned to anyone that he had been threatened or that he owed anyone money.

The status of that scenario in the case was not known. If police were to uncover actual evidence supporting the theory that Biggie Smalls's murder was the result of a personal financial dispute with a Los Angeles–area gang member, it would torpedo the conspiracy theory that Biggie Smalls's murder was payback for Tupac Shakur's death. That, in turn, would mean the hype about the East Coast–West Coast feud escalating to violence was just that: hype.

At that point in the investigation, detectives had already interviewed more than a hundred witnesses and looked at several dozen separate pieces of videotape in their attempts to solve the crime. Two years later, they had interviewed nearly three hundred people in connection with the case. But just like in the Tupac Shakur investigation, witnesses wary of retribution were hesitant to come forward. Because of this, authorities made little progress in their investigation—that is, until they turned their attention toward Suge Knight.

Making an appearance at the Petersen Automotive Museum party, police later learned, was Orlando Anderson—the same Orlando Anderson and reputed Southside Crip member who had been roughed up by Tupac and Suge Knight just hours before Tupac was shot in Las Vegas. Orlando had been named as a potential suspect in Tupac's murder by Las Vegas police, but he was never charged with the crime. When Detective Fred Miller was asked what he thought of Orlando's attendance at the party, he said, "It's interesting but not noteworthy."

Orlando, who had no known ties to the music industry, was accompanied to the party by his uncle, Keefee Davis, who according to Compton Police is an alleged Crip. Detective Miller confirmed that Davis and Orlando attended the same party as Biggie the night he was killed. "They were at the party. Whether they had any contact with Mr. Wallace, other than maybe saying hi, we're not aware of," Miller said.

As evidenced by the release of the composite sketch and the interviews of scores of witnesses, LAPD detectives appeared to have conducted a thorough and extra-careful investigation of the Biggie Smalls case.

They had reason to be careful: No other agency in California has withstood as much public examination as the LAPD. And when an evidence-planting scandal at the Rampart police station came to light in 1999, causing scores of cases to be overturned and inmates wrongly convicted to be released, the department came under even closer scrutiny. About corruption within the rank-and-file of his police department, the top cop, Chief Bernard Parks, told MSNBC: "People need to understand that there are some bad officers in a very large department. This department found the indiscretions [and] worked diligently . . . to remove them from the department."

LAPD has also been one of the most-featured law-enforcement

agencies in television shows and in movies. The year 1992 was a watershed year for the Los Angeles Police Department. After the verdict in the Rodney King trial and subsequent riots, police, under a microscope of public scrutiny, were especially careful while investigating high-profile cases. Biggie's murder qualified as an extremely high-profile case. Police didn't want to make any mistakes.

This was a major case. Twenty-two officers, mostly detectives, were originally assigned to the Biggie Smalls investigation. A year later, two lead investigators—Detectives Russ Poole and Fred Miller—were actively on the case with full-time backup detectives at their disposal. In May 1998, Poole and Miller traveled to New York City to conduct more interviews of witnesses. All told, investigators traveled to twenty cities interviewing witnesses and digging for clues.

At the time, Detective Poole told reporters, "We've put more man-hours on this case than we had, by this point, on the [Ennis] Cosby case, and just as much or more than the O. J. Simpson case. See, it's been a year, and we're still working hard on it, still chasing clues."

Then, several months into the case, Detective Miller was assigned full-time as the sole lead detective. Miller, a thirty-year LAPD veteran who logged more than twenty-five of those years in Homicide, didn't work the case alone. He had three investigators working full-time with him. An unassuming, pleasant-looking man, Miller worked the case from the third floor of Parker Center; LAPD's headquarters, named after former chief Bill Parker, is in the heart of L.A.'s downtown command center at 150 North Los Angeles Street.

The Robbery-Homicide Division is where the murders in this city are chronicled by investigators. Biggie's murder was assigned to LAPD's Robbery-Homicide Special Section, which handles cases involving serial killers, high profiles, and other homicides requiring extensive time. In this case, the investigation would turn into years.

Detective Miller noted that he preferred working in the Robbery-Homicide Division over other assignments because he enjoyed solving murder cases. "It takes special people to want to work it all the time," he said. Detective Miller, a career cop, retired from the LAPD in October 1999; lead detective Dave Martin and his assistant, Detective Steve Katz, then officially took over the Biggie Smalls murder investigation.

Seventy-six sworn detectives and five civilian personnel are assigned seven sections within the Robbery-Homicide Division, the headquarters unit that investigates particularly complex or high-profile cases. Included within that division was the Hitman Section. The Hitman Section provided high-tech support for the Robbery-Homicide unit, a citywide LAPD detective division that tracked major crimes, such as officer-involved shootings, serial rapes, bank robberies, and high-profile murders.

For weeks following Biggie's murder, Wilshire District detectives called to the scene the morning of the shooting stayed on the case and continued investigating it. But about two months after it opened, the case was handed over to Robbery-Homicide and the initial detectives' work ended.

At that point, the Biggie Smalls case joined the ranks of one of the Hitman Section's most notorious. Since 1985, the Hitman Section has had its share of famous cases: the North Hollywood bank shootout; the O. J. Simpson case; the Symbionese Liberation Army shootout; Robert Kennedy's assassination; the Charles Manson murders; the Night Stalker crimes (just those committed in L.A.); the Ennis Cosby murder; and the most recent, the Biggie Smalls drive-by.

The same month Biggie was murdered, sixty-one other people were killed in LAPD's jurisdiction within the city limits of Los Angeles. The total murders for that year were 569. For the Wilshire District within the West Bureau—the same bureau that originally investigated Biggie's case—there were thirty-two murders that year.

Initially the police said they believed Biggie's shooting was gang-related. More than eighteen months later, they left open the possibility of several different scenarios, only ruling out a few during the length of the case. Also, investigators believed there may have been accomplices. But only one man, the lone shooter, was in the car at the time of the slaying. That meant one or more things. There could have been accomplices on foot acting as lookouts; or there could have been someone in another car helping box-in Biggie's vehicle. Or could it have been someone in a nearby car helping to maneuver the shooter's car to pull up next to Biggie's GMC? Whatever the work of the accomplices, the crime was considered by police to be a professional and preplanned

one. A professional hit. The murder weapon, a 9-millimeter semiautomatic handgun, was never recovered by police.

Investigators repeatedly publicly urged anyone who might know
the identity and whereabouts of the man in their composite sketch to
call their twenty-four-hour toll-free number: 1-888-800-LAPD. If the
gunman were caught, he would undoubtedly be charged with murder
one, or "premeditated criminal homicide," which means special circumstances of planning the murder in advance, such as a planned hit,
and would be cause for the prosecution to seek the death penalty.

Early on, Detective Miller agreed with investigators who said they
were not able to find a connection between the Tupac Shakur and Biggie Smalls cases. "I wish we could have," Miller said. "Police in Las
Vegas have more to go on [in that case] than we do in ours."

Still, the media reported that the murders may have been linked,
much to Miller's chagrin. "Misinformation and innuendoes [reported
by the media] have slowed us down, to be perfectly honest," Miller said
during an interview on the third floor at Parker Center. But Miller
wouldn't release too many details about the case—to protect the investigation, he said. "You know what? We're not going to tell you things
that only the suspect and us know."

Early on in the case, Lieutenant Moen told reporters that one angle
detectives were looking into was that it could have been gang-related.
"There have been a number of murders in the rap community, and a
link may be a possibility." Moen said. That scenario has not been substantiated. It also, however, has not been ruled out."

Detective Poole added, "I think these people knew exactly what
they were doing. I don't think it was like a regular drive-by by some
inexperienced gang-bangers, otherwise, we would have found out a
long time ago. I think it's a little bit more sophisticated and complicated than most people think."

While it appeared LAPD investigators were working hard on the
case, even so, nine months after the murder police were openly criticized in some news reports for not solving the case. "Much like the Las
Vegas slaying of Tupac Shakur several months prior, LAPD Homicide
Division detectives are blaming a lack of cooperation by witnesses
(more than two hundred have been interviewed) to the March 9 shoot-

ing for bogging down the case," reporter Daniel Frankel wrote in a December 16, 1997, news article. According to friends and family members of Biggie's, Frankel reported, "police simply aren't interested in solving the murder."

Also, the *Los Angeles Times* quoted Biggie's mother as saying, "I'm fed up with the police just pussyfooting around. I really am beginning to believe what others tell me: that the police don't care about solving the murders of young black men—especially rappers."

Detective Russell Poole, who was taken off the case in April 1998, earlier discussed Voletta's concerns about the investigation with the *Los Angeles Times*. "We are trying to do everything in our power to solve this murder," Poole said. "It is our top priority. I understand that Mrs. Wallace is upset, but I've tried to explain to her that you can't just throw a case like this together. You need eyewitnesses, and we have none. We've interviewed hundreds of witnesses, and the majority of them are not being totally candid with us. It's very frustrating." Detective Miller said rappers didn't want to talk about the murder, "because they can rap about the details instead and make money off of it. It's not to their advantage to talk to you or me." After the fact, months later, "if they did talk now, their credibility would be lacking, especially with the rap singers," Miller noted.

Sometime later, however, Voletta Wallace said she was in regular contact with LAPD detectives who kept her apprised of their efforts in solving her son's murder. Her earlier frustration, she said, came from not having an end in the case. "I hope they solve it," Voletta Wallace said in August of 1998. "That's the only way I will find some peace and some closure. I know somebody out there needs to be exposed and that person isn't exposed. That's the only way I can go on with my life. They took something very special from me and I want to know who the hell took it from me. I spoke to the police last week. They said they are still working on the case."

Voletta Wallace has not been shy about openly criticizing Puffy Combs for appearing not to be one-hundred-percent forthcoming with information about her son's death.

"There are a lot of people who know things who are willing to talk, and L.A. police aren't coming into [New York to] interview them," she said of other possible witnesses.

On Tuesday, March 11, two days after the murder, Puffy had issued a statement expressing his sorrow over the loss of the Notorious B.I.G. The brief press release read, "B.I.G. was one of my closest friends. Words can't express my pain. He was one of the greatest artists I've ever had the pleasure to work with. I love him and will always miss him."

A few days later Puff Daddy released a second statement, this one debunking the alleged East Coast–West Cost rap feud, saying: "Christopher Wallace was my friend and I love him. I miss him so much. I have spent the last week trying to make sense of what our lives have become. Every day I try to make sense of why my friend is not here. It isn't easy. . . . From the beginning, all Big and I wanted to do was make music people could dance to and laugh at while at the same time keeping it real with lyrics that talked about life in the ghetto. The trials we go through as people are not easy. Our music was supposed to encourage us to see life for what is, then make a change. What it was never meant to be was some competition with the West Coast. Though I have said this many times before, I feel I need to repeat it today: In my heart there is no East Coast–West Coast rap war. I do not want it. I do not like it. I will not fuel it. There are enough obstacles we face as a people already. There is no reason for us to turn on one another."

On Wednesday, March 19, the day after Biggie Smalls was buried, Puffy Combs sat in a posh suite at the Surrey Hotel on Manhattan's Upper East Side. He sat on a corner sofa and talked with reporter Anita Samuels of the *New York Daily News* in a rare interview where he actually talked about what he saw the night Biggie was killed.

He said that when he realized the crack of gunfire had hit Biggie, it frightened him. At the hospital, as Biggie's lifeless body was being wheeled into the emergency room, Puffy said he prayed. "I was just praying over him, praying to God to please pull him through," he said. "I was scared, real scared. I was just praying, and for some reason I just dropped to my knees right there and I prayed that he was going to be all right, that he was going to make it. We really didn't see a lot of blood or anything, but he was not conscious. I was saying the Lord's Prayer and Hail Marys. I was talking to God, asking Him to help him and be strong for him. I was begging God to help him out. I was touching him and talking to him in his ear." But those prayers, he was later told, were in vain. "They told me that he was already deceased, that he had died immediately," Puffy said.

Puffy told the *Daily News* he didn't see the gun, the gunman, or the getaway car. He also denied that the killing was a result of what he called the "nonexistent East Coast–West Coast feud" between Bad Boy and Death Row.

A year after the March 1997 murder, Puffy told *MTV News*, "I know that, definitely, it had to be more than one person involved."

The so-called feud had, once again, appeared to turn deadly. Puffy blamed the media for hyping the rap war. "Me and Biggie have been fighting to let people know from the very beginning that we were never with that whole East Coast–West Coast thing. We were not about that," he told the *Daily News*. Puffy went so far as to say in that interview that Biggie's killing could have been a random act of violence.

But if Puffy didn't see the shooter, as he told the *Daily News* in New York in a March 21, 1997 article, how could he for certain rule out the rap feud as a motive? The police, on the other hand, while saying they couldn't find any evidence linking the so-called rap feud to the murder case, also did not rule it out. So how was it that Puffy could rule it out? How could he make such a determination—that the shooting was a random act—if, as he claimed, he didn't even see the shooter's face? Upon what was he basing this opinion? Puffy refused to elaborate. After Biggie's death, for whatever reason—grief or fear—Puffy lay low, quitting work for several months.

Given Death Row's intimidating reputation, *MTV News* asked Puffy if he believed he was in physical danger. "I never knew of my life being in danger," he answered. "I'm not saying that I'm ignorant to the rumors. But if you got a problem and somebody wants to get your ass, they don't talk about it. What it's been right now is a lot of moviemaking and a lot of entertainment drama. Bad boys move in silence. If somebody wants to get your ass, you're gonna wake up in heaven.

There ain't no record gonna be made about it. It ain't gonna be no interviews. It's gonna be straight-up, 'Oh shit, where am I? What are these wings on my back? Your name is Jesus Christ?' When you're involved in some real shit, it's gonna be some real shit.

"But ain't no man gonna make me act a way that I don't want to act. Or make me be something I'm not. I ain't a gangster, so why y'all gonna tell me to start acting like a gangster? I'm trying to be an intelligent black man. I don't give a fuck if niggahs think that's corny or not. If anybody comes and touches me, I'm going to defend myself. But I'm a be me—a young niggah who came up making music, trying to put niggahs on, handle his business, and make some history."

During the many months of investigating the case, Detective Miller noted, "Lots of theories have surfaced. We have ruled out a couple of theories and haven't ruled out the others." One scenario police had not ruled out, according to Miller, was that Puffy may have been the target, not Biggie. "We haven't ruled out the theory that Puffy was the intended target," he said. "This is a little more than a typical drive-by shooting. The target was well known to whoever did it. We haven't eliminated that theory."

Biggie's friend Lil' Cease disagreed. "I was right behind him in the backseat," he told the *Los Angeles Times*, "but not one bullet hit my door. Not one bullet hit any other window. Every single shot fired hit B.I.G.'s door. They was after him for some reason I don't understand. I told the police. I said, 'Man, I will do anything I got to do to catch that dude.' We all want the police to get this guy."

One nagging theory, however, was not eliminated, and that was the report that Biggie had owed a gang member money and refused to pay it. As the reports were surfacing, MTVs Kurt Loder came out directly and asked Puffy point-blank about the widely circulated reports that Biggie's murder was actually an L.A. gang-deal-gone-bad, and that he had owed one gang member a large sum of money. Puffy's response? "That's all wrong," he told Loder.

Referring to reports that had appeared on MTV, the *Los Angeles Times*, and national magazines such as *Time, Newsweek*, and *People* Kurt Loder asked Puffy, "A number of reports have come out . . . that have pointed out—people we've talked to, also—that Bad Boy Entertainment had actually hired Crips for security work out on the West Coast. Is that true?"

"We've never hired Crips," Puffy responded, "or any other gang faction, to do security for us. But the misconception is that because we're young and we're black, like we're not handling business like anybody else. We're trying our best to handle our business just like any other businessman that's out there in the world. And it would be extremely unintelligent to hire gangs to do security for you. We have never, never, hired any gangs for security."

Loder pressed further. "I know Compton police say that's what they've heard from gang informants."

"It's not the truth. I'm here to make sure I tell you the truth," Puffy responded.

Loder persisted: "Is it possible someone below you could have done this? I mean, maybe—"

"No," Puffy said, cutting him off. "It's not possible. I have a small boutique label, and I take responsibility for everything that comes from my label, and I know for a fact that this is something that has never happened. And I heard y'all report about an affidavit filed by the Compton police, but I'm just here to say that it's not the truth. No one, and I see everything I sign off on, everything that's done, and I know the security that we hired were bonded security men and also off-duty California police officers. Just like—that's the same route Madonna would take or anybody that's in entertainment too, you know. Sylvester Stallone would hire bonded security people. And that's what we did."

The affidavit Puffy was referring to was signed by Compton police detective Tim Brennan. The court paper, prepared by police to obtain search warrants for a gang raid, was unsealed in February 1997. "There is . . . an ongoing feud between Tupac Shakur and the 'Bloods-related' Death Row Records with rapper Biggie Smalls and the East Coast's Bad Boy Records, which employed Southside Crips gang members as security," the affidavit said.

Police investigators, in contrast to what Puffy said, never indicated that they believed the shooting to be a random act of violence. "The way it went down," said Lieutenant Ross Moen, "it was a targeted hit."

Bad Boy's spokeswoman at the time, Maureen Connelly, released this statement: "Bad Boy Entertainment employs full-time security personnel and they [are] supplemented by off-duty members of the Los Angeles police force."

Puffy's attorney, Kenny Meiselas, had this to say: "That [Puffy] hired gang members is absolutely false. It's when he goes into other cities that he uses the off-duty or ex–police officers. Somebody alleged that Puffy used gang members as security, which he never did. He was able to demonstrate that he used off-duty police officers. In fact, some of those officers got in trouble because he used the officers. It was against their department's policy. I think that Puffy's not worried about safety any more than anybody else. He utilizes bodyguards in public where other people would also utilize them—a Madonna or a Prince or a Mary J. Blige. These people all have their own security and their own bodyguards. That's the case with Puffy. Until his own album came out about a year ago, he was not that big. He was more well-known as a producer. Now he's known as a recording-artist superstar in the same light as Michael Jackson or Madonna. He's much more visible now. It's appropriate security."

Police urged witnesses to Biggie's murder to come forward. On Thursday, May 15, 1997, the city of Los Angeles and Biggie's family jointly announced approval of a $50,000 reward—$25,000 from Biggie's mother matched with a $25,000 donation from the city of Los Angeles—for any information leading to the arrest and conviction of the killer of Biggie Smalls.

In early 1999, Voletta said from her New Jersey home that she was in regular contact with LAPD detectives investigating her case. Detective Miller, the lead investigator, and three other detectives were eventually assigned full-time. "I can't say we have a suspect at this point," Miller said. "It's very active. We're full-time on this case. If a big case came in, we'd shelve it for a couple of days, then come back to it. . . . There's nothing I can comment on because I don't want our suspects to read it, but there is definitely a light at the end of the tunnel."

10

NOTORIOUS B.I.G.'S FUNERAL

On Wednesday, March 12, 1997, the body of slain rapper Biggie Smalls was flown from Los Angeles, where he was gunned down, to New York City, where he grew up.

The day after his murder, on Monday, March 10, the headline in the *New York Daily News* had read, "BLOWN AWAY." "That wasn't right," said Wakeem Widdi, who owned a neighborhood market in Clinton Hill where Biggie once lived. A stack of that day's newspapers was delivered to the market where Biggie was once a bag boy. "That's how we found out," Wakeem said. "The first thing I thought of when I read it was his mother. He was her only kid. I felt bad."

On Tuesday, March 18, nine days after he was fatally wounded, hordes of fans lined the Brooklyn neighborhood streets of Clinton Hill on the edge of Bed-Stuy to bid one last farewell to the late rapper. Fans showed up in droves—literally thousands of them—to pay their final respects. Biggie's music blared from ghetto blasters. Many fans held photos of him. People stood on the streets and openly wept for the slain rapper they revered. A long procession carried his body from the chapel to his old neighborhood for his final trip home to Brooklyn.

That morning, Biggie's body had lain in state at the Frank E. Campbell Funeral Chapel at 1076 Madison Avenue on Manhattan's posh Upper East Side where 350 invited guests attended an emotional private, hourlong, open-casket memorial service.

Handed out to attendees was the program for the service. The pallbearers were Damien "D-Rock" Butler, Lance "Un" Rivera, and Lamont Mosely. It read: "Ms. Wallace would like to thank the Bad Boy Family for their love and support, Puffy for being a dear friend, Mark [Pitts, his manager] for being like a brother and Wayne for being a good friend. She also extends her gratitude to the people she hasn't met yet, who've lent their support, given her positive feedback and helped her to remain strong through this difficult time.

"Love, peace, health and prosperity to Christopher's children, T'Yanna, Chyna, Christopher Jordan and his wife Faith Evans-Wallace."

Biggie's body was laid out in an extra-large mahogany, white velvet–lined coffin (valued at $15,000) that was half open, displaying his upper torso and face. Biggie could have been dressed for one of his video shoots. He was decked out in a double-breasted white suit, cream-colored silk shirt, blue-gray tie, and white, derbylike playa hat.

Mourners who filed into the chapel included a host of rap stars. But before they were allowed in, they had to show identification and be checked off of the exclusive list of invitees. Among the most famous invited guests were Spinderella and Pepa of Salt-N-Pepa, risqué female rapper and fellow Brooklynite Foxy Brown, Run-D.M.C., DJ Kool Herc, R&B diva Mary J. Blige, Queen Latifah, Dr. Dre, Sistah Souljah, Bustah Rhymes, Flavor Flav of Public Enemy, Treach of Naughty By Nature, and Lil' Cease, Lil' Kim, and their fellow Junior M.A.F.I.A. members. Also attending were former New York City mayor David Dinkins, who had never met Biggie, and Arista Records founder and head Clive Davis. News reporters were not allowed to attend. Instead, they crowded Madison Avenue, along with the fans. Lil' Kim and Mary J. Blige reportedly sobbed uncontrollably during the service. The song "We'll Always Love Big Poppa" played as mourners filed past the casket to pay their last respects.

During the service, Voletta Wallace read biblical scriptures to her son, as she had done since he was a child. Puffy Combs delivered a eulogy. Faith Evans, his estranged wife, sang the gospel song "Walk With Me, Lord." On the service's program was this quote from Biggie: "I want to see my kids get old."

Juanita Preudhomme, a friend of the family, described the ceremony to an Associated Press reporter: "It was a peaceful event. It wasn't all sorrow. Everybody was hugging and kissing, just like Biggie would have wanted." Mary J. Blige was seen weeping and leaving the church supported by friends. Mase, a Bad Boy Entertainment headline rap artist, was also in tears as he walked down Madison Avenue away from the chapel.

The motorcade to follow started out peacefully enough but ended in arrests. There was a heavy police presence that day. About noon, when the funeral service was completed, a procession of twenty black stretch limousines were led by four flower-filled cars (one bearing the letters "B.I.G." spelled out in red carnations and another bearing a yellow ribbon with "For Daddy" written on it), and a hearse carrying Biggie's body. The funeral procession was meant to give fans a chance to say good-bye to the performer. Faith Evans told reporters the funeral procession through Brooklyn was a family tradition.

The motorcade wound its way from Manhattan along FDR Drive and over the Brooklyn Bridge. Biggie's body passed through downtown Brooklyn, then moved onto Fulton Street where it passed along the streets of Fort Greene, Clinton Hill, and Bedford-Stuyvesant. The convoy made stops at Biggie's old apartment on St. James Place. Neighbors and fans created a shrine of flowers, candles, CDs, and pictures at Biggie's apartment stoop. Partially emptied bottles of champagne and cognac were placed at the shrine alongside malt-liquor bottles—reminders of good times, mourners explained. Dollar bills and coins were also scattered at the makeshift altar. Across the street from Biggie's old apartment, two little girls sat on a car roof clutching a sign that read, "We love you Biggie. Save our youth. Stop the violence." Three other young girls carried a sign that said, "We're your future rap stars." Some people danced atop parked cars. Vendors hawked T-shirts with Biggie's image on them, and fans chanted, "B-I-G forever!"

It took the motorcade more than ten minutes to move past Biggie's former apartment building on St. James Place before it moved on to stops at Fulton and Washington Streets and finally at Nostrand and Gates Avenues, where it ended.

The crowds chanted and cheered, waiting for the motorcade. Lil' Cease, Randy, and Nino, members of Junior M.A.F.I.A., waved and flashed peace signs out of their limousine windows as the procession slowly wound its way past boarded-up and graffiti-covered buildings, then down St. James Place. One boarded-up building was plastered with posters promoting Biggie's second album.

Thousands of people packed the procession route, with the largest crowds gathered near Biggie's former home. Fans stood on the crowded sidewalks, hung out of tenement windows, perched on lampposts, and climbed onto cars hoping for a glimpse of the cortege. Thousands thronged the streets chanting, "B-I-G forever," as the hearse paraded by. Then the hearse left, heading up Fulton Street, leaving the crowd behind with Biggie's music blasting from a storefront loudspeaker.

One mourner, Carol Williams from Brooklyn, told *People* magazine that fans showed up to celebrate Biggie's life. "They're here to express love," she said. "It's like when John F. Kennedy passed on. Biggie may not have been presidential material, but to the extent that he was able to come from this way of life and succeed, he means a lot to people."

It was a day of mourning and healing, but it was also a day marked with rioting when fans and police clashed. The crowd along the procession route was generally peaceful—that is, until the motorcade left. As the procession left, the trouble began. Fans came out in droves, and so was the New York City Police Department. Minutes after the motorcade rounded the corner away from Biggie's old neighborhood, a scuffle between police and mourners broke out.

From the start, the police presence was heavy. Squads from NYPD SWAT teams, clad in riot gear and armed with rifles, with their stealth vehicle by their side, were set up on the periphery of the procession route. They were there just in case havoc broke out.

It did.

When some onlookers got rowdy, the NYPD officers intervened. SWAT officers sprayed some in the crowd with Macelike pepper spray. Police pulled out their nightsticks. When the dust cleared, several people suffered minor injuries and ten people—seven during the procession and three in the aftermath—were arrested, including *New York Times* reporter Julia Campbell. Police claimed she pushed an officer, so they charged her with disorderly conduct. She said she was Maced. Campbell, a part-time stringer for the *Times*, told The Associated Press that she was arrested after asking a police officer why he had used pepper spray on her. The police declined to provide details of the arrest. Campbell was handcuffed and ushered away. She was released after the officers wrote her a citation for a misdemeanor violation. She told AP that she had had an earlier verbal altercation with the same officer who ended up detaining her.

Many onlookers accused police of using excessive force. The officers said they used the pepper spray to disperse the crowd. Four officers and two civilians were hospitalized for burns from the pepper spray during a scuffle between cops and some of those in the crowd. Seven cars were damaged during the melee.

While all of this was going on, the hearse carried Biggie's body to the Fresh Ponds Crematory in Middle Village, Queens where he was cremated. The next day, his ashes were turned over to his mother.

Meanwhile, Biggie's murder thrust the now infamous rap war into the national spotlight and created a call for peace from all sides. Could it be that the so-called feud had, in fact, manifested itself into a brutal rap war? Rappers from both coasts, including Snoop Doggy Dogg, Chuck D, and Doug E. Fresh attended a summit held by Minister Louis Farrakhan in Chicago, pledging their support for a unity pact that would include a joint peace tour and an album.

11

ORLANDO ANDERSON AND THE COMPTON INVESTIGATION

Fourteen months after Biggie Smalls's murder and nineteen months after Tupac Shakur was gunned down, another black-on-black killing took place, leaving the man widely suspected of being connected to Tupac's murder dead on a Compton, California, street.

It was just after three P.M. on a spring afternoon on Friday, May 29, 1998, when a car drove up to a crowded car wash on a street corner in the heart of Compton, on Alondra Boulevard and Oleander Avenue. An argument broke out between two groups of men. Moments later the sound of gunfire erupted. When the smoke cleared, four men were sprawled out on the ground, bleeding from gunshot wounds. Two were already dead. A third died early the next morning.

The United States is a nation long hardened to the idea of black-on-black murder. Although a shooting in a white rural school is cause for a national outcry (as witnessed by a rash of killings in schools in the late 1990s), a gun battle in an African-American ghetto barely raises an eyebrow. The bloodshed at the car wash would have been quickly forgotten with little mention but for the notoriety of one of the dead— twenty-three-year-old Orlando Napoleon "Little Lando" Anderson, a member of the Los Angeles street gang known as the Southside Crips.

The shooting of Orlando Anderson was but the latest in a string of murders that blighted the reputation of rap culture and the image of young African-American men. What was perhaps most intriguing was that Orlando was the man widely suspected of actually pulling the trigger nineteen months earlier and killing Tupac.

After police in Las Vegas and Compton all but named Orlando, a Lakewood resident, as being involved in Tupac Shakur's death,

Orlando's family released a statement denying he was connected to the Tupac shooting. The statement read: "Tupac Shakur, the talented musical genius, fell at the hands of a violent cruel drive-by shooter or shooters in Las Vegas. That's a fact. That person, however, is not Orlando."

In March 1997, *MTV News* reported that Tupac's murder had touched off a gang war in Compton and that Compton police informants had heard that Orlando was the trigger man in Tupac's killing.

The day after MTV aired its report, Orlando's attorney arranged for him to appear on CNN to dispute the accusation to a national audience. Orlando, who sat quietly on a studio set next to his attorney, spoke briefly to a CNN reporter. "I just want to let everybody know that I didn't do it," he said.

Orlando also told CNN that he was afraid for his life and rarely left his house for fear of retaliation for being accused of killing Tupac. What critics, however, couldn't forget was the look on his face as he spoke on CNN. It looked like he was smiling almost the entire time. Was it out of shyness, embarrassment, or of guilt?

To the *Los Angeles Times*, Orlando said, "I wish they would hurry up and catch the killer so my name could be cleared."

Ironically, while some associates may have wished for Orlando's death because they believed he was a passenger in the Cadillac from which the gunman fired, Orlando's murder case was unrelated to Tupac's, according to Captain Danny Sneed with the Compton Police Department. "Apparently, one of the guys involved in this owed Anderson some money," Sneed said. "An argument ensued, guns came out. It had nothing to do with Shakur's murder. Anderson was a known gang member. [But] as it related to this case, it had nothing to do with gang affiliation or Tupac Shakur."

Orlando, whose careful and guarded demeanor of late was down when he left his house that day, was unarmed when he was killed. It was his good friend, Michael Reed Dorrough, twenty-four at the time, who, while sitting in the passenger seat of Orlando's black sport-utility vehicle, started the gunfight, Sneed said. Sneed conceded that Anderson was a known gang member. "He *is* a gang member, I can tell you that."

What did happen that spring afternoon was that Orlando drove his friend Dorrough to the car wash, located at the center of Compton and down the street from a high school. They were there to collect a financial debt that was owed to Orlando. Michael Stone, forty-one, had left his vehicle at the car wash so it could be hand-detailed. Orlando and Dorrough, tipped off that Stone would show up there, sat in Orlando's vehicle, patiently waiting for Michael Stone to return for his car.

Just after three P.M., Michael Stone arrived. Orlando and Dorrough thought he was alone, but a few feet away stood Stone's nephew, twenty-four-year-old Jerry Stone. As Michael Stone walked to his car, Orlando drove up next to him, and the three began to argue. Then Dorrough, in the front passenger seat, started firing, Captain Sneed said. Jerry Stone, who was standing a few feet away, returned fire, blasting Orlando's utility vehicle.

"When one man began firing his weapon, another returned the fire with a handgun. Four people were shot," said Sneed, who said he was at the scene of the shootout minutes after it occurred.

Orlando Anderson, twenty-three, tried to drive away from the spray of gunfire. Bleeding from several gunshot wounds, he managed to drive about two-hundred yards down the street. When Compton police officers arrived, they found his car up on a curb against a pole. He was slumped over the steering wheel, dying. Dorrough was still in the car. Both were taken by ambulance to the hospital. Dorrough suffered minor injuries. Orlando was dead on arrival.

Michael Stone was also taken by ambulance to a hospital. He died the next day. Jerry Stone, who was taken to Martin Luther King Hospital by a friend, died of his wounds a short time after his arrival.

Dorrough, the one who allegedly started the altercation, was the only one to survive. He was initially booked on two counts of murder and one count of attempted murder. After Michael Stone's death the next day, Dorrough's charges were upgraded to three counts of open murder.

At the completion of the police investigation, Sneed, a media relations officer for the Compton Police Department, issued this press release, dated Wednesday, July 22, 1998:

On May 29, 1998, at 3:11 P.M., the Compton Police Department received several 911 calls of shots fired at a car wash located in the area of Alondra Boulevard and Oleander Avenue. Upon officers' arrival in the area, they discovered three gunshot victims. Compton Fire Department paramedics responded and administered treatment prior to transporting victims to local area hospitals. Victim Jerry Stone was located at Martin Luther King Hospital, after having been transported to the hospital by private vehicle.

The investigation has revealed that four subjects became involved in an altercation over a previous monetary dispute. Suspect Dorrough removed a handgun and began shooting. Victim Jerry Stone removed a handgun and returned fire. Numerous shots were fired and all four subjects involved were shot.

Anderson drove off, with Dorrough as the passenger, and both were found by police a short distance away. Dorrough was treated and released for minor injuries and booked at Compton Police Department. Anderson, Jerry Stone, and Michael Stone died at Martin Luther King Hospital.

Although this incident did occur near a high school, this was in no way connected to the high school or its students. No persons injured or involved were connected to the high school in any way.

Although gang members may have been involved, this does not appear to be gang-related.

A team of homicide and gang detectives have concluded an investigation in this matter. Suspect Michael Dorrough has been charged with three counts of murder and is awaiting trial. Anyone having information regarding this shooting is encouraged to call the Compton Police Department at (310) 605-6505.

SUSPECT: Michael Reed Dorrough, male African-American, DOB 2-9-74, resident of Long Beach.

VICTIMS: Orlando Anderson, male African-American, DOB 8-13-74, resident of Compton, DECEASED. Michael Stone, male African-American, DOB 12-18-56, resident of Compton, DECEASED. Jerry Junior Stone, male African-American, DOB 8-20-73, resident of Compton, DECEASED.

Even though Michael Dorrough didn't personally shoot all of the victims, he was charged with all three murders just the same because police contended he was the one solely responsible for the shootout. "He started the gunfight," Captain Sneed said. "That's why he's being charged with all the murders."

Investigators with the LAPD confiscated Orlando Anderson's utility vehicle, hoping it would help them in their investigation of the Biggie Smalls murder. "We stood by while LAPD recovered the car," Sneed said. Later, when the LAPD crime lab didn't turn up any evidence connecting Orlando to Biggie's case, the LAPD returned the vehicle to Compton police, Sneed said.

The Compton gun battle marked an end to a stormy nineteen months for Orlando Anderson. In October 1996, two Las Vegas Homicide investigators were dispatched to Compton to interview several gang members arrested in a raid. One of them was Orlando.

According to California law-enforcement sources at the time, investigators believed Orlando may have had information regarding Tupac's death. Orlando always maintained that he had nothing to do with Tupac's slaying.

In the end, Las Vegas police agreed, saying there was no direct evidence linking Orlando to Tupac's murder. "Essentially, we have two to four black males who were inside the vehicle and we have no further description," LVMPD sergeant Kevin Manning told reporters. Later Manning said, "We've never had a definitive suspect."

Tupac's mother, Afeni, however, was unconvinced. According to her lawsuit against Orlando, the rapper's shooting was precipitated by the scuffle between Tupac's entourage and Orlando Anderson at the MGM Grand hotel-casino just hours before Tupac was killed.

The affidavit, filed in Los Angeles Superior Court by Compton police investigating gang-related crimes, gave a description of the vehicle driven by Tupac's murderer. The affidavit claimed it was taken to an auto shop in Compton two days after the Las Vegas shooting. Then, about a week after Tupac was shot, police confiscated bullets from a house where Orlando was living with his uncle, Dwayne Keith "Keefee D" Davis, also identified by police as a Crips gang member.

It was the second time police had seized materials from the residence associated with Keith Davis and Orlando Anderson. The house was owned by Davis. Police confiscated a cache of weapons from the house during a gang sweep a month after Tupac's murder, as revealed in the affidavit. Davis, however, was never charged with a crime. At the time Orlando denied living in the house, even though a high-school diploma with his name on it hung on one of the bedroom walls.

The affidavit filed in court by Compton police also contended that Orlando was seen several days after Tupac's shooting carrying a Glock .40-caliber handgun—the same type of semiautomatic weapon rumored to be the type used to kill Tupac.

Orlando's family continued to deny that Orlando murdered Tupac. Although Orlando had clear links to the Crips and he was anything but a Boy Scout, he didn't come across as an archetypal gang-banger. He graduated from high school and even attended Compton College for a time. He was never convicted of a crime. His half-brother Pooh graduated in 1999 from Berkeley. Also, friends say that Orlando didn't drink, didn't take drugs, didn't smoke, and didn't sport tattoos. Orlando had two girlfriends simultaneously and had fathered four children by the age of twenty-three. He didn't appear ever to have been gainfully employed, and never filed a federal tax return. He lived a lower-middle-class life despite having no obvious means of support. In an interesting twist, Orlando was starting up his own record label at the time of his murder but it wasn't known how he planned to finance the venture.

The probable-cause affidavit from Compton police for Orlando's arrest was thrown out of court. Thus, Orlando was never prosecuted. In it, Orlando was identified by Travon "Tray" Lane as being at the scene of an L.A. murder. He was suspected of killing Edward Webb in April 1996. He was also identified as being seen carrying a Glock .40. And he was allegedly behind the retaliatory attack on Bloods following the murder of Bobby Finch, a bodyguard who grew up with the Southside Crips. Finch was shot to death during the drive-bys that erupted after Tupac was shot in Las Vegas. Finch was shot September 11, 1996, four days after Tupac. According to the Compton police affidavit, Las Vegas police told Compton detectives that Bobby Finch was riding in the assailant's Cadillac when Tupac was gunned down. Captain Danny Sneed said the April 1996 murder case against Orlando was closed without solving it. "We were never able to prosecute Orlando Anderson for that murder," Sneed said. "We had probable cause for an arrest warrant but we were never able to prove it. The case against Orlando Anderson is closed."

If the Compton PD's arrest warrant is to be believed, because it was based primarily on informants, on September 9, 1996, three separate Blood sects convened at Lueders Park, a gang hangout in Compton, and retaliation for Tupac's shooting was hatched. Compton police were told by their informant that five sites for drive-by shootings were chosen. At 2:58 that afternoon on East Alondra, one unnamed man was shot in the back. Two days later, at 9:05 on the morning of September 11, Southside Crip Bobby Finch was gunned down on South Mayo. The next day, Vegas police were told by Compton cops that they'd received calls that Finch had been riding in the white Cadillac used in Tupac's shooting. By early morning on the fourteenth, five more people had been shot in what Compton police regarded at the time as related assaults.

Meanwhile, three Bloods were fired on and wounded in two separate shootings. On September 13, the day Tupac Shakur died, two more Bloods were shot and killed by an assailant who fled on foot. As the gang war raged, police in Compton and Las Vegas continued to receive unsubstantiated tips that "Keefee D's nephew" or "Baby Lane" (Orlando Anderson) was the one who shot Tupac. On September 13, the affidavit stated, an eyewitness fingered Orlando Anderson as the triggerman in the April 1996 homicide. Around the same time, the affidavit stated, another informant told a police officer that Orlando had been spotted with a .40-caliber Glock handgun.

With the account presented in the affidavit, the confidence Compton police had had for an early resolution in the April 1996 murder case against Orlando, soon evaporated when then District Attorney Janet Moore insisted that Orlando be released because there wasn't enough evidence to hold him.

Former DA Moore left the city of Compton and went to work for the city of Torrance. She has never given the specific reasons or a detailed explanation—other than there wasn't enough probable cause—as to why she threw out the April 1996 murder case against Orlando Anderson.

12

PUFF DADDY AND THE FAMILY

THE *NEW YORK TIMES* once called Sean "Puffy" Combs, or Puff Daddy, "a rapper, a dancer, a mourner, a preacher, a trash-talking homeboy." He is also one of the most successful music artists of our time. As CEO of the hottest, most controversial label of the decade—Bad Boy Entertainment—he took hip-hop out of the underground with the birth of powerhouse artists such as the Notorious B.I.G., Faith Evans, Craig Mack, and Total. He was the producer of choice for top sellers like Mariah Carey, Aretha Franklin, and Boyz II Men. And if that weren't enough, following the death of his top artist, Biggie Smalls, Puff Daddy appeared to overcome his grief by taking center stage.

So just how did this young, black, connection-less kid from East Harlem end up as CEO and creator of a multimillion-dollar record label?

Puff Daddy often refers to himself as "the black Sinatra." Some would argue that his voice doesn't come close to the quality of the 1950s crooner; Puffy's lavish and excessive lifestyle, however, probably would stand up to scrutiny against Sinatra's in his heyday. Besides playing a superstar, however, Puffy's reputation is also one of a workaholic.

Puffy—also known as Big Daddy, Puff Daddy, P-Diddy, P.D., and Puff—has always kept a sign at his desk that reads: "Sleep is forbidden." That's because he has always been known as a workaholic who survived on very little or no sleep. "24/7" (twenty-four hours a day, seven days a week) was the credo by which he lived. It's what those who knew him well contended transformed him into the head of the hottest and largest R&B recording label in the country, if not the world. The headquarters at Daddy's House—the studio that made Biggie

Smalls and Puff Daddy famous—was located on Nineteenth Street just off of Fifth Avenue in Manhattan.

But Puffy was also said to not always be the easiest person to get along with. During a Fox-TV interview in 1997, an angry Puffy Combs pulled off his mike and stormed off the set and out of the studio. He was angry about the questions *Fox News* anchor John Norris was asking. The questions focused around the Biggie Smalls murder case, a topic about which Puffy has remained steadfastly and relatively silent.

It was obviously a topic Puffy didn't want to talk about. Puffy turned down most interviews when reporters asked to talk about the shooting that had killed his top-selling artist. Puffy's assistant, Gwen Quinn, noted that "Puffy isn't doing any interviews" when told that part of the discussion would be Biggie's murder.

One of Puffy's attorneys, Kenny Meiselas, echoed those sentiments: "Puffy's thinking is that talking to reporters has not necessarily changed what they print. It's been frustrating for him." Meiselas noted that Puffy had "moved on" beyond the Biggie Smalls murder case. "This is a non-story. No one's interested anymore."

In a rare moment of candor about the murder, Puffy did tell *MTV News* this: "I want them to resolve it. Every day I hope that it gets resolved and the case gets solved . . . So somebody's gonna get loose lips one day and it's all gonna come out to light because Biggie was just too big. I know how he gets down. He's gonna haunt whoever did it to him until they speak up. But to be honest, there's young men and women that are murdered every day and it's two, three, four years down the line and they don't have no leads, they don't have no nothin'. So the only thing you can do is hope and pray. It's basically in God's hands now."

God, however, wasn't an investigator in the murder. Like it or not, interest in the case has centered around Puff Daddy and his Bad Boy family. Because Puffy has so adamantly refused to discuss the murder in detail, some, including Biggie's mother, have questioned why. After all, Puffy was an eyewitness. If Puffy were truly interested in solving the case, Voletta Wallace opined, he'd cooperate and talk openly and freely about what he saw and what he knew, in hopes of shedding light on the events of that March night.

Voletta also wondered if Puffy knew more about her son's slaying than he shared with investigators. "Does Puffy know something about my son's death?" she asked. "Maybe he's afraid to talk. Maybe he's intimidated. But at least do something. Give a hint. Don't just sit back and act as if he was my son's best friend and confidant. Believe me, it's not the buddy-buddy thing that the media says their relationship was. They had a beautiful relationship. But it was a business relationship. Damien Butler was Christopher's best friend.

"There are a lot of people out there who know something about my son's death. But they're afraid to come forward."

Attorney Meiselas defended Combs, saying he cooperated from the start with police investigating the Smalls case. "Puffy and Bad Boy have fully cooperated with the Los Angeles Police Department," Meiselas said from his New York City offices, "and [Puffy] has sat down on more than one occasion and provided the police with all the information he was aware of."

Still, Puffy appeared to have gone to great lengths *not* to talk about Biggie's murder during his Fox-TV interview. From Puffy's vantage point, Fox anchor Norris pressed too hard. After Puffy stormed off the set, Meiselas once again defended his actions. "Puffy loved Biggie like a brother," he said. "He has done everything possible to assist police in finding the person who took his friend and creative partner away."

The Fox segment was part of a lengthy piece John Norris was doing on Puffy: a day in the life of a superstar record producer. The segment included Norris driving around the city in Puffy's limousine as Puffy went about his typical day-to-day business. Moments before the two were to go on the air in a live segment, Norris told Puffy that the audience was "not your constituency" and that they didn't know who he was. He forewarned Puffy that he would be asking him some "newsy" questions and that if he didn't want to answer them, he should simply say he didn't want to answer.

That short preamble set the stage for what happened next. Once on the air, Norris opened the segment by mentioning the murders of Tupac Shakur and Biggie Smalls and that "the public still knows very little of what goes on in the lucrative world of the rap-music industry."

Puffy responded dryly, saying that in previous interviews, "I think that people have been a little bit more sensitive from asking me stupid questions. I haven't gotten that many idiot questions."

Norris asked, "Do you know why your friend Biggie was killed? Do you have any idea?"

Puffy responded, "No, it wouldn't be fair for me to speculate on why he was killed."

Then, anchor Norris pressed harder, interjecting a personal note about a friend of his who had died in a helicopter crash and that he had wanted to find out why his friend was killed.

Puffy responded, "Oh, I definitely want to find out, and in my mind have certain feelings about that situation, but I would never just put those feelings out in the public and not be sure—that would just be unfair—without me knowing the truth. I think that would be reckless."

Combs, still maintaining his calm, but by now visibly agitated, added, "I try to just talk to intelligent people, people that want to talk about something of substance."

Then, before the segment was finished, Puffy stood up and pulled off his mike. The cameras were still rolling. At the station break and off-camera, Puffy said to his publicist, who accompanied him to the set: "I'm so heated right now, I don't want to talk right here. I'm feeling nothing, there's nothing going on, I don't want to argue with the dude. I need to . . . Woooeee!" He turned to Norris and said, "This is what you have to deal with, young black entertainers. It's a war zone, but you have to know how to handle yourself."

As Puffy was leaving, Norris asked him what the rest of his day would be like. Puffy was incredulous. "After this, you want to really honestly know what I'm gonna do after this?" he asked. "I'm gonna go to the bathhouse. I got to get some steam, because I'm gonna have a breakdown." Then, a calmed-down Puffy said, "I think it's going to be real emotional for everyone when '98 drops. I think it's going to be a load off my shoulders. I just think I need a new year. I think a lot of people need a new year just to get a fresh start, and I think it's going to be a good year in '98."

Indeed, even before the year was out Puffy's luck was changing. For thirty-five weeks in 1997, from January to September, he ruled the rap charts as either the producer or the performer of number one singles.

The year also included the October 1997 opening of Puffy's restaurant, Justin's Bar and Restaurant in Manhattan's Flatiron District where he serves up Southern soul and Caribbean fare. "It's food that represents the black culture," Puffy told a reporter at the eatery's opening. "But it's food that everyone can enjoy, no matter what race you are." The restaurant was inspired by Puffy's grandmother, Jessie, and named after his son Justin by ex-girlfriend Misa Hylton, Puffy's longtime friend from Mount Vernon. Kim Porter, his girlfriend at that time, was named the marketing director for the restaurant-bar. The opening was a VIP party. Donald Trump attended; the Donald told MTV, "The food is absolutely great. The Puffman did a great job."

Also showing up were Mike Tyson, Heavy D, the Reverend Al Sharpton, and Mariah Carey. Later, Puffy opened a second Justin's, on Peachtree Road in Atlanta's trendy Buckhead district.

For opening that restaurant, Puffy was recognized by the Georgia House of Representatives with Resolution HR39, authored by Georgia state senator Vernon A. Jordan and adopted January 14, 1999, by the legislature. The resolution read:

NOW, THEREFORE, BE IT RESOLVED BY THE HOUSE OF REPRESENTATIVES that the members of this body recognize Sean "Puffy" Combs and congratulate him for his many achievements.

BE IT FURTHER RESOLVED that the Clerk of the House of Representatives is authorized and directed to transmit an appropriate copy of this resolution to Sean "Puffy" Combs.

Puffy, at age twenty-seven, made *Entertainment Weekly*'s 1998 Power List at number 41, as one of the most powerful people in Hollywood. The year before, he had been number 40 on the list.

Another recognition came on March 6, 1999, when Puffy was named one of four Howard University alumni-award recipients; this, even though Puffy left Howard University after just eighteen months, without a degree in hand. The same weekend he was honored, he gave his alma mater a donation of $500,000.

In 1999, *Rolling Stone* magazine named Puff Daddy the 1998 Artist of the Year.

During that time, Puffy's name had been linked with several women, including Mariah Carey, who denied any romantic connection to Puffy. "We have fun laughing about all the rumors about us," Mariah laughed to a reporter at the opening of the first Justin's Bar and Restaurant. "I'm just here to support him with the restaurant." When asked by *Vibe* about her relationship with Puffy, she responded, "That stuff is all ridiculous and hoopla and hype. We were at one club one time. Every single article is the same picture [of us]."

One woman—Janet Jackson—resisted Puffy's attempts to work with her. It was Puffy's wish to produce a record for Janet Jackson. That dream never came true. "I've been saying this on every interview. Janet Jackson," Puffy told MTV. ". . . I want to get in the studio with Janet, produce with Janet." Still, his public campaign didn't make it happen.

Later Puffy conceded, telling MTV, "I've worked with everybody I've wanted to work with. There was one artist I mentioned before. But I mentioned her name and she didn't want to work with me. She didn't want none of the hits. So I got to move on. . . . Everybody has their own . . . decisions they have to make. I love, you know, I love Janet Jackson's music. . . . It was just a fantasy to one day work with Janet Jackson. Now I don't want to do it. I don't want to work with her anymore. I'm moving on. My heart has been broken and I am moving on."

After Janet Jackson's next album was released—the album Puffy wanted to work on—she responded to Puffy's comments, telling MTV: "The album's finished. Not that he's begging, but I do hear that he keeps [asking]. . . . I don't know if it ever will happen. Maybe in the future, I don't know. I'm probably the only one who hasn't worked with him." At the 1997 VH-1 Awards show, on her way to the stage to pick up an award, Janet stopped to acknowledge Puffy, who was sitting in the front row. He was hard to miss in his midlength white Versace coat and white hat.

When asked about Puff Daddy during a *Wall of Sound* music magazine interview to promote her new album, *The Velvet Rope*, Jackson admitted she'd had reservations about his agenda, including his actions following Biggie's death. "I was very cynical in the beginning," said Jackson. "I was sittin' back [thinking], 'How much pain is he really in?' It seems like he's taken his and ran with it. Part of me wondered if [his grief] was really real, but only he knows that, and God. He's doing really well and he seems to know what the kids really want and they're lovin' it. Good for him."

The Bad Boy label has dominated the charts, and not just with the late Notorious B.I.G., but with other standout artists like Mase and L.O.X. But Biggie was the first at Bad Boy to make it really big. With his gangsterlike persona, he had topped the charts. After his death, in 1998 Bad Boy won two Grammy awards: Best Rap Group Performance, with Faith Evans (Biggie's widow) for a remix of the Police's hit "Every Breath You Take" and Best Rap Album for *No Way Out*. The album, released July 22, 1997, sold four million copies.

Following Biggie's death, Puffy kept an insulated tight circle of friends and working associates around him. Today, inside his midtown Manhattan lobby, on the first floor, visitors still must have a key to access the elevator, or be buzzed up, to get to the ninth floor of Daddy's House studios and offices at Bad Boy Entertainment. Once upstairs, visitors are instantly greeted by a security guard and a receptionist.

While Puffy declined to be interviewed by some publications, he did, however, model clothing and sunglasses with his then girlfriend, Kim Porter, a cover story in *Notorious* magazine's April/May 1998 edition, the third issue. Puffy liked the magazine so much that in November 1998 he bought an interest in it and stepped in as co-publisher. The journal, which in its first four issues dealt with "sex, love and romance for men and women," changed its focus to "people breaking the rules and changing the world." Editor-in-chief and co-publisher David Anthony told *Newsweek*, "I think Puffy is almost the quintessential *Notorious* individual."

Also in November of 1998, Puffy was on the cover of *The Source*. He told his story to the editor of the magazine, who happens to be his godmother.

Puffy has a reputation for being a clotheshorse. And he had a say-so in what his girlfriend Kim Porter wore during their photo shoot for *Notorious* magazine. After seeing what the magazine had selected for her, Puffy said that they looked like "the shit my mother wears around the house. Why isn't there anything short and tight?" To make him happy, the stylists quickly requested a better selection.

While Puffy may have been demanding, he was also extremely successful. A self-proclaimed workaholic, he was all but married to Bad Boy, going so far as to sport a Bad Boy tattoo on his right arm. And he became wealthy. As a record producer, he received two Grammy Awards.

Puffy, surrounded by the trappings of wealth and glamour, has said it's family life that makes a man rich. And although Puffy and his counterpart, Suge Knight, the CEOs of the two top-selling gangsta-rap labels in the U.S., have been compared with each other; Puffy, in his interview with Norris, strongly disagreed with that comparison. "Right now, the media is so sensationalized," he said. "They like to play with people's lives by jumping on a story quick, trying to bring something or going with an accusation or a speculation. If you let it, it could ruin you."

Puffy, considered a music mogul, planned to expand even more by branching out into filmmaking. In 1998, he signed a deal with Dimension Films (the people behind the *Scream* franchise) to form his own movie company, Bad Boy Films. At the time of the signing, Puffy had already decided on his first production: a big-screen adaptation of the George Pelecanos novel *King Suckerman*, a violent crime story about a Vietnam vet, set in Washington, D.C., during America's bicentennial. While the script was still being hammered out, Puffy was planning to star in it. He was also planning to perform on the film's soundtrack.

He was also scheduled to shoot his movie acting debut as the quarterback in Oliver Stone's football drama *Any Given Sunday* (the film was released in 2000), with Al Pacino cast as the coach. But the deal fell through. Producer Stone replaced Puffy's part in the film, which was shot in late 1998, because, he told reporters, Puffy's schedule conflicted with filming.

Puffy also competed to become a sports agent. The *Los Angeles Times* reported in 1998 that Combs was believed to be in the running to become Heisman winner Charles Woodson's agent. The Michigan cornerback signed with brothers Carl and Kevin Poston as his agents for the NFL draft in April 1999, and not with Puffy.

Puffy has been criticized by some—including Tupac Shakur when he was alive, and by Suge Knight—for jumping onstage with his artists and for appearing in music videos with them. Puffy explained, however, in an MTV interview that he always wanted to be the best that he could be. "One reason why I liked being a performer," he said, "was because I got the chance to do it and experiment with it, with my artists just out of being young. I jumped on the stage with Biggie just out of being young and not wanting to be left out of the mix, you know what I'm saying, even though I was the CEO of the company. . . . I like seeing people, everybody rockin'."

Immediately following Biggie's murder, Puffy Combs hit a slump. He told MTV's Kurt Loder that the future no longer seemed bright to him. "It doesn't—I mean, to me it doesn't feel bright," he said, "and that's just honestly speaking. . . . I'm just trying to make sense out of it. You can't get to no brightness until like . . . It's just so hard trying to make sense out of, you know, why he's not here. To not be here, I just have to get past that and I can't. I don't know when I'm be able to get past that . . . but I'm gonna have to. It's just that when something like this happens, you sit up. I wake up every morning and I just can't believe it. I wake up thinking that it's a dream, but it's reality. It's just like when you're used to speaking to somebody, it's things that people are going through, there are millions of people all over the world right now that are going through things that I'm going through. It's like you wake up and you're used to that person calling and they're not calling. You're used to laughing with that person, used to the good times, and they're not there. So it's hard to even think about anything else. It's just like a state where I'm stuck. But, you know, I'm not gonna give up."

In October 1997, Puffy eventually broke down and talked about the East Coast–West Coast feud. "I haven't figured out what it was all about," Puffy told MTV. "I just know that it was something that was negative, that I would say fans ran with, the media ran with, a lot of artists ran with, and it's just something that got out of control. Also, as far as a divide-and-conquer situation, it would be self-defeating for me as a person having a record company, and a person that's trying to be successful all over the world, to alienate half of the country I'm making music for. It just wouldn't—It would be unintelligent, and the whole time we were going through it we were so embarrassed."

Puffy emphasized that he and Biggie had nothing to do with Tupac being shot in New York City. After Tupac's song "Hit 'Em Up," in which he called Biggie names and claimed to have slept with his wife, Puffy said Biggie was hurt "not because of the words, but because he didn't really understand why this man had so much hatred for him, you know what I'm saying? Biggie nor myself had nothing to do whatsoever of Tupac being robbed or shot in New York City at the studio.

"[We] had no knowledge of him going to be robbed. And that's just a fact. Anything else is a fantasy. And when Biggie heard it, he was hurt by it, because he really regarded Tupac as a friend. They had good times; that's how they met. Their relationship before that situation is that they were friends, and he would never do nothing, nor myself or anybody associated with me, would have never done nothing to hurt him. And, in fact, he had helped us when Biggie was first getting out there. They were together. He would let Biggie open dates for him and he was appreciative and I was appreciative. And it was a shock to us and it's something that we tried our best to do anything to alleviate any type of negativity as far as that situation. . . . We never made any negative statements, and the statements that we did say were that we wanted a resolution to it in a positive way."

And while 1997 and 1998 were tough years for Puffy because of Biggie's death, professionally he peaked. His singles topped the charts for months, including the number one on the National ARIA chart for eight weeks; number one on the *Billboard* Hot 100 chart for eleven weeks; number one on the *Billboard* Hot R&B chart for eight weeks; number one on the *Billboard* Hot Rap chart for eight weeks; number one on the *Billboard* Hot R&B Airplay chart for eight weeks; number one on the *Nightlife* Music Video Top Ten for four weeks; and the Hot Club Single of the Month and *Nightlife* Music Video pick from DJs. In 1998, Puff Daddy knocked Hanson from the number one position as the most popular music video being played in Nightlife clubs around Australia and New Zealand.

Bad Boy Entertainment became one of the most successful and controversial labels of the decade. Bad Boy sold nearly $100 million worth of records; that amount was a tie with Suge Knight's 1996 annual sales record for Death Row Records, before Suge was incarcerated. The artists Puffy had recorded and produced in Daddy's House included Faith Evans, Craig Mack, the Notorious B.I.G., New Edition, Method Man, Babyface, and Mariah Carey.

In 1996, rap music accounted for fifty-six million albums sold and more than $1 billion in sales in the U.S., constituting 9 percent of all domestic record sales. Sales of rap rose 5 percent during the first six months of 1997. Puffy Combs tapped in to those sales with a vengeance. And Puffy was being credited as being the man to make rap go global. "I'll Be Missing You" sold more than seven million copies worldwide. For a roughly two-year period in 1998 and 1999, Puffy's record label, then co-owned by Bertelsmann AG's BMG music-and-video unit, generated about $200 million in revenue.

In Puffy's childhood lay the seeds for his success. From the day he was born, on Wednesday, November 4, 1970, Sean John Combs was programmed to be a success. His parents, Janice and Melvin Combs, both grew up in a tough section of Harlem, one of New York City's oldest communities and located at the northern tip of Manhattan. But they wanted better things for their firstborn. After Puffy was born, the family moved to a better section of Harlem. But it was still Harlem, a predominantly poor, black neighborhood.

His father, Melvin, was a drug dealer and a street hustler; he died when Sean was just three and shortly after his baby sister Keisha was born. Melvin was fatally shot in the head in 1973 in a drug deal gone bad near Central Park. But their mother, Janice, kept the truth from her children and told them he was killed in a car accident. She tried to make a fresh start for her family. They moved into their grandmother's government-subsidized apartment. Janice enrolled Puffy in an all-white Catholic school. He became an altar boy. He mostly played with white kids, though he still attended an after-school program in Harlem.

When Puffy was eleven, his mother moved him and his sister to suburban, middle-class Mt. Vernon, New York, in Westchester

County. By the time he was twelve, Puffy had landed two paper routes in the well-manicured neighborhood so he could earn his own spending money. He attended Mt. Saint Michael's Academy, an all-boys' prep school, which then was a private high school in Manhattan (today it's coed). It was rumored that while he was a high-school football player, he had earned the nickname Puffy for his habit of puffing out his chest to make his then skinny body look larger; it's also been said that Puffy's nickname refers to his mercurial personality, which can puff up in anger. Whichever way he got the moniker in his youth, it stuck—he was called Puffy from then on. Those in his employ call him "Puff Daddy" out of respect.

It was when he was still in high school, at seventeen, that Puffy learned the real cause of his father's death. In the public library he located some old newspaper clippings. "[Melvin] was a drug dealer, a street hustler," Puffy would later say. "But he was a good street hustler. He was a successful street hustler."

After high school, Puffy attended Howard University for two years and majored in business administration. During his sophomore year, in 1990, Puffy convinced childhood friend Heavy D to sign him up as an intern at the label he recorded for, Uptown Records; Andre Harrell, head of the R&B label in New York City, hired Puffy as an unpaid intern at Uptown.

Puffy desperately wanted to be in the music business. It was his dream. "He begged and convinced Andre Harrell at Uptown Records to give him a chance," said Puffy's attorney, Kenny Meiselas. Puffy commuted by train—three hours up and three hours back—from college in D.C. to the internship position in New York, just for the opportunity to work in the business.

Puffy didn't return to college. Instead, he was promoted by Harrell as director of A&R at Uptown, replacing Kurt Woodley, who stepped down. Puffy's new responsibilities included finding new artists and marketing the existing ones. Harrell even gave Puffy a room in Harrell's own house in a tony New Jersey suburb.

Also in 1991, Puffy met Kim Porter, who also worked for Uptown. She would be his girlfriend until 1999. The couple split up before their son Christian, who was born April 1, 1998, turned one.

Puffy had his first hit when Jodeci's debut album, *Forever My Lady*, topped the *Billboard* charts in 1991. In July of 1992, Puffy produced R&B singer Mary J. Blige's debut album, *What's the 411?*

With the success of Mary J. Blige and other young singers and rappers, Andre Harrell promoted Puffy once again, this time to vice president. The appointment in December of 1992 made Puffy the youngest A&R vice president in music-business history. Sean Combs was twenty-two years old in 1992, and starting to reap the benefits of his hard work.

But Puffy wanted to expand; with his promotion, Andre cut a deal with Uptown for a production, management, and record company through which Uptown would distribute albums. It was called Bad Boy Entertainment, so named after parties Puffy used to have that he dubbed "Bad Boy."

But Puffy demanded more artistic license, and tensions between himself and Harrell escalated. Harrell fired Puffy from Uptown in 1993 for what some say was insubordination. Puffy was twenty-three at the time. He took Bad Boy Entertainment with him and tried to keep it afloat. His goal was to expand Bad Boy and turn it into his own vision, not Uptown's. His plan was realized a few months later when he landed a reported $15 million distribution deal with Arista Records for the Bad Boy Entertainment label. Bad Boy was renegotiated in 1995 as a fifty-fifty joint venture with Clive Davis and Arista Records for a reported $70 million five-year deal.

Over the next two years, Bad Boy continued to expand, with the additions of such artists as Faith Evans, 112, Total, and Craig Mack. He expanded his business ventures as well—from recording star, producer, and restaurateur, to clothing designer, and children's nonprofit organizer. In 1995 Puffy founded the Daddy's House Social Programs, a not-for-profit children's group; in 1997 he reimbursed himself for expenses in the sum of $50,000 from the proceeds, according to a tax form filed with New York State in 1998.

In the summer of 1996, before the Tupac slaying, Puff Daddy organized Hoodstock '96. Puffy, Biggie, Lil' Kim, Junior M.A.F.I.A., and others performed on a stage erected at 125th Street and Adam Clayton Powell Boulevard in the heart of Harlem, in the 'hood. Thousands of rap fans filled the streets.

In 1997, Puffy launched his own solo career with *No Way Out* by Puff Daddy and the Family. It debuted number one on the R&B album charts. A week later it debuted at number one on the pop side and was immediately certified a double-platinum, two-million seller. Puff Daddy and Notorious B.I.G. occupied the number one positions on the pop and R&B charts for a twenty-eight-week run. And six other songs produced by Puffy added up to forty-two weeks at number one on the *Billboard* Hot Rap Singles chart. The *No Way Out* album generated nearly two dozen industry award nominations and two 1997 Grammy Awards, including Best Rap Album of the Year and Best Rap Duo or Group.

In 1998–99, Puff Daddy organized the Bad Boy Tour, a Harlem-style cabaret on a grand arena scale that showcased virtually the entire Bad Boy artist roster along with some of the biggest names in hip-hop, including Lil' Kim, Nas, Jay-Z, and Busta Rhymes. Shows were sold out across the country and, without a single incident of violence, the tour resurrected the concept of touring for hip-hop artists, beleaguered for a decade by promoters' fears of violence and low ticket sales.

Things could not have been better for the Bad Boy family, with their chart-topping songs. Puffy's success continued with appearances on cuts with new artists like Da Brat, Junior M.A.F.I.A., 112, Total, Jay-Z, and Lil' Kim.

Puffy's attorney, Kenny Meiselas, explained: "He is an entrepreneur who has put together a staff of college graduates who are urban specialists. Puffy is generally recognized throughout the industry as a major figure in the industry who knows what he's doing, who is a very special person, a creative person, who gives back to charities."

Puffy Combs, while in his mid-twenties, became one of the youngest record-company CEOs in the history of music.

But controversy continued to surround Puff Daddy. Faith Evans, Biggie's widow, who moved to Matewan, New Jersey, after Biggie's death, told *Elle* magazine in late 1998 that she wasn't paid any royalties for her part in the smash hit single "I'll Be Missing You." Faith also complained that three years after her solo album was released by Bad Boy Entertainment, she had not been paid "a dime."

An unnamed Bad Boy spokesman responded that proceeds from the

"I'll Be Missing You" single went to charity and to a trust fund for Biggie's two children, one of whom he had had with Faith. The spokesman went on to say that royalties from the singer's solo album, on the other hand, had been withheld during what was called a "negotiations" period, but that all issues had been resolved. Everyone, according to Bad Boy, was "as happy as can be." In the magazine, Faith also noted that after she learned that rapper Lil' Kim had had an affair with her husband, she went down to Puffy's studio and "beat Kim up for the first time." Lil' Kim's camp refused to comment on that story.

Relations between Faith Evans and Puffy Combs had become even more strained by November 1999. Considered the "first lady" of Bad Boy Entertainment, Faith was attempting to leave the record label. "I'm disappointed. I am not happy," she told the *New York Daily News*. Under her contract with Bad Boy, Faith was obligated to deliver several more albums. Her attorney, L. Londell McMillan, who successfully helped The Artist Formerly Known as Prince get released from his Warner Music Group contract, said that Faith, seeking to regain control over her music-publishing and songwriting interests, wanted to be treated with the multiplatinum status she deserved.

Faith was also upset about a press leak purporting that she had undergone liposuction surgery, an item she has said came from inside Bad Boy Entertainment.

Puffy was mentioned in a controversial $700 million lawsuit alleging that eleven major talent agencies and twenty-nine promoters conspired to prevent them from promoting white performers and top-selling black acts. Puffy was the client of a promoter who claimed the unfairness had affected the black business community since black-owned caterers, transportation, and security companies were not hired. The suit, filed November 1998 in U.S. District Court in Manhattan, made civil-rights claims against some of the biggest names in the business.

As his star became brighter, Puffy's excesses became more pronounced. He was mostly chauffeur-driven around New York City, in a Mercedes-Benz or limousine. "I work hard," he told *People* magazine. "I want to live good. I want to live like a king." In late 1997, he purchased an Upper West Side brownstone and had it renovated.

During the summer of 1998, Puffy bought a $375,000 Bentley which he described to friends as his first gift to himself. He also invested $1.5 million in the style magazine *Notorious*, and purchased a $10 million twelve-story apartment building on Park Avenue. He would later move into the building when he split with live-in girlfriend Kim Porter.

During the fall of 1999, Puffy signed with Ballantine Publishing to write an autobiography co-authored by Mikal Gilmore. He received a reported $1 million advance. At the time, Judith Curr, Ballantine's publisher, told reporters that "Sean 'Puffy' Combs's remarkable story is an inspirational saga of triumph over adversity . . . about how a person can transform not only his own life and legacy, but how others might realize their own dreams of empowerment." It was supposed to hit bookstores sometime in 2000, but the deal fell through. In March 2000, Ballantine spokeswoman Ki Groh said there was no such book in the works at Ballantine. "There have been a lot of changes here," she noted.

Puffy's life story has included lavish parties and hobnobbing with the rich and famous. For his twenty-ninth birthday, he threw a gala bash for himself. It was held Wednesday, November 4, 1998, at Manhattan's posh Cipriani Hotel on Wall Street. The invitation was in the form of a videotape. On it, a cavalcade of celebrities made cameo appearances. It opened with Chris Rock saying, "Be in New York City." Then Oprah Winfrey with, "You're cordially invited to celebrate the birth of . . ." then Chris Rock saying, ". . . Sean 'Puffy' Combs." Penny Marshall admonished, "Remember, this invite admits only the recipients of this invitation, plus one guest." Celebrities from Magic Johnson, to Ellen DeGeneres, to Robin Leach appeared. The video ended with Shaquille O'Neal saying, "Be there or hear about it on the fifth."

The birthday bash cost Puffy $600,000 and featured go-go girls on a $50,000 Lucite dance floor. *People* magazine dubbed it Puffy's "hip-hop happy birthday party." The invitee list was twelve hundred guests long—so lengthy that not everyone who was invited was allowed in. The crush of an estimated three thousand crashers and the overambitious guest list prevented many guests from getting past the doormen to the party room, which accommodated about one thousand people.

THE MURDER OF BIGGIE SMALLS · 177

Among those who did make it inside were Muhammad Ali, Donald Trump, Mariah Carey, Kevin Costner, Henry Winkler, Penny Marshall, Duchess of York Sarah Ferguson, and supermodels Veronica Webb and Naomi Campbell. Those stranded outside, stuck behind a police line even though they had invitations, were Minnie Driver, Jon Bon Jovi (who also appeared on the videotaped invitation), and, for a while, Christie Brinkley, Chris Rock, and Donna Karan.

In 1999, Puffy rented a $2.5 million estate in the Hamptons where he spent that summer. He threw more lavish parties for guests that included Donald Trump, Martha Stewart, Costner, and other high-profile friends.

Puffy's extravagant taste was also marked by the purchase of a $375,000 powder-blue Bentley. He also sported pricey clothes and accessories, such as Versace furs, Prada shoes, and diamond earrings. His excesses were becoming legendary.

In 1999 comedian Jerry Seinfeld posed with Puffy for the cover of *Forbes* magazine, which did a feature on the top 100 power celebrities. While Seinfeld drove his own Mercedes to the shoot with only a publicist in tow, Puffy arrived in a specially requested white stretch limo, and with an entourage, including a security guard in charge of a black case containing Puffy's diamonds. Puffy arrived with two racks of garment bags containing fifteen suits—platinum, sharkskin, and cream-colored—even though Puffy ended up posing in jeans and a T-shirt. While Seinfeld requested just mineral water and fresh fruit, the *New York Post* reported, Puffy's office had faxed the magazine a list of Puffy's favorite foods. According to the *Post*, the list included filet mignon and lobster, and reminded them that Justin's, Puffy's restaurant, was in the city. After ordering Puffy's favorite menu selections (fried chicken and collard greens) from Justin's, two of his eatery's waiters were hired to serve it to him.

In November 1998, *Essence* magazine named Puffy as its Man of *Essence*. But readers criticized the designation for honoring an unmarried father of two. Puff Daddy had joined a select group of black men honored by the magazine, including Denzel Washington, Danny Glover, Michael Jordan, and Kenneth "Babyface" Edmonds. About the criticism, Puffy issued this statement: "I'm proud to be a responsible

single father and I take pride in being a responsible role model."
Essence threw a small private party at a midtown restaurant November 16 to celebrate its 1998 honoree.

Still, for all his Hollywoodlike excesses, fans loved Puffy's music just the same. Puffy, after all, had boasted that "my company right now is one-hundred-percent black." That, apparently, was "keepin' it real" to him.

At the same time Puffy was seemingly on top of the world, his star was tarnished when he was arrested in April and later admitted to beating Steven Stoute, an Interscope Records executive. Steven suffered a broken arm, a broken jaw, and cuts and contusions to his head, arms, legs, and back. The rift between Puffy and Steven occurred after Puffy appeared in a video with rapper Nas that featured Puffy on a crucifix. Puffy had second thoughts about the crucifix scene and asked that it be edited out; but when he watched the debut on MTV, the scene remained intact. So Puffy and two bodyguards stormed Steven Stoute's office and pummeled him with their fists, a champagne bottle, a telephone, and a chair. Puffy was charged with second-degree assault and faced up to seven years in prison, but later he publicly apologized and made a reported $500,000 payment to Stoute.

During a hearing on the ninth floor in Manhattan Criminal Court, Stoute told prosecutors that the two had worked out their differences and that he didn't want Puffy convicted of a crime.

During his hearing, dressed in a dapper pinstripe suit, Puffy apparently irritated Judge Martin Murphy. The judge snapped at Puffy to take his hands out of his pockets. Then he asked, glaring, "Mr. Combs, do you remember me?"

"Can't say I do," a somber Puffy responded.

But Judge Murphy didn't hold that against Puffy. He quickly disposed of the case after Puffy pleaded guilty to a lesser charge of misdemeanor harassment. He paid a fine and the judge sentenced him to a mandatory day of "anger-management" class. It was a mere slap on the wrist. In a statement released after the hearing, Puffy said, "I handled myself inappropriately. I made the wrong decision. . . . I'm glad to get this whole incident behind me. And it's now time for me to do what I do best, [to] concentrate on my album and give back to my fans."

Puffy had appeared before Judge Murphy in 1998 over a fatal 1991 stampede at a New York City College concert promoted by Combs. And in the earlier hearing the judge alluded to Puffy was called as a witness to testify in a New York City courtroom in a lawsuit filed against the city and state of New York.

In January 1999, Puffy and rapper Heavy D (Dwight Myers), were found half responsible for a 1991 event in which nine students were crushed to death during a stampede in a stairwell at the Nat Holman Gymnasium at City College of New York. Eight people suffocated in the crowd; a ninth died a few days later. They had been there for a celebrity basketball game and after-party sponsored by Puffy and Heavy D. Among the celebrities stopping by the 138th Street gym were, according to witness testimony, Mike Tyson, LL Cool J, and basketball player Walter Berry; more people than expected had showed up for the December 28, 1991, event. Judge Murphy, however, ruled that Combs and Myers oversold the event.

When Police Officer Sean Harris reached the bottom of the crowded stairwell leading to the gym by climbing down the banister, he had to push aside the table to get into the gym. "After falling through the door [and] into the gym, [Harris] saw Combs standing there with two women, and all three had money in their hands," Judge Louis C. Benza of the State Court of Claims in Albany wrote in his December 1998 ruling. "This revelation places a strain on the credibility of Combs's testimony that he was caught up in the melee and attempted to help the people who were trapped in the stairwell." The City University of New York was held responsible for the other half of the damages. "It does not take an Einstein to know that young people attending a rap concert camouflaged as a 'celebrity basketball game,' who have paid as much as $20 a ticket, would not be very happy and easy to control if they were unable to gain admission to the event because it was oversold," Benza ruled in a seventy-three-page decision against the City University of New York.

The Court of Claims deals only with cases against the state, so the ruling had no legal effect on Puffy and Heavy D. The judge blasted Puffy anyway. He said Puffy's security people had been responsible for the fatal mistake of closing the stairwell door to the gym. "Combs's forces, who were fully aware of the crowd uncontrollably pouring down the stairwell, created something akin to a 'dike,' forcing the people together like 'sardines' " and "squashing out life's breath from young bodies," the judge wrote. The families of the dead concertgoers were given the go-ahead to begin settlement negotiations with Puffy, Heavy D, and the college. In the end, Puffy settled for an undisclosed amount.

"It was a very hard thing for me to do," Puffy told *Vanity Fair*, of his testimony at the state hearing. "The City College tragedy is something that I live with every day. I was one of the promoters of that event, and my heart continuously goes out to the family and the children that lost their lives, and I constantly pray every day for them, and that's definitely the way my day started, and I just got here right now. I was a witness," Puffy added, "it wasn't like I was on trial, but I had to go back and tell everything that happened, so it was definitely something that was hard for me to do."

It would get worse for Puffy. He was arrested December 27, 1999, with his celebrity girlfriend, Jennifer Lopez, for criminal possession of a weapon after a shooting erupted inside the packed Club New York hip-hop venue, sending panic-stricken clubgoers into the frigid air outside the hot night spot at 252 West Forty-third Street. Three people—a bouncer and two bystanders—were wounded. Puffy, his chauffeur Wardel Fenderson, bodyguard Anthony "Wolf" Jones, and Jennifer— an A-list film star, singer, and dancer, as well as a part of 1999's successful Latin-invasion contingent—then left the midtown night spot. According to police, the four fled in a gray 1999 Lincoln Navigator registered to Bad Boy Entertainment. The driver ran eleven stoplights before he was pulled over by police. Detectives found a loaded 9-millimeter Smith & Wesson model 915 pistol, later found to be stolen, on the floor next to the passenger seat. Puffy and Jennifer were passengers in the backseat of the sport-utility vehicle. The gun found in the Navigator was reported in August as stolen from a Georgia man, police said.

The shooting went down like this: The weekly "Hot Chocolate" party at Club New York, was in full swing when Puffy and his entourage arrived just after midnight. Unlike hundreds of other guests jammed inside the club, Puffy and his entourage were not subjected to body searches by guards when they passed through the copper-colored doors, witnesses said. Inside, disc jockey Goldfinger was spinning R&B, hip-hop, and reggae, and about six hundred people on the dance floor moved beneath swirling colored lights as loud music played. Combs's crew were having a good time in the VIP section near the DJ's booth, witnesses said.

Eric S. Funk, the club's general manager told reporters that Puffy and Jennifer had arrived with about thirty people sometime after midnight and spent most of the evening in a VIP section set off by velvet ropes from the rest of the club patrons. He said customers at the door were searched and screened with a metal detector, but neither he nor the club's owner, Michael Bergos, could say how the guns got past the doormen and inside the night spot.

Assistant District Attorney Matthew Bogdanos's version of the shooting was that Puffy and rapper Shyne, whose real name is Jamal Barrow, got into an argument with an unidentified man, who allegedly tossed a wad of money at the pair. Quoting eyewitnesses, Bogdanos said both Puffy and Shyne pulled semiautomatic pistols. Shyne allegedly fired as he fell backward. One shot hit club bouncer Julius Jones, twenty-seven, in the shoulder. Another struck guest Natanya Ruben, twenty-nine, in the cheek and lodged in her nose. A third round hit bouncer Robert Thompson, thirty-nine, of Danbury, Connecticut, in the shoulder. Natanya and Julius were from Brooklyn, Ruben, shot in the face, and Jones, also from Brooklyn, were taken by ambulance to St. Vincent's Hospital and Medical Center, according to Mark Ackermann, a hospital spokesman.

Inside the club, police investigators recovered four shell casings: two from a 9-millimeter pistol and two from a .40-caliber gun. The 9-millimeter casings were believed to have come from the weapon allegedly carried by Shyne, nineteen, a Belize-born rapper on Puffy's label. Barrow was arrested outside the club and charged with three counts of attempted murder and reckless endangerment. It was not clear who fired the .40-caliber bullets. No .40-caliber pistol was recovered.

The judge released Anthony Jones on $20,000 bail and Wardel Fenderson on $2,000 bail. Shyne, twenty-one at the time, was held on $1 million bail after his arraignment on three counts of attempted murder. Prosecutors said that a ballistics test on the gun Barrow was carrying when he was arrested matched some of the spent shell casings found in the club.

Jennifer Lopez, who was twenty-nine at the time of her arrest, told police she didn't know anything about the gun and that she wasn't aware the police had been trying to pull them over. She was released after thirteen hours of detainment, some of which were spent handcuffed to a bench outside a holding cell inside the Midtown North Precinct station house. There were reports that Jennifer was hysterical and sobbed for hours while she was held. No charges against her were ever filed.

According to court papers filed during Puffy's incarceration in the New York City jail, where he was booked at 3:09 A.M., he expressed more concern for his girlfriend than anyone else. Puffy "repeatedly and spontaneously . . . asked officers why Jennifer Lopez was being arrested," the documents revealed.

Puffy was arraigned early in the morning in Manhattan Criminal Court before Judge Gabriel W. Gorenstein, and charged with illegal gun possession. During his arraignment, Puffy's attorney, Harvey Slovis, accused the witnesses—who had told police Puffy had drawn a gun—of lying.

"I don't know if you know this, Judge, but this person Jennifer Lopez is a very famous actress," Slovis said. "To think that Mr. Combs is walking around with her with a loaded gun and then going to pull it out, it's so ridiculous that it stretches the imagination."

After the arraignment, Slovis told reporters, "There's no reason to charge people in the backseat" when the weapon was found in the front seat. "So many people make false charges against [Puffy]—it's the price [he pays for fame]," Slovis said.

Prosecutors testified that following the nightclub shooting, Puffy and Jennifer ran out and jumped into the SUV chauffeured by Wardel Fenderson. The Navigator, allegedly with Wardel at the wheel, sped down West Forty-third Street toward Eighth Avenue and swerved around a marked police car, its dome lights flashing. Officers had parked there, in the middle of the street, to close off the block. The Navigator, with chauffeur Wardel Fenderson behind the wheel, sped north on Eighth Avenue. The chauffeur led police on a high-speed chase through midtown Manhattan, allegedly running eleven red lights before he was pulled over on the northeast corner of West Fifty-fourth Street and Eighth Avenue, twelve blocks away. All four occupants climbed out of the car and the police found the gun under the front passenger seat, where Anthony Jones had been riding, court papers said.

Curiously, Wardel, the alleged driver who had led police on the high-speed chase, was never charged with a crime. Puffy's attorneys would later learn that was because Wardel Fenderson was offered immunity in exchange for his testimony against Puffy, which would include an allegation of bribery.

Meanwhile, Shyne had been arrested by two uniformed police officers called to the scene after a call was placed to 911. He had been approached by the officers as they arrived outside the club. The officers reported finding a second gun in Shyne's waistband.

A weary-looking Puffy, wearing a black leather jacket, baggy black denim pants, a long, oversized white T-shirt, and his trademark diamond stud earrings, was released about twenty hours later, at 10:45 P.M., after posting $10,000 bail. Puffy was greeted by a battalion of reporters who had waited for hours outside the courthouse. He held a brief news conference that night. Nothing, of course, required him to do that. In fact, most defense attorneys will tell their clients not to talk to the press. But Puffy obviously wanted to tell his side of the story, at least briefly. Looking exhausted and disheveled, Puffy denied to reporters that he had ever possessed or drawn a pistol. "I do not own a gun," he told them. "I do not carry a gun. The charges against me are one-hundred-percent false, and I feel confident that in the next couple of days I'll be vindicated and everything will be all right."

But he wasn't vindicated. Instead, more than two weeks later, he was indicted.

The fracas allegedly began this way: Witnesses told police that at 2:55 A.M. an unidentified man at Club New York threw a wad of bills at Puffy, which, they said, irritated Shyne—an aspiring rapper described as having a voice oddly similar to Biggie's, and part of Puffy's thirty-person entourage that night—and prompted him to allegedly pull out a semiautomatic pistol and fire off several rounds. The bullets hit three victims. Police said at least one witness claimed Puffy also pulled out a gun. Puffy denied the accusation.

It wasn't until a few days later, after a grand-jury inquest, that the District Attorney's Office filed an affidavit saying Puffy had had two stolen guns in his possession that night.

Jennifer, who was released at about four P.M. from the Midtown North Precinct station house, did not speak with reporters, but her lawyer, Larry Ruggiero, said: "They established she did nothing wrong. Jennifer had nothing to do with the gun or the shooting."

After Puffy's release, the couple checked into room 801 at Manhattan's Peninsula Hotel under the last name "Rios."

On December 30, Jennifer and Puffy each testified before a grand jury. Jennifer told the grand jurors that she did not see Puffy with a gun. She was called back by the District Attorney's Office for further questioning. Hundreds of fans showed up on the street, turning the scene into something out of a Hollywood premiere.

District Attorney Robert Morgenthau, who at that point had been in the office twenty-five years, later described the fan frenzy as "the biggest crowd I've ever seen here." He noted that it surpassed the media frenzy during the trial against mafia don John Gotti.

Camera-clutching fans shouted out Jennifer's name and chased her vehicle as she sped away after more than four hours of questioning by investigators. Jennifer, wearing a long white coat and dark glasses, with her hair pulled straight back, rushed past hordes of reporters, photographers, and fans to an interrogation room across the street from where Puffy was appearing for questioning at the same time.

Jennifer's lawyer, Lawrence Ruggiero, said in a statement: "Jennifer Lopez does not own a firearm nor does she condone the use of firearms."

When Puffy emerged from questioning by grand jurors, he told reporters at the courthouse that he came before them "to tell the truth, and hopefully we can get down to the bottom of this."

Tom Morganthau with *Newsweek* once said that Puffy's song "Fake

Thugs" was a reminder of who Puffy really was. The headline to that article described Puffy as a "hip-hop socialite." Life, once again, was imitating art. Puffy, once considered squeaky-clean, was himself reflecting the very thug image from which he professed he tried so hard to distance himself.

To help him out of the Club New York legal mess, Puffy put together a team of lawyers. Puffy hired a top legal team comprised of Johnnie Cochran, Harvey Slovis, and Benjamin Brafman. Cochran was O. J. Simpson's ex-lawyer; Slovis was a Brooklyn attorney; Brafman once defended mob killer Salvatore "Sammy the Bull" Gravano, John Gotti's former underboss in the Gambino crime family.

On Thursday, January 13, seventeen days after the shooting, Puffy Combs, in a six-page affidavit, was indicted on charges that he had two loaded guns in his sport-utility vehicle as he fled the nightclub shooting. He was formally charged with possession of a weapon, meaning he had a loaded gun with intent to use it. He was also charged with third-degree, which is simple possession of a gun. Along with Puffy, Shyne was indicted on attempted murder charges, and bodyguard Anthony Jones on a weapons charge. Jones was also charged with possessing marijuana.

One gun, a 9-millimeter pistol, was found by police on the floor at the front seat of the vehicle, and the other, also a 9-millimeter, was thrown from the vehicle, Manhattan district attorney Robert Morgenthau said. Both guns had been fired, but the district attorney could not say where or when the weapons were fired. Until that day, prosecutors had not accused Puffy of having the gun they say was thrown from the car. Both weapons—Smith & Wesson semiautomatic pistols—showed signs of having been recently fired, Morgenthau said. Each gun had a sixteen-bullet capacity. The one found inside the car at the front seat contained twelve bullets. The gun allegedly thrown from the window contained eight rounds. The ammunition was a mix of hollow-point and regular round-nosed shells.

In court, Morgenthau described the existence of front- and rear-seat "traps"—or hidden storage compartments—custom-built into the Lincoln Navigator's cab. "It does not come with the car," Morgenthau testified. "You can hide your jewelry, your gun." None of the guns were found in the traps. Morgenthau said investigators were still seeking a fourth handgun, after shells from a .40-caliber gun were found inside the club.

Puffy faced a sentence of up to fifteen years in prison for the gun charges, if convicted. From the outset, he maintained his innocence.

"The decision to indict me is wrong," he said in a statement. "I'm innocent and we will prove it. I am putting my faith in God and I know my name will be cleared."

Jennifer released a statement after Puffy was indicted, saying she never saw Puffy with a weapon on the night of his arrest. "I am surprised and saddened to learn of the indictment against Sean Combs," she said. "I support him wholeheartedly throughout this difficult time." Even so, Jennifer and Puffy spent New Year's Eve apart. Jennifer went to her mother's house in Miami while Combs stayed in New York.

Attorney Johnnie Cochran added his statement to the mix: "We ask the public, Sean's millions of fans, and those with whom he is involved in various business ventures to withhold judgment until the case is over. Mr. Combs, like any other citizen accused of a crime, is presumed to be innocent. Mr. Combs looks forward to his day in court where he can respond to these charges and demonstrate that he is not guilty of these crimes, once and for all." Cochran added that Puffy's fingerprints did not show up on either weapon.

No one in this case has been convicted and the outcome of the case is pending.

In late January 2000, Puffy reportedly laid off employees at Bad Boy Entertainment.

On Valentine's Day—February 14, 2000—Puffy went back to court. The nightclub's bouncer, Robert Thompson, who was a victim of the shooting, had filed a $100,000 million lawsuit against Puffy.

Then, another indictment, this one for bribery, was filed on February 23, 2000, the same day Puffy attended the Forty-second Annual Grammy Awards show at the Staples Center in Los Angeles. Puffy had been nominated for Best Rap Performance by a Duo or Group, for his song "Satisfy You" featuring R. Kelly. The song "You Got Me" by the Roots, featuring Erykah Badu, won the category. A somber, unsmiling Puffy Combs was shown sitting in the audience with girl-friend Jennifer Lopez. But Puffy left about thirty minutes before the three-hour show ended. The vacated seat, prominently in the front row, didn't go unnoticed by Grammy-show emcee Rosie O'Donnell. "Good news, everyone," Rosie said at one point, "Puffy Daddy has left the building. He was in the front row, and it's a comfort to me, trust me."

Backstage, when asked how he was holding up, Puffy told re-porters, "It's unbelievable. There's something new every day. The truth will all come out eventually."

Two days later, on February 25, Puffy issued this statement: "I am outraged by this new (bribery) charge. I am not guilty. From the outset, I have firmly believed that the Manhattan District Attorney's Office has unfairly targeted me for baseless charges. This was done . . . on the night of the Grammy Awards in an attempt to embarrass me. I intend to fight these groundless charges with all my heart."

Officials denied there was any connection between the Grammys and the timing of the indictment. "The grand-jury schedule was set without any relation to the Grammy Awards," a spokesman for Man-hattan district attorney Robert Morgenthau said.

The indictment claimed Puffy tried to bribe his chauffeur, Wardel Fenderson, with $50,000 and a diamond ring as collateral. The ring—which the deputy district attorney told the court cost $40,000, but that Puffy told his chauffeur cost $300,000—was a birthday gift to Puffy from Jennifer. In return for the money, the driver would allegedly claim ownership of the gun found in Puffy's car.

At a February 10 bail hearing, Assistant District Attorney Matthew Bogdanos told the court that Puffy had offered Wardel $50,000 to take the blame "at the front desk in front of dozens of police officers." Bog-danos also claimed that Fenderson was offered the diamond ring as collateral for the deal. Bogdanos said Puffy's bribery attempts contin-ued "in the holding pen, the limousine ride home after his release from court, and at his [Puffy's] Park Avenue residence." Prosecutors con-tended that Combs continued the bribery attempts for days. Fenderson was not charged with a crime, and was reportedly cooperating with prosecutors.

Puffy's attorney, Benjamin Brafman, released a statement saying that the new indictment would "prove to be a terrible abuse of prosecutorial discretion. There is no basis in fact for this charge, and we are completely confident that this charge, like the weapons charge, will be categorically rejected by a jury."

Puffy appeared in court February 29. He pleaded not guilty.

After his plea, Puffy again proclaimed his innocence at the courthouse to waiting reporters. "Every day they are trying something new," he told them. "It's not me. I'm innocent. The way they are acting in court is outrageous."

Then, in a written statement, he said, "I am outraged by the new bribery charge. As I have said before, this charge is completely baseless. I did not bribe anyone at any time, anywhere. I look forward to my day in court and being completely exonerated on all the charges."

The prosecution asked that Puffy's bail be increased from $10,000 to $150,000. No ruling was made. The bribery charge carried a penalty of seven years; the gun possession charges, fifteen. Puffy faced being imprisoned like his nemesis, rap producer Suge Knight. At the time of this writing, the final outcome of the nightclub shooting was pending.

The December 1999 nightclub shooting wasn't the first time Puffy had found himself in trouble with the law. In 1996, Puffy was found guilty of criminal mischief for threatening a *New York Post* photographer with a gun the year before; he was fined $1,000. The court records on that case were sealed.

Also in 1995, Puffy was arrested for allegedly flashing a silver gun and smiling threateningly during a January 23 confrontation with a man in a parking lot at Georgetown University in Washington, D.C., according to a court affidavit.

The arrest warrant claimed an indignant Puffy was confronted by staff inside a university dining hall. After Puffy and an unidentified man entered the cafeteria, at a university they did not attend, and started distributing magazines with Puffy's photo on the cover, a worker approached to ask "if they needed help," according to the arrest warrant. Puffy allegedly swore at the man, identified as Mario Cruz, and left the hall, returning soon thereafter to ask what time Cruz got off work. When Cruz emerged from his job at four P.M. January 23, 1995, Combs and his friend were allegedly waiting for him, the affidavit said. Puffy allegedly lifted his shirt to reveal a gun on his belt, then got into a car and drove away. The student, Cruz, reported the incident to police.

A District of Columbia Superior Court judge issued a warrant for Puffy's arrest on a threat charge. Puffy later surrendered to the FBI in New York. He was released on his own recognizance. The case was dropped for lack of evidence and never prosecuted. Whether it would be revisited by prosecutors in the Club New York case remains to be seen.

Just prior to the nightclub incident, there was a shooting episode on Halloween 1999 which didn't involve Puffy, but put Bad Boy Entertainment back in the spotlight. On the afternoon of October 31, an unknown gunman blasted the lobby door of Puffy's Manhattan recording studio with at least four shots from a 9-millimeter semiautomatic pistol, shattering the glass lobby door. Puffy, who at the time owned the second-floor studio, was out of town in Florida. About seven musicians, including Lil' Kim and Lil' Cease, were recording upstairs. Puffy had leased the studio to Atlantic Records, which was Lil' Kim and Lil' Cease's label. No one was reported injured. But a woman on the street was badly cut by glass shards as she fled the gunfire outside 321 West Forty-fourth Street. The woman received thirty-five stitches at St. Luke's–Roosevelt Hospital.

Police couldn't find anybody else who was injured, although it was reported that they found blood outside the studio. The *New York Post* reported that Bad Boy artist Shyne was the intended target of the shooting, after having gotten into an altercation earlier that evening at a nightclub. Police, however, could not confirm that report. Lil' Kim and Lil' Cease released a statement denying any involvement in the shooting. Police did say, however, that the shooting stemmed from a fistfight on the street that may have begun in a nearby bar. But no arrests were ever made in the case.

By mid-1999, Puffy had moved out of the Park Avenue apartment he had shared with his longtime girlfriend Kim Porter, to an apartment in midtown inside his recording studio. Instead of being seen with Kim, he had been spotted with Jennifer Lopez on his arm. The couple went public by holding hands for the cameras at the September 1999 MTV Awards.

For Christmas 1999, two days before the shooting at Club New York, Puffy gave Jennifer a white mink coat and an antique diamond bracelet.

Puffy's success and wealth has been emphasized by excesses. His music has been described by critics as "candy rap," and he has made himself his own label's main attraction. On the other hand, Suge Knight, until he was jailed, appeared to stay close to his roots. "I love Compton," Suge told the *New York Times*. "Compton's like the ocean. It's real pretty, but any time something can happen. Somebody getting eaten. Somebody fighting. Something's always going on." He criticized those in the business who acted fake. "Everybody's Hollywood," he said. "They all have their move. People think I'm making all this money and I have to give autographs, but what's cool is to sit in your neighborhood and get some chili-cheese fries and eat your food and deal with your homeboys. . . . I ain't got no problems. I don't see no shrinks. I remember where I'm from. That keeps me straight."

By 1999, Andre Harrell was president of Bad Boy Entertainment, freeing up Puffy to record more. Puffy told BET that Andre's involvement allowed him to be a CEO 20 percent of the time and a performer 80 percent. It also allowed him, in 1999, to record an album of his own.

The fans turned out in droves for Puff Daddy's Family Tour. The show was packed with tributes to the Notorious B.I.G. Los Angeles was the only major city that was left off of the tour itinerary. "We're not gonna do L.A. just because of personal feelings of mine," Puffy told *MTV News*. "I mean, I love all the fans in L.A. I love all the people in L.A. I can't blame L.A. for . . . I ain't got no hard feelings with Los Angeles. I go there a lot myself, but I'm traveling with a group of people, and everybody here has mothers and fathers and kids and stuff like that, and I just really can't guarantee nothing almost nowhere." The world tour's European leg was canceled because "doctors told me to take a rest," Puffy told *People* magazine. "I was tired. I was wearing myself down, and it was killing me. I have to be able to perform without getting sick or hurting myself, because it would be really bad if I wasn't able to work."

During his Puff Daddy and the Family World Tour in early 1998, Puffy repeatedly implored the crowds to remember Biggie Smalls. This could have been a sincere gesture, of course, or the memorial could simply have been cynical showbiz. Either way, it sold albums.

Puffy tried to distance himself from hardcore gangsta/playa rap. He still, however, produced Biggie's gangsta raps.

After Biggie's death, Puffy acknowledged that violence surrounded the rap industry. Inevitably, the murders of Tupac Shakur and Biggie Smalls raised questions about whether gangsta rap promoted violence—questions that have troubled industry executives and musicians. Even a dictionary definition for *gangsta* included violence. The online *A–Z Dictionary* defines "gang'sta rap" as "a type of rap music whose lyrics feature violence, sexual exploits, and the like."

"The music's so personal, so directed, so violent," said Bruce St. James, program director for Los Angeles's largest rap station, KPWR, "that we wondered [when] someone would take it too far."

The violence surrounding Biggie's death lingered for Puffy. He claimed during a BET interview that he wasn't a part of it. "Every day, I try to make sense of why my friend is not here," he said. "It isn't easy. In my heart and in my mind there is no East Coast–West Coast rap war. I do not want it. I do not like it. I will not fuel it."

"In a sad way, Puffy's the reigning champ," rapper Heavy D, who has known Puffy Combs since their childhoods, told *Playboy* magazine in a January 1998 article. "He's a very spiritual person. Puff is a good guy. Puff ain't never been a punk, you know. He's a hustler. He went to college and learned to throw parties. He's got that brilliant energy."

While gangsta/playa rap music has been a political target because of the violence that has appeared to surround it, Biggie's music has impacted rap in a positive way, Puffy told MTV. "I don't know if he changed rap," he said. "I'd say he took it to the next level. I think every MC, or rapper, or producer, anybody involved in the industry of hip-hop, they gonna be involved with helping taking it to another level. I just think he helped take it to another level. I don't think that's nobody's mission, to change hip-hop or change rap, 'cause there ain't nothin' wrong with it. I just think that he was one of the people that helped to take it to the next level."

Biggie also helped to carry Puffy Combs and his Bad Boy family to a new level—a lucrative one. Biggie's music continued topping the charts and selling millions after his death, assisting in Puffy Combs's multimillionaire status. In 1998 alone, Puffy earned an estimated $53 million through his rap empire.

13

BIGGIE'S ESTATE AND LEGACY

NO ONE WILL EVER KNOW what more Biggie Smalls could have accomplished, had he survived; whether he, like successful rappers before him, would have tapped into lucrative clothing endorsements, movie roles, and TV ads. Or, at the other end of the spectrum, if he would have, like his rival Tupac Shakur and Biggie's record producer Puffy Combs, continued having brushes with the law, or, worse, landed in jail.

What *is* known is that Biggie's music, after his death, topped the charts and sold millions of CDs. Like Tupac Shakur before him, he was bigger in death than in life. Three weeks after his murder, the Notorious B.I.G.'s second album, *Life After Death*, was released, debuting at number one on the *Billboard* charts. Like Tupac Shakur before him, Biggie left behind a legacy that was based almost as much on his bad-boy lifestyle as it was on his music. With the success of *Ready to Die* and *Life After Death* the Notorious B.I.G. became the most visible figure in East Coast hip-hop.

His death was the result of a vicious attack, whether it was the result of a Crips-Bloods feud, or an East Coast–West Coast rap war, or a random killing. Looking back, Biggie appeared to be simultaneously headed for tragedy and fame.

In January 2000, the Notorious B.I.G. was inducted into the Recording Industry Association of America's Diamond Club. The distinction was awarded after Biggie's album *Life After Death* reached the RIAA's Diamond Award sales plateau of ten million.

Biggie's estate was valued in the multiple millions of dollars. In December 1998, previously unreleased songs in an album long anticipated by fans were produced. It was a joint release by Bad Boy, Voletta Wallace, and Faith Evans.

Voletta and Faith share in Biggie's estate, along with his two children, T'Yanna and Christopher Jordan (or "C. J."). A third child, Chyna, who has often been written about as also being fathered by Biggie, was actually Biggie's wife Faith Evans's daughter from a previous relationship.

Although Biggie and Faith had initiated divorce proceedings, the papers were never formally filed in court. Faith and Biggie were still technically married at the time of his death. "They were separated," Biggie's mother said. "They never got a divorce. Christopher signed the paper but it was never sent in. I blame [Bad Boy] management for Christopher and Faith not getting a divorce." Faith voluntarily made Voletta a joint heir with her in Biggie's estate. Faith acknowledged Biggie's dedication to his mother and split the estate with Voletta.

Voletta emphasized that it was Biggie, not Faith Evans, who had provided her with her son's Teaneck, New Jersey, condominium, which she described as being decorated in green and black "as if it were meant for the *Rich and Famous*." When Biggie died, Voletta was still working as a teacher. After he became successful, Biggie gave his mother a monthly allowance to supplement her income. He was protective of her and wanted to provide for her the way she had provided for him when he was growing up. Once, when he was a boy, he told his mother that when he became old enough he wanted to be her husband so he could take care of her.

"There are rumors that Faith [Evans] has been very kind to me and very generous," Voletta said. "Whatever Faith gave to me, whatever I inherited, I got from my son. My son was a very generous son. He had made it for about two and a half years before his death. The big money had started to come in." Even though they were separated at the time of his death, because the divorce was never made final his property reverted to Faith. And he didn't have a will.

Also, Voletta said, Puffy Combs had publicly said that he was "taking care of Biggie's mother." Not true, she said. "Puffy's not taking care of Biggie's mother," Voletta said. "Biggie is taking care of Biggie's mother. Puffy's been very outspoken that he's taking care of Mrs. Wallace and the children. Puffy doesn't buy my food, pay my mortgage. Everything was in Christopher's name. He died a very rich man and a very smart man. He made his mother a rich woman."

As for Puffy's contention that Biggie was his best friend, Voletta said it was nothing more than a business association.

"Christopher had a good working relationship with Puffy," she explained, "but they were not friends. They were *business* associates. My son was smart enough to do his business himself. He had plans for the future."

Some of those plans included future music production with Lance "Un" Rivera. Biggie owned half of the production company, Undeas Records, with Lance, which had produced Junior M.A.F.I.A.'s albums.

Puffy Combs lived up to a promise he made after Biggie's death, and that was to open a trust for the rapper's children. The money—$3 million—was generated from the release of two songs: "We'll Always Love Big Poppa" and "I'll Be Missing You."

The release of those songs premiered on more than two hundred radio stations across the country simultaneously at noon Wednesday, May 14, 1997 (declared Notorious B.I.G. Day), followed by a thirty-second moment of silence. "The reason we did two songs, we felt that everybody wanted to be involved," Puffy said during a news conference the same day. "The L.O.X. started out with the song first, and they were a catalyst for us making the second song. And we shot two videos, because Biggie deserved to get that type of tribute." Also, rapper Ice Cube canceled two shows he had scheduled in Los Angeles that day, out of respect for the slain rapper.

After his death, the Notorious B.I.G. was nominated for MTV's Best Rap Video for "Mo' Money Mo' Problems." At the 1997 MTV Awards ceremony in New York's Times Square, Puff Daddy teamed with Sting for a tribute to Biggie, dueting on "I'll Be Missing You," the song Puffy built around the Police's hit, "Every Breath You Take." The memory of Biggie resounded throughout the event. Puffy Combs received Best R&B Video for "I'll Be Missing You." Puffy wore a black shirt with Biggie's photo emblazoned on it and the word "Remember."

Biggie was awarded Best Rap Video for "Hypnotize." With Puffy Combs by her side, Voletta Wallace accepted the award for her son.

For his acceptance speech, Puff Daddy said, "B.I.G., we'll never forget you. Everybody that's passed away this year, we'll never forget you. God bless us all." In an interview afterward with MTV, Puffy noted, "What '97 was, it was overwhelming. We lost so many people. All over the world, people have felt pain, and 'Missing You' is a song to try to help you deal with the pain."

On Tuesday, June 3, 1997, ASCAP's Rhythm and Soul Music Awards featured a special tribute to Biggie. The ceremony, at the Manhattan Center in New York City, celebrated the tenth anniversary of its Rhythm and Soul Music Awards. More than five hundred guests attended. The musical tribute to Biggie featured 112, Faith Evans, rap act the L.O.X., and Puffy all performing their hit song, "I'll Be Missing You." Again, Voletta Wallace accepted the award on behalf of her son. Voletta said she considered her son "a rapper for the fans, a rapper for the people. The people loved him when he was alive and cherished him when he died."

Biggie was given another posthumous award for 1997, this one at the *Billboard* Awards, held in Las Vegas at the MGM Grand. Puffy Combs was on his world tour at the time and interrupted it to attend. He met Voletta Wallace in Las Vegas, where she stayed for two days at the Hard Rock Hotel. Voletta brought Biggie's oldest child with her from New Jersey. They all walked up on the stage together to accept the award on behalf of Biggie.

A large part of the legacy Biggie left behind lies with his children—a daughter and a son—and his mother. When Voletta Wallace talks about her son's murder, even after so much time has gone by, she still fights back tears. But when she speaks of her grandchildren, the children her son left behind, she speaks with hope. She makes sure her grandchildren know who their father was. Voletta said she is helping to raise Biggie's children, who stay with her on weekends, with the knowledge of their father and his success. T'Yanna was old enough to remember him. "T'Yanna loved her father and Christopher loved his daughter," Voletta said. "She still thinks that one day he's going to walk through this door." Even though his son C. J. was only a few months old when Biggie was killed, "he knows who he is," Voletta said. "I make sure he knows who his father was." Their mother,

Faith Evans, also keeps him alive for their children. When C. J. sees Biggie on TV in a video, he yells, "That's Daddy, there's my daddy."

There has been wide speculation that Biggie's murder, after three and a half years, and Tupac's homicide, after more than four years, will never be solved. The LAPD was optimistic in the beginning; Las Vegas police were less so about their case, saying witnesses were uncooperative and that until someone came forward to finger the gunman, the crime would go unsolved. The LAPD was more optimistic and actively seeking closure in the year 2000.

That optimism was music to Voletta Wallace's ears. She said she won't return to Los Angeles where her son was killed until his murderer is caught and brought to justice. When that occurs—and she emphasized "*when*," not "if"—she plans to attend every day of the trial. "I'm not only hoping," Voletta said, "but I am praying that they will catch the dog who killed my son. I can't wait. I know that's a trip I'm waiting to take. That's the only way I'll go back to L.A., to look the murderer in the face."

With sales of ten million copies, Notorious B.I.G.'s 1997 Bad Boy/Arista title *Life After Death* became what the RIAA called the first hardcore rap album to reach the sales landmark.

In his mother's words, "All his albums, to me, were a celebration of his life."

Biggie's last words to his fans, included as a biography that accompanied his *Life After Death* album, were prophetic, given that they were released after his murder, in an album that became a huge success: "I want this to be the biggest record ever," Biggie Smalls wrote. "I want it to hit the streets harder than any record before. I want to live up to my name and prove to everybody that there really is life after death."

APPENDIX

A MORGUE LIST of fatal shootings during a period the Compton Police Department described as a rap-war "bloodbath":

- Randy "Stretch" Walker, a witness to Tupac Shakur's being shot in a 1994 New York City shooting/robbery, was shot to death during a high-speed chase in Queens on November 30, 1995, exactly one year to the day after the New York City shooting.
- Kevin Gaines, an LAPD officer living with Sharitha Knight (Suge Knight's ex-wife), was shot to death March 18, 1997, by a fellow off-duty cop during a traffic dispute.
- Jake Robles, an employee of Death Row Records and a close friend of Suge Knight, the label's CEO, was shot outside an Atlanta party on September 24, 1995. He died a week later.
- Tupac Shakur, a Death Row rapper, was shot September 7, 1996, in a drive-by, on his way to a Las Vegas party. He died September 13, 1996.
- Bobby Finch, a reported Crips gang member, was shot to death on September 11, 1996, in a drive-by in Compton, California.
- Marcus Childs and Timothy Flanagan were both shot to death on September 13, 1996, during a drive-by in Los Angeles.
- Yafeu "Yak" Fula, who performed as "Kadafi" in the Outlawz, and who was the only willing witness to Tupac Shakur's murder, was shot to death in a housing project in Orange, New Jersey, on November 10, 1996.
- Biggie Smalls, a rapper for Bad Boy Entertainment, was shot to death in a drive-by after an L.A. party on March 9, 1997.
- Orlando "Little Lando" Anderson, was shot to death during a dispute over money in Compton, California, on May 29, 1998.

Brooklyn: life on street in, 108, 110; Shakur in, 31; Smalls's early years in, 17-27, 28, 31-32; and Smalls's funeral, 148; Smalls's loyalty toward neighborhood in, 44, 50; Smalls's popularity in, 28. *See also specific neighborhood*
Bugsy (Junior M.A.F.I.A. member), 22
Bullet (film), 49
Busta Rhymes, 5, 149, 174
Butler, Damien "D-Rock": identification of Mack by, 120; at Los Angeles party, 6; and motive for Smalls's murder, 137; moves in with Smalls, 37; as pallbearer at Smalls's funeral, 148; and Smalls's death, 15-16; and Smalls's early career, 31-32; and Smalls's murder, 9, 10, 12; Smalls's relationship with, 6, 163; and surveillance photos of Smalls, 128-29

C, Father, 29
C, Matty (aka Matt Life), 28
"California Love" (Shakur song), 41
Camden, New Jersey: Smalls's cancelled concert at, 33-34
Campbell, Julia, 151-52
Capone (Junior M.A.F.I.A. member), 22
Car accident: Smalls and Lil' Caesar in, 37-38
Car door: auction of bullet-riddled, 135-36
Carey, Mariah, 91, 161, 165, 166, 171, 177
Carrier, C. Scott, 114, 115
Casey, Phil, 110-11
CC's Club (New York City), 31
Cedars-Sinai Medical Center (Los Angeles), 12-14, 126, 131, 132
Cee, Mister, 28-29, 30
Central Intelligence Agency (CIA), 111-12
Cflo (aka Chris Elliott), 105
Chaka Zulu, 57
Chesnoff, David, 81, 83-84, 95, 96, 98, 99, 130
Chicago, Illinois: rap summit in, 56, 152
Childs, Marcus, 79, 199
Chuck D, 56-57, 68-69, 109, 152
Clinton Hill (Brooklyn), 19, 20, 22, 27, 28, 36, 148, 150
Club 662 (Las Vegas), 72, 73, 74
Club New York: Combs at, 180-88, 189
Cochran, Johnnie, 185, 186
Cohn, Marc, 68
Coker, Cheo Hodari, 2, 37, 38-39, 42, 108
Combs, Sean "Puffy": alleged Federal investigation of, 129; autobiography of, 176; awards/honors for, 165-66, 168, 170, 174, 186; and awards/honors for Smalls, 195-96; bribery charges against, 186-88; as CEO of Bad Boy Entertainment, 1,

161; and Chicago rap summit, 56; childhood/youth of, 171-72; and Club New York case, 180-88, 189; conspiracy law suit against, 175; criticisms of, 169; and drugs, 185; and Dupri birthday party, 55; early career of, 172; Evans discovered by, 35; excesses of, 175-77, 190; fans of, 184; filmmaking by, 168; Fox-TV interview of, 162, 163-64, 168; and gangs in Los Angeles, 110-11; and gangsta rap, 191; gun possession charges against, 180-88, 189; Heavy D's comments about, 191; as intended target in Smalls's murder, 14-15, 125-26, 145; and Jackson (Janet), 166-67; and Knight, 55, 58, 93, 168, 169, 190; LAPD interview of, 163; and *Life After Death* album, 45-46; and Los Angeles party, 3, 5, 6, 7, 9; and New York City College concert, 179-80; nicknames for, 161, 172; as performer, 165, 168, 169, 174, 178, 190-91; as in physical danger, 143-44; and Quad Studio shooting, 51, 60, 63, 66, 67, 70; and rap feud, 55, 58, 70, 97, 98, 143, 144, 169-70, 191; and *Ready to Die* album, 32; reputation of, 161, 167-68; restaurants of, 165, 166; and safety for Smalls, 3-4; security guards for, 94-95, 115-16, 128, 147, 167, 177, 180; and Shakur's murder, 33, 97-98, 170; Shakur's ridiculing of, 53; Smalls first meets, 29; and Smalls's alleged financial dispute with Crips, 107; and Smalls's death, 13, 15; and Smalls's demo tapes, 28-29; and Smalls's disillusionment with rap business, 41-42; and Smalls's European plans, 1; and Smalls's funeral, 148, 149; on Smalls's impact on rap, 191-92; and Smalls's mobster image, 29; and Smalls's murder, 8-10, 11-12, 115-16, 142-44, 161, 162-63, 169; as Smalls's producer, 30; Smalls's relationship with, 163, 195; Smalls's role in success of, 30; and sports, 23, 168-69; statement about Bad Boy security guards by, 143, 145-46; and Stoute beating, 8, 178; as success, 165, 170-71, 174, 178, 190, 192; surveillance of, 94; as "taking care" of Voletta Wallace, 194-95; Thompson lawsuit against, 186; threats against *New York Post* photographer by, 188; thug image of, 184-85; tributes to Smalls by, 190, 191, 195, 196; twenty-fifth birthday party for, 176-77; and Uptown Records, 28-29, 30; Wallace's (Voletta) views about, 30, 126,

Kadafi (Yafeu "Yak" Fula), 88-89, 90,
    199
Kane, Big Daddy, 28
Kelly, R., 32, 186
Kenner, David, 81, 88, 92, 95-96, 98
Kessler Institute for Rehabilitation (New
    Jersey), 37-38
King Suckerman (Pelecanos novel), 168
Knight, Marion "Suge": and
    Anderson-Shakur confrontation, 5, 6, 76,
        80-82, 83, 87, 88, 95; arrests of and
        lawsuits against, 80, 82, 92; attorneys for,
        81, 83-84, 92, 95-96, 98, 99, 121, 130; and
        Bloods, 78, 82, 93, 107, 109; business
        savvy of, 97; and Combs, 55, 58, 93, 168,
        169, 190; Compton childhood/youth of,
        109; contracts on life of, 97; and Dupri
        birthday party, 55; and Evans-Shakur
        relationship, 53-54; and events leading to
        Shakur's murder, 74-75, 76; and gangsta
        rap, 52; as intented victim in Shakur's
        murder, 77; Justice Department
        investigation of, 93-94; LAPD
        questioning of, 117, 136; LAPD search
        of locations linked to, 117, 118-19; Las
        Vegas mansion of, 130; Las Vegas Police
        Department questioning of, 98-99, 100;
        Mack relationship with, 116- 22, 136;
        parole violation of, 6, 76, 80-82, 83, 88,
        95; personal and professional
        background of, 84, 91, 92, 93; and
        plans/future of Death Row Records,
        91-92, 96-97; in prison, 6, 57, 83-84,
        85-88, 92, 95, 97, 108, 116, 122- 24; and
        rap feud, 55, 58, 97; reputation of, 92, 97;
        security guards for, 9; Shakur's argument
        with, 74; Shakur's bond posted by, 52,
        69, 92; and Shakur's murder, 72, 98-99,
        102; as Shakur's record producer, 9;
        Shakur's relationship with, 92; and
        Smalls's murder, 57, 116-23, 136, 138;
        and *Soul Train* Music Awards, 55; as
        uncooperative, 122; and wrongful-death
        suit against Anderson, 87-88. *See also*
        Death Row Records
Knight, Sharitha, 84, 96, 122, 199
Knight, Terri, 85-86

Lane, Tiffany, 40
Lane, Travon "Tray," 78, 88, 158
Las Vegas, Nevada: Tyson-Seldon fight in, 72,
    73. *See also* Las Vegas Police Department
Las Vegas Police Department: and
    Anderson-Shakur confrontation, 75-76;
    and Compton Police Department, 159;

and Finch as suspect in Shakur's murder,
    159; and Fula murder, 88-89; Knight
    questioned by, 98-99, 100; and Quad
    Studio shooting, 67; and Shakur's
    murder, 67, 77-80, 83-90, 98-100, 157,
    159, 197; and Smalls's murder, 141; and
    uncooperativeness of witnesses, 98-99,
    100
"Last Day" (Smalls song), 54
Latore, George, 18
Leach, Robin, 176
Leaphart, Walter, 56, 68-69
Lee, Spike, 112
Life After Death ... 'Til Death Do Us Part
    (Smalls album), 1, 5, 13, 41, 42-43, 45-46,
        109, 193, 197
Life, Matt (Matty C), 28
Lil' Kim (Kimberly Jones), 22, 39, 70, 94-95,
    149, 173, 174, 175, 189
Little Caesar (Lil' Cease) (aka James Lloyd):
    car accident of Smalls and, 37-38; and
    gunman's blast of lobby door at Bad Boy
    Entertainment, 189; as image of Smalls,
    44; as Junior M.A.F.I.A. member, 22; at
    Los Angeles party, 6; moves in with
    Smalls, 37; and Smalls's funeral, 149, 150;
    and Smalls's murder, 9, 10, 12, 121,
    145
Little Shawn, 62, 64
LL Cool J, 2, 49-50, 179
Load (Metallica album), 68
LoadTV, 97
Loder, Kurt, 145-46, 169
Lopez, Jennifer, 180-88, 190
Los Angeles, California: life on street in,
    107-13; as not on Combs tour, 190;
    Smalls in, 1-10, 108-9, 110-11, 115;
    Smalls's views about, 45. *See also* Los
    Angeles Police Department
Los Angeles Police Department: and
    Compton Police, 157; corruption probe
    of Rampart station of, 119, 121, 138;
    criticisms of, 141-42; Death Row offices
    searched by, 117, 118-19; and
    high-profile cases, 138-39; and Hip-Hop
    Music Awards, 112-13; Hitman section
    of, 140; New York trip by officers of, 125,
    139; and officers as security guards,
    127-28, 130; press releases/conferences of,
    131- 33; sealing of Smalls records by,
    114-15, 118-19; and Smalls's murder, 11,
    13, 14, 90, 113, 114-47, 157, 163, 197;
    Texas trip of, 133, 134; and
    uncooperativeness of witnesses, 141-43.
    See also specific person

Pinkett, Jada, 40
Pitts, Mark, 11, 14, 15, 148
Platinum House (Atlanta club), 55
Playboy magazine, 56, 191
"Player's Anthem" (Junior M.A.F.I.A.), 44
Poetic Justice (film), 49
Police, 167, 195
Poole, Russell, 116, 139, 141, 142
Porter, Kim, 165, 167, 168, 172, 176, 189-90
Prince, 147, 175
Priority Records, 97
Puff Daddy and the Family, 174, 190-91, 192

Quad Studio shooting: Combs denial of
    Smalls having anything to do with, 170;
    and controversy about whether Shakur
    was armed, 65-66; impact on recording
    of rap music of, 68-69; and media, 64;
    police investigation of, 53, 62-71; and rap
    feud, 53, 55, 67-68, 70; robbery in, 63;
    Shakur blames Smalls and Puffy as
    setting up, 33, 51, 53, 55, 60, 62, 66, 69;
    and Shakur-Smalls friendship, 51- 52;
    Shakur's actions immediately following,
    64-66, 70; and Shakur's murder, 67;
    Shakur's uncooperativeness in, 66-67;
    Smalls's views about, 53, 70; and Smalls's
    "Who Shot Ya'" song, 53, 69; as
    unsolved, 66-67
Quest: as Smalls stage name, 27, 30
Qwest Records, 5

R U Still Down? (Shakur album), 105-6
Randy (Junior M.A.F.I.A. member), 150
Rap business: Smalls's disillusionment with,
    41-42; violence surrounding, 191
Rap feud: and Bad Boy Entertainment, 146;
    and Bloods-Crips, 146; and Chicago
    summit, 56, 152; and Combs, 55, 58, 70,
    97, 98, 143, 144, 169-70, 191; and Death
    Row Records, 146; and Dupri birthday
    party, 54-55; Evans role in, 38- 39, 53-54,
    70; intensification of, 52-61; and Lil'
    Kim, 70; and lyrics, 60; and media, 55,
    56-57, 60-61, 70, 144, 169; as out of
    proportion, 49-50; and Quad Studio
    shooting, 53, 55, 67-68, 70; and Robles
    murder, 55; of Shakur and Smalls, 38-39,
    48-61; and Shakur's murder, 4, 50, 76, 78,
    97, 98, 137; and Smalls in Los Angeles, 2,
    4; and Smalls's murder, 2, 3, 50, 56, 58,
    115, 117, 133, 137, 143, 144, 191; and
    Smalls's notoriety, 45; Smalls's views
    about, 45, 70, 111; and *Soul Train* Music
    Awards, 2, 55

Rap music, 26-27, 58, 59, 109-10, 171, 191-92.
    See also specific performer, song, or album
Ready to Die (Smalls album), 23, 32, 43-44, 51,
    193
Rhyme and Reason (documentary), 41
Ritz (New York club), 50
Rivera, Lance "Un," 2, 148, 195
Robles, Jake, 55, 71, 199
Rock, Chris, 176, 177
Roots, 186
Ross, Diana, 101
Rourke, Mickey, 49
Run-D.M.C., 72, 149

Samuels, Anita, 143-44
"Satisfy You" (Combs song), 186
Scream (film), 168
"Scream/Childhood" (Michael Jackson song),
    32
Sealing of records: about Smalls's murder,
    114-15, 118-19
Security guards: for Bad Boy Entertainment,
    126, 129, 143, 145-46, 147, 179-80; for
    Combs, 94-95, 115-16, 128, 147, 167, 177,
    180; Crips as, 107, 115-16, 126, 135, 137,
    146; and intensification of rap feud, 54;
    for New York City College concert,
    179-80; police as, 3-4, 6, 9, 14, 15, 127-28,
    130, 147; for Shakur, 72, 73-74; for
    Smalls, 3-4, 6, 9, 14, 15, 107, 115-16, 127,
    128, 129, 130, 135, 137; for Snoop Doggy
    Dogg, 93; and *The Source* awards, 54
Seldon, Bruce, 72, 74
Shakur, Afeni, 48, 80, 83, 86, 87-88, 90, 91, 92,
    104-6, 157
Shakur, Mutula (aka Jeral Wayne Williams),
    90-91
Shakur, Tupac: arrests/questionings of, 48;
    aspirations of, 50; awards/honors for, 2-3,
    48, 49, 55; banned videos of, 97; in
    Brooklyn, 31-32; as characteristic of West
    Coast rap, 33; childhood/youth of, 48, 50;
    Combs criticized by, 169; death of, 100,
    102; Giovanni poem about, 104; guns of,
    53, 65-66; in jail, 51-52, 66-67, 69; Mack
    shrine to, 121; Makaveli pseudonym of,
    103-4; and money, 48, 50, 96, 105, 106;
    posthumous releases of, 193; as prolific
    writer and performer, 104-5, 106;
    romanticism surrounding, 104; and
    rumors of Shakur seeking revenge
    against Smalls, 46-47; as
    security-conscious, 69; sexual- assault
    charges against, 51, 62, 66, 92; Smalls
    compared with, 33, 48-49, 50, 56, 109;

and violence in rap industry/society, 58, 191; witnesses to, 10, 14, 120, 121, 125, 127, 130, 138, 139, 142-43, 147. *See also* Cedars-Sinai Medical Center (Los Angeles); *specific person*

Sneed, Danny, 78, 79, 154-56, 157, 159

Snoop Doggy Dogg (aka Calvin Broadus), 2, 4, 55, 56, 92-93, 96, 152

Soul, 27, 33

Soul Train Music Awards, 2-3, 4-8, 55, 58, 110-11, 115.

SoundScan, Inc., 45

The Source Magazine, 28, 41, 54, 61, 97, 112-13, 167

Sticky Fingers, 32

Sting, 195

Stone, Jerry, 155, 156, 157

Stone, Michael, 155, 156-57

"Stop the Gunfight" (Smalls-Shakur single), 58

Stoute, Steven, 8, 178

Street gangs, 107-11, 154-60. *See also* Bloods; Crips

Strictly 4 My N.I.G.G.Z. (Shakur album), 49

Sugar Hill Records, 58

Sugarhill Gang, 58

Sure, Al B., 35

Sway (KMEL DJ), 57

Teaneck, New Jersey: Smalls's condominium in, 6, 34-35, 37, 194

Television: Smalls on, 32

Texas: LAPD officers trip to, 133, 134

Tha Dogg Pound, 96

Theo, DJ, 110

This Is for My Dead Homiez (film), 50

Thompson, Robert, 181, 186

Thrust (aka Chris France), 58

Thug Life (Shakur album), 49

Too Short, 33

Total, 161, 173, 174

Trump, Donald, 165, 177

Tucker, Chris, 5

Turner, Zayd, 62-63, 64, 66

2Pac: Greatest Hits (Shakur album), 103

2Pacalypse Now (Shakur album), 49

Tyson, Mike, 46, 72, 73-74, 81, 101, 165, 179

U2, 45

Undeas Records, 195

Uptown Records, 28-29, 30-31, 172-73

The Velvet rope (Janet Jackson album), 167

VH-1 Awards, 166

Vibe magazine: and Combs-Carey relationship, 166; Evans' reflections on Biggie in, 38; on Evans-Shakur relationship, 54; on Evans-Smalls relationship, 36, 37; on Junior M.A.F.I.A., 44; party thrown by, 3, 4-8; and Quad Studios shooting, 64; and rap feud, 61; on rap music, 59; and reactions to Shakur's murder, 89-90; and Shakur-Smalls controversy, 38, 39; Shakur's (Afeni) criticism of police in, 91; Shakur's interviews with, 104; on Shakur's murder, 14; and Smalls's disillusionment with rap business, 41; Smalls's interviews with, 14, 36, 37, 38, 41, 44, 89-90, 108; and Smalls's plans to go to California, 108; and Smalls's settling down, 38. *See also* Coker, Cheo Hodari

Violence, 43, 46, 49, 58, 109, 110, 174, 191

Virgin Music Canada, 58

Wade, Cornell: Shakur interview with, 74

Walker, Randy "Stretch," 51, 62-63, 64, 65-66, 70-71, 103, 199

Wallace, Christopher George Latore. *See* Smalls, Biggie

Wallace, Christopher Jordan (son), 13, 36-37, 41, 149, 175, 194, 195, 196-97

Wallace, Chyna (daughter), 149, 175, 194, 195

Wallace, T'Yanna (daughter), 13, 35, 41, 149, 175, 194, 195, 196-97

Wallace, Voletta (mother): aspirations for Smalls of, 25- 26, 30; and awards/honors for Smalls, 195-96; and Combs, 30, 126, 142-43, 162-63, 194-95; divorce of, 18; and Evans-Smalls relationship, 36, 194; on LAPD, 142, 147; on Lil' Kim-Smalls relationship, 39; mastectomy of, 33; and posthumous release of Smalls music, 106, 193-94; and Quad Studio shooting, 53, 55;on Shakur-Smalls friendship, 50-51; and Shakur's murder, 56, 76, 126; and Smalls- Banks case, 34; and Smalls's childhood/youth, 17, 18, 20- 21, 22, 23, 24-25; and Smalls's estate, 194; and Smalls's first break as rapper, 29-30; and Smalls's funeral, 148, 149, 152; Smalls's last telephone call to, 1, 2, 3; and Smalls's legacy, 196-97; on Smalls's lyrics, 43; and Smalls's murder, 4, 13, 15-16,'114, 126, 142-43, 147, 162-63; and Smalls's relationship with, 21, 22, 26, 33, 36, 43, 194

"Warning" (Smalls video), 32, 63

Watson, "Tex," 124

Webb, Edward, 78, 158